The Alchemical Mercurius

The figure of the alchemical Mercurius is ubiquitous and radical in Jung's later works, but despite this, there has been little research concerning Mercurius in Jungian studies to date. In this book, Mathew Mather explores the figure of the alchemical Mercurius and contextualises and clarifies its significance in Jung's life and works.

Placing the alchemical Mercurius as a central concern reveals a Jungian interpretation in which the grail legend, alchemy and precessional astrology, as three thematic threads, converge. In such a treatment, Jung's belief in the dawning of a new platonic month emerges as a central consideration and an esoteric perspective on Jung's life and works is brought more fully to light, constructing a life-myth interpretation.

The book is composed of three parts:

- Aurea catena: locating the figure of the alchemical Mercurius within the western esoteric tradition.
- Daimonic encounter: the relevance of this figure in Jung's personal life.
- Magnum opus: the portrayal of this figure in Jung's key texts such as *Synchronicity*, *Aion* and *Mysterium Coniunctionis*, and Emma Jung and von Franz's *The Grail Legend*.

The Alchemical Mercurius is a unique contribution to analytical psychology, substantially revealing 'esoteric Jung' and providing valuable perspectives on the theme of his myth for our times. The book will appeal to researchers and academics in the field of analytical psychology as well as postgraduate students.

Mathew Mather is Lecturer in Media at the Limerick School of Art and Design, Limerick Institute of Technology, Ireland. His research interests include Jung's later works, synchronicity, alchemy, esotericism, art and the psyche.

Research in Analytical Psychology and Jungian Studies Series

Series Advisor: Andrew Samuels

Professor of Analytical Psychology, Essex University, UK

The *Research in Analytical Psychology and Jungian Studies* series features scholarly works that are, broadly speaking, of an empirical nature. The series comprises research-focused volumes involving qualitative and quantitative research, historical/archival research, theoretical developments, heuristic research, grounded theory, narrative approaches, collaborative research, practitioner-led research, and self-study. The series also includes focused works by clinical practitioners and provides new research-informed explorations of the work of C. G. Jung that will appeal to researchers, academics, and scholars alike.

Books in this series:

Time and Timelessness
Temporality in the theory of Carl Jung
Angeliki Yiassemides

Apophatic Elements in the Theory and Practice of Psychoanalysis
Pseudo-Dionysius and C. G. Jung
David Henderson

C. G. Jung and Hans Urs von Balthasar
God and evil – critical comparison
Les Oglesby

Bridges to Consciousness
Complexes and complexity
Nancy M. Krieger

The Alchemical Mercurius
Esoteric symbol of Jung's life and works
Mathew Mather

The Alchemical Mercurius

Esoteric symbol of Jung's life and works

Mathew Mather

Routledge
Taylor & Francis Group
LONDON AND NEW YORK

First published 2014
by Routledge
2 Park Square, Milton Park, Abingdon, Oxfordshire OX14 4RN

and by Routledge
711 Third Avenue, New York, NY 10017

First issued in paperback 2016

Routledge is an imprint of the Taylor & Francis Group, an informa business

British Library Cataloguing in Publication Data
A catalogue record for this book is available from the British Library

Library of Congress Cataloging in Publication Data
Mather, Mathew
The alchemical Mercurius : esoteric symbol of Jung's life and works/Mathew Mather.
pages cm
Includes bibliographical references and index.
1. Jung, C. G. (Carl Gustav), 1875–1961. I. Title.

BF109.J8M3456 2014
150.19'4092–dc23   2013037316

ISBN 13: 978-0-415-36576-5 (pbk)
ISBN 13: 978-0-415-70525-7 (hbk)

Typeset in Bembo
by Sunrise Setting Ltd, Paignton, UK

For my parents
Brian and Maeve

Contents

Figures

Foreword

Roderick Main

C. G. Jung was deeply interested in and influenced by western esotericism – especially Gnosticism, alchemy and spiritualism, but also astrology, magic and a host of other traditions and thinkers – throughout his long professional life. His engagement with these areas was both theoretical and practical, providing him with cultural parallels for some of his psychological notions, such as the process of individuation, and for some of his therapeutic techniques, such as active imagination. For many, especially clinicians and academics, these scarcely concealed interests of Jung's have been grounds for suspicion of his work as a whole; for others, especially at a more popular level, they have been a factor contributing to Jung's appeal; and for yet others, especially esoteric practitioners, they have led to Jung's being variously co-opted as a supporter of esoteric traditions or rejected as a distorter of them (Main 2010: 167–9).

It is only within the past twenty or so years that western esotericism has established itself as a respectable field of academic research, mainly within religious studies (Hanegraaff 2012). The significance of Jung's work within this field has been clearly acknowledged. Antoine Faivre, Emeritus Professor of History of Esoteric and Mystical Currents in Modern and Contemporary Europe at the Sorbonne, cites Jung and Jungian concepts when presenting his influential formulation of the essential and non-essential characteristics of esotericism (Faivre 1994: 10–15, 107). Wouter Hanegraaff, Professor of History of Hermetic Philosophy and Related Currents at the University of Amsterdam, devotes lengthy sections to Jung in both of his main surveys of western esotericism (1998: 496–513; 2012: 277–95). And Jung is the only modern psychologist to be assigned a main entry (Maillard 2006) in Brill's encyclopaedic *Dictionary of Gnosis and Western Esotericism* (Hanegraaff *et al.* 2006). With his interest in a worldview based on correspondences (synchronicity), animated nature (the *anima mundi*), imagination and mediations between a seen and an unseen world (archetypes and symbols) and the experience of psychological and spiritual transformation (individuation), Jung easily satisfies Faivre's essential criteria for indemnification as an esotericist (Main 2010: 169–70). And when Hanegraaff updates Faivre's criteria to take account of how modern esotericism has transformed from the late nineteenth through the twentieth century under the influence of secular thought – specifically, under the influence of a causal worldview, the comparative study of religions, evolutionism and psychology itself – Jung again fully fits the picture that emerges (Hanegraaff 1998: 411–511; Main 2010: 170–1). Furthermore, Jung's contribution has been seen not only as that of someone who has drawn on and in turn influenced western esotericism but also as that of someone who has helped to shape the academic study of the field, albeit controversially, especially through his pivotal role in the first two decades of Eranos conferences (between 1933 and 1953), where a select group of outstanding religious scholars gathered each year to explore the relevance of myth, symbolism and other topics marginalised in post-Enlightenment western culture (Hanegraaff 2012: 277–95).

Identifying esoteric currents in modern thought is not just an exercise in historical curiosity. As Hanegraaff has argued – and he is avowedly speaking for academics and intellectuals such as himself who, when confronted with esotericism, 'tend to smile about it, feel embarrassed, or look the other way' (Hanegraaff 2012: 1): 'our perceptions of "esotericism" or "the occult" are inextricably intertwined with how we think about ourselves: [. . .] our very identity [. . .] depends on an implicit rejection of that identity's reverse mirror image' (Hanegraaff 2012: 3). So, if we were to come to think differently about how we imagine esoteric otherness, we should also have to question our own identities. As a result the field of western esotericism has, in Hanegraaff's view, 'potentially explosive implications for academic research as a whole' (Hanegraaff 2012: 3).

Academic and intellectual responses to Jung's work are often not dissimilar to the responses to esotericism noted by Hanegraaff, and this may in no small part be because of the pervasiveness of esotericism in Jung. It is notable, for instance, that Jung's work tends to alienate both scientists, for whom it seems too dependent on religious assumptions and attitudes, and religious adherents, for whom it seems too naturalistic and psychologically reductive. Part of the underlying reason for this double rejection may be that the form of science in which Jung is interested is one which, like alchemy, engages the symbolic imagination and includes intuition and feeling as well as sensation and thinking (Jung 1944; cf. Pauli 1952: 206, 212); while the form of religion in which he is most interested is one which, like most forms of western esotericism, involves a panentheistic understanding of God as permeating and giving structure and meaning to the world, including to humans, who therefore have an inborn capacity for obtaining direct, experiential, salvific knowledge of the divine ('gnosis'). Such an outlook is in fundamental tension both with mainstream theistic religion, in which the Creator is seen as separate from the creation and knowledge is obtainable only through faith and reason, and with mainstream science, in which the world is viewed independently of any supposition about the divine and knowledge is obtainable only through empiricism and reason (Hanegraaff 2012, pp. 370–3).

Against this background, it is timely that Mathew Mather has addressed head-on the esoteric dimension of Jung's thought. Focusing on the figure of the alchemical Mercurius, the symbol *par excellence* of esotericism itself, Mather meticulously tracks the extensive role played by this figure both in Jung's published writings and in what Mather, following Jung but also extrapolating beyond him, identifies as the mythic dimension of Jung's own life. Mather is careful to ground his researches in detailed, critical scholarship, including close textual reading and some fascinating historical contextualisation. But he does not shrink from also empathically entering the thought-world of esotericism and advancing, on the basis of what he finds from that perspective, a bold case for Jung's own esoteric beliefs – on alchemy, on the legend of the Holy Grail and, most provocatively, on precessional astrology and the imminence of a new Platonic month.

The range of Jung's interests and the complexity of his personality mean that it will remain debatable how central a place western esotericism occupies in his overall identity (see Main 2010). But that Jung's serious engagement with esotericism does play a role of considerable importance not only for understanding his psychological model but also for appreciating his place in the development of western culture is becoming increasingly difficult to dispute. Mather's book contributes substantially to illuminating this most occulted, discomfiting, yet potentially significant aspect of Jung's work.

References

Faivre, A. (1994) *Access to Western Esotericism*, Albany, NY: State University of New York Press.

Hanegraaff, W. (1998) *New Age Religion and Western Culture: Esotericism in the Mirror of Secular Thought*, Albany, NY: State University of New York Press.

Hanegraaff, W. (2012) *Esotericism and the Academy: Rejected Knowledge in Western Culture*, Cambridge: Cambridge University Press.

Hanegraaff, W. (ed.), in collaboration with A. Faivre, R. Van den Broek, and J.-P. Brach. (2006) *Dictionary of Gnosis and Western Esotericism*, Leiden: Brill.

Jung, C. G. (1944/1968) *Collected Works*, vol. 12, *Psychology and Alchemy*, 2nd ed., trans. R. F. C. Hull, London: Routledge & Kegan Paul, 1968.

Maillard, C. (2006) 'Jung, Carl Gustav', in W. Hanegraaff *et al.* (eds.) *Dictionary of Gnosis and Western Esotericism* (pp. 648–53), Leiden: Brill.

Main, R. (2010) 'Jung as a modern esotericist', in G. Heuer (ed.) *Sacral Revolutions: Reflecting on the Work of Andrew Samuels – Cutting Edges in Psychoanalysis and Jungian Analysis* (pp. 167–75), London and New York: Routledge.

Pauli, W. (1952/1955) 'The influence of archetypal Ideas on the Scientific Theories of Kepler', trans. P. Silz, in C. G. Jung and W. Pauli, *The Interpretation of Nature and the Psyche* (pp. 147–240), New York: Pantheon.

Preface and acknowledgements

The present book is based on a PhD thesis completed at the Centre for Psychoanalytic Studies, Univesity of Essex. A memory from my first supervisory board stands out. Professor Andrew Samuels asked: '. . . and does your thesis involve dragons?' After I acknowledged that indeed it does, he replied 'that's nice, I like dragons'. His unique and sophisticated 'trickster-like' personality afforded a role model, of sorts, toward better understanding my thesis topic. I am also indebted to Matt ffytche, my other board member, for bringing a touch of luminosity to my work. Most thanks, however, go to my supervisor Roderick Main, who (whom!) gave my 'wild-card' project a chance in the first place. Not only did he help to get the 'spirit back in the bottle' on many an occasion, but he also sensitively and ingeniously guided a transformation within the 'academic bottle' that greatly enhanced my presentation of Mercurius – no easy task!

I would also like to thank my parents, brother and sister. My mother would often tell me that 'only Allah is perfect', and that is why the makers of Persian carpets would intentionally include a missed stitch before completing a carpet. Being far from perfect, I take responsibility for all the 'missed sitches' in the book. I would also like to acknowledge my mother as being of primary inspiration for my interest in the psyche. Similarly I would like to thank my father. Perhaps his agnosticism might nudge a little closer toward a gnosis. My brother and sister being on different continents from myself precluded the possibility of lively discussions.

I also thank Andreas Jung for accommodating my afternoon visit to Kusnacht, for his time in discussing Jung and the family and for allowing me to peruse Jung's alchemical books. Ulrich Hoerni also enabled a trip to Bollingen Tower, for which I am also very grateful.

I am also indebted to Nic Stratton for kindly hosting my many visits to the university. I will miss our many conversations and differences of opinion. Perhaps we will yet solve that mystery of the light beam, and other serendipitous (or is it synchronistic!) phenomena. I also appreciate the many new friendships made during the years, as well as my longstanding friends who have shared such arcane interests.

Finally, I would like to thank my wife Lyn and my two lovely daughters, Katie and Karla. Lyn shared many a sympathetic moment of 'madness and revelation' during the years of following the tracks of Mercurius. I thank her for her interest and enthusiasm for the project, for assisting in numerous proof-readings, and for graphic illustrations of Dee's *Hieroglyphic Monad* and the Pisces–Pegasus–Aquarius constellations. Finally, I thank Katie and Karla for bearing with their father, who was sometimes 'lost with the fairies'. I celebrate their lighthearted joyfulness that was so welcome amidst the gravitas that characterised much of this project.

* * *

The author and publishers are grateful to the British Library Board for permission to reproduce the frontispiece of John Dee's *General and Rare Memorials* (shelfmark 48.h.18.); also to Bayerische Staatsbibliothek München for 'The Extraction of Mercurius', from Pandora's *Reusner* 1598 (shelfmark ESlg/Alch. 205, S. 253) and to the National Gallery of Art, Washington D.C., for 'Saint George and the Dragon' by Sodoma 1518, and to the Germanisches Nationalmuseum Nürnberg for woodcut IV from the *Rosarium Philosophorum* Secunda Pars Alchimiae 1550.

It might be said that the secret of Merlin was carried on by alchemy, primarily in the figure of Mercurius. Then Merlin was taken up again in my psychology of the unconscious and – remains uncomprehended to this day!

(Jung 1963/1995: 255)

Introduction

In a letter dated 1942, in the midst of World War II, Jung wrote: 'For the time being I am still immersed in Mercury who, as he will always try to, has dissolved me almost and just failed to separate me limb from limb' (footnote 5, in Jung 1973–75: 319). During this time he was working on two lectures on the theme of 'The Spirit Mercurius' subsequently presented at Eranos during the summer of 1942. The first lecture is an interpretation of Grimm's fairytale 'Spirit in the Bottle'. The second lecture is a more general thematic compilation on the figure of Mercurius.

Concerning the first lecture, Jung admonishes the reader that his treatment is a 'general survey' and that it makes 'no claim to completeness' (1943/1948: footnote 193). What follows is a fairly detailed analysis of the fairytale. Toward the beginning he enticingly states that this German fairytale 'contains the quintessence and deepest meaning of the Hermetic mystery' (195). He then proceeds to interpret it as a transformation mystery whereby the boy, lost to the world and led by a strange calling, enters the darkness of his unconscious. He goes to the very ground and root of his being and there discovers a numinous being bottled up within the physiology of his body. Releasing this chthonic spirit, Mercurius, results in him almost losing his life. Fortunately though, by virtue of his wits, there is a favourable resolution for both himself and the spirit.

Jung effectively portrays the fairytale as a timeless archetypal mystery applicable to a multitude of historical and cultural contexts, as a paradigm of psycho-spiritual transformation and renewal.[1] On another level, he also locates the story within the western Christian tradition by interpreting it as a cultural evolution at a particular stage of individuation. From this point of view, he identifies the magician or alchemist with the Christian God and the spirit in the bottle with the quintessential pagan god, as the 'serpent of paradise' in the garden of Eden. In this sense God 'banished' the pagan spirit which gets bottled up and hidden in the depths of matter.

Such a theme is central to Jung's broader critique of modern Christianity, as it portrays a 'split archetype' into instinctual and spiritual polarities. The instinctual, bottled and buried, gets contaminated with the feminine, pagan and malefic; whereas the spiritual conflates to the masculine, Christian and benevolent. Thus, in his opinion, such a split has resulted in a specifically Christian wound as reflected in such narratives as the grail legend, and as portrayed in the dreams and psychopathology of his patients. In this context, the spirit Mercurius is portrayed by Jung as a dynamic and compensatory figure to the collective consciousness of Christianity (1943/1948: 245).

He further clarifies that it would be incorrect to equate the alchemical Mercurius with the Devil. Although essentially a dark and chthonic god, he opposes dogmatic definition and opposition at all costs: he is a real trickster who 'drove the alchemists to despair' (1943/1948: 203). Jung then relates that releasing the spirit Mercurius is alchemically incorrect. The more usual procedure would be to keep such a spirit bottled up and to transform him by means of various alchemical procedures (ibid.). In this context we also witness an earlier work, 'Wotan', inflected as the spirit Mercurius, as the 'awakening of the blonde beast' in the German soul. Jung explicitly identifies the spirit Mercurius with Wotan, national pagan god of Germany, but offers no expansion of the topic (ibid.: 198).

Moving to the second lecture (a good example of Jung's problematic writing style), we get a monologue on Mercurius arranged thematically around a number of categories. Jung utilizes a fairly vast array of text citations to 'draw a picture of this versatile and shimmering god' (1943/1948: 204). In the midst of this lecture, in seeming exasperation, he notes that 'the concept swells dangerously and we begin to perceive that the end is nowhere in sight' (ibid.: 211). Its confounding properties, seemingly decoupled from the substance itself, lead him to the conclusion that it is a projection of the unconscious. Finally, toward the end of this lecture, Jung attempts to 'pin the concept down' by means of a six-point summary:

1 Mercurius consists of all conceivable opposites. He is thus quite obviously a duality, but is named a unity in spite of the fact that his innumerable inner contradictions can dramatically fly apart into an equal number of disparate and apparently independent figures.
2 He is both material and spiritual.
3 He is the process by which the lower and material is transformed into the higher and spiritual, and vice versa.
4 He is the devil, a redeeming psychopomp, an evasive trickster and God's reflection in physical nature.
5 He is also the reflection of a mystical experience of the artifex that coincides with the *opus alchymicum*.
6 As such, he represents on the one hand the self and on the other the individuation process and, because of the limitless number of his names, also the collective unconscious.

(Jung 1943/1948: 237)

Jung ends by further elaborating the relevance of the spirit Mercurius to Christianity and contemporary times. For example, he highlights this figure as having 'the very qualities we so urgently need to heal the split in ourselves' (1943/1948: 246).

Such a notion takes us into the very heart of what we might consider Jung's 'alchemical myth'. Von Franz, in a dramatic moment in the film *Matter of Heart*, clarifies the key features of such a myth:

> civilization needs a myth to live by . . . And I think that the Christian myth, on which we have lived, has degenerated and become one-sided and insufficient. I think alchemy is the complete myth. If our Western civilization has a possibility of survival, it would be by accepting the alchemical myth, which is a richer completion and continuation of the Christian myth . . . The Christian myth . . . does not include the dark feminine . . . treats matter as dead and does not face the problem of the opposites – of evil. Alchemy faces the problem of the opposites, faces the problem of matter, and faces the problem of the feminine.
>
> (von Franz, quoted by Marlan, in Papadopoulos [ed.] 2006)

* * *

Jung's more serious interest in alchemy began in 1928 and lasted for the remainder of his life (Jung 1963/1995: 234). During these final decades of his life, he also related that 'the question of the chthonic spirit has occupied me ever since I began to delve into the world of alchemy' (ibid.: 192). Within this body of work he makes copious references to the figure of Mercurius. A look at selected words from the index of the *Collected Works* is illustrative:

word	**index content (pages)**
synchronicity	0.5
individuation	1
self	4.5
Christ	5.5
Mercurius	7.5

Here we see an alchemical word (Mercurius) taking up 7.5 pages of index content. It features more prominently than analytical psychological concepts (for example synchronicity, individuation and the self) or a theological word (Christ). Based on this anomaly, I queried the extent to which this phenomenon has been dealt with in Jungian studies.

An extensive literature review revealed that with the exception of work by Marie-Louise von Franz and Emma Jung, this phenomenon gets relatively thin coverage by first-generation followers and in the post-Jungian literature. As far as I am aware, apart from von Franz and Emma Jung's work, we do not see a single book, article or even chapter dedicated to this theme, despite the centrality of this figure in Jung's primary writings. This said, a fair amount has been written on Hermes and also on 'trickster' themes; however, a simplistic Hermes–Mercurius substitution is problematic. Such interpretations are often biased toward a mythological, as opposed to an alchemical, perspective. The emphasis has been mostly on the Greek Hermes, and less so on the Egyptian Thoth. Jung's tendency to conflate Mercurius with figures such as Wotan and Merlin and his interpretation of this figure as a compensatory symbol to the Christ figure, for example, have also been under-represented in the literature.

I thus claim there is a clear discrepancy in the significance placed on this figure between Jung (primary writings) in comparison with first-generation followers and post-Jungians. Indeed, a singular work of sizeable magnitude focused on this particular theme is absent in the literature. The present work is thus an effort to retrieve and contextualise the alchemical Mercurius and to 'redeem' it from what would appear (in some circles at least) to be its present status as a 'curious notion' (Stevens, cited by Mogenson 1999: 132).

Furthermore, an investigation of the alchemical Mercurius in Jung's oeuvre (including posthumous publications) inevitably leads us to not only his alchemical worldview, but also his astrological worldview. Many find this aspect of his thinking unpalatable. We might add that most contemporary Jungians would consider their inspired leader's interest in astrology to be a step too far, an embarrassment best swept under the carpet. Yet there is no doubt that Jung's astrological worldview, his 'secret knowledge', profoundly influenced not only his *Red Book*, but also his mature thought such as appears in such watershed works as *Aion* and *Mysterium Coniunctionis*. Indeed, if we are serious about a fuller understanding of his life and works, then it is imperative to both acknowledge and better understand this side of him, lest we 'auntify' him.

In redressing such omissions, a hoped-for impact would be a revitalised interest in 'original Jung'. A drifting away from the 'big thing' of his oeuvre has been voiced: 'If one looks around in today's Jungian world, one gets the strong impression that Jung's heritage has been forfeited ... the psychologist has got out of the *magnum opus* (or has never had access to it)' (Giegerich 1999: 81).

The most notable finding is that placing the alchemical Mercurius as a central concern reveals a Jungian interpretation in which the grail legend, alchemy and precessional astrology, as three thematic threads, converge. In such a treatment, Jung's belief in the dawning of a new Platonic month emerges as a central consideration. An esoteric perspective on his life and works is thus brought more fully to light and a life-myth interpretation is constructed. My opinion is that such an esoteric perspective is both fundamental and timely, especially in light of the recent publication of *The Red Book*, if we are to grasp the deeper significance of Jung's esoteric identity and of key aspects of the relevance of his myth for our times.

* * *

For such a venture, a few methodological considerations are also in order. Apart from obvious translation issues, these include: dating and differing versions of texts in the *Collected Works*; limited publication of letters; errors in the seminar series, the authenticity of *Memories, Dreams, Reflections* (*MDR*); and concerns around the portrayal of Jung by his biographers.

Many of Jung's writings have both published and unpublished antecedents (see Bair 2004: 582). The final published versions may have omissions and be changed by edits, in comparison with unpublished (archival) versions. 'The Spirit Mercurius', for instance, was originally delivered as two lectures at Eranos in 1942 as 'The Hermetic Principle in Mythology, Gnosis and Alchemy' (Jung 1943/1948: 191). The following year it was published as *Der Geist Mercurius*. We then discover there is an unpublished document, discovered posthumously, titled 'The concept of Mercurius in Hermetic Philosophy' (ibid.: 136; see footnote).

Moving to the *Letters*, we need to be cognisant that those published have been selected from a fairly large collection. The Pauli/Jung collection (the English version of which was published in 2001), for instance, illustrates the extent to which the original two volumes are deficient. Indeed, for the present research, these letters proved significantly more valuable than the voluminous original letters publications. Future access to as yet unpublished letters (such as those to Herbert Silberer relating to alchemy) is direly needed.

Concerning the various seminar series, we should flag that these were transcriptions and subject to error. On this score, we will never know exactly what Jung said in the seminars. We also read, in a letter dated 1955, 'I must warn you that I have never been able to go through them [the seminar notes] and correct minor errors . . . It is also expected that you wouldn't use them for quotations in printed papers without special permission' (Jung 1973–75: 227).

Progressing to Jung's so-called autobiography, we then discover that this is actually a highly edited document based on a much larger volume of autobiographical notes known as 'The Protocols'. The editors of MDR apparently tampered with the more controversial aspects. Jung himself called this *tantifizierungen* (auntification)[2] (Bair 2004: 626–40). For example, he 'insisted his remarks about alchemy during the "biographical hours" were vital, even though many were little more than unfocussed ramblings'[3] (ibid.: 599). As his 'autobiography' was also published posthumously, we have no final approval from the actual 'author'. There was 'considerable editing after his death' (Shamdasani 2005: 30). In essence, 'what was indeed a remarkable biography has been mistakenly read as an autobiography' (ibid.: 38).

Apart from the dubious origins of *MDR*, there is also the unique style of this book. Peter Homans, taking Jung's cue that it is a *personal myth*, describes it as being of a unique genre: what he terms 'automythology' (Homans 1979/1995: 29). Jaffé, Jung's secretary, described it as a self-confessed expression of his No. 2 personality as 'inner man' and, in a spirit of compensation, goes on to contribute a brief version of the so-called 'No. 1 Jung' (Jaffé 1989: ix, xx). Vincent Brome, Ronald Hayman and Deirdre Bair largely share this compensatory emphasis, compared with earlier more hagiographic accounts by Barbara Hannah, Marie-Louise von Franz and Laurens van der Post.

Not surprisingly, constructing biography on Jung is problematic. Robert Smith, for example, notes that 'there is a recognizable need for Jung's interpreters to embark upon a new quest for the historical rather than the mythical Jung. Some have so "spiritualized" Jung that they have made him into a cultural hero, mythologized beyond all recognition' (Smith 1997: 6). Along similar lines, Richard Noll has pointed out that 'MDR and its imitators have actually obscured the story of Jung who is much more interesting – and at times terrifyingly flawed – because of his humanity, and not his semi-divinity' (Noll 1997: xiii).

Considering the biographers, Sonu Shamdasani warns of further pitfalls. He even coined the word *interprefaction*[4] to signify 'the manner in which interpretations and constructions are treated as facts. When interprefaction prevails, the requirement of evidence recedes' (Shamdasani 2005: 4). By way of example I point out how, in his *Cult Fictions*, Shamdasani exposes Noll's work such as *The Aryan Christ* and *The Jung Cult* as being not only sloppy but also 'excessively speculative and inferential' (Shamdasani 1998: 7). He also points out a number of critical flaws and errors in the latest work by Bair (Shamdasani 2005: 102–3). His conclusion is that, of all the biographies, it is Hannah's that is the 'most reliable and important' (ibid.: 117).

Further, in constructing Jungian biography, and in light of the above, one should be ever mindful of Shamdasani's observation that '[t]he most curious aspect of the reception of Jung's work is that there have been few figures in twentieth century intellectual history who have been subject to such a high level of misunderstanding' (Shamdasani 1998: 12).

In addressing these problems I veer toward caution when using biography (thereby avoiding the possibility of 'interprefaction'). I also depend, as far as possible, on primary sources, yet also acknowledge the inherent limitations of this. For key information, I attempt to find corroborative evidence. For example, the timing of the beginning of the New Age, derived from a seminar, is corroborated with a letter (see chapter 4). Ultimately though, even the primary sources (especially the seminar series) do not pass as 'solid evidence'. Thus the goal of finding a 'perfectly sound' construction is elusive, and will probably remain so. Despite such problems, I venture and 'risk' an interpretation that does justice to an 'intuitive' and 'felt' sense derived from many years of reading Jung and related materials, yet grounded, as far as possible, in reliable data. My chosen methodological approach is thus more that of construction than critique. In addition, my use of concepts such as myth, symbol, and so on should be understood in a Jungian sense, as my primary goal is to better locate Mercurius within a Jungian conceptual framework and within his biography.

* * *

In identifying the key literature consulted, I follow the sequence: primary materials, first-generation followers, biographies, post-Jungian literature.

Many of Jung's later writings appearing in the *Collected Works* (post-1928) feature the alchemical Mercurius. 'The Spirit Mercurius' (1943/1948) is the principal text.

Other essential works include *Psychology and Alchemy* (1944), *Psychology of the Transference* (1946), *Aion* (1951) and *Mysterium Coniunctionis* (1955/1956). Interestingly, Mercurius features prominently in a number of writings related to Jung's magnum opus.

The *Letters* (Volumes I and II, 1973–75) have few references of specific interest. Indirectly, however, they were invaluable due to their bias toward later Jung and preciseness of dating. The *Pauli/Jung Letters* (2001) were crucial, as the figure of Merlin–Mercurius is found on a number of occasions and especially in Pauli's letters.

Mercurius features less prominently in the various seminar series compared to the *Collected Works*. However, the timing of these, mostly post-1928, allowed for corroborative evidence that informed a number of my arguments. The *Visions Seminars*, in particular, were invaluable in ascertaining Jung's astrological worldview and as a means of amplifying key images in *The Red Book.*

A primary work of especial note, despite its completion by 1928, is *The Red Book*. Although Mercurius does not feature here (pre-alchemical period), the work was invaluable for establishing pre-figurations of this character. The nature of this work also added depth to my argument of esoteric Jung and of my construction of him as New Age prophet.

Concerning first-generation writers, Emma Jung and von Franz covered this topic more than others have. Emma Jung's *The Grail Legend* (1970/1998; completed by von Franz) includes a chapter on the subject, 'Merlin and the Alchemical Mercurius', and also scattered mentions elsewhere in the text. In these texts we see conflation between Mercurius and Merlin, as well as a variety of guises such as the grail itself, the contents of the grail, the grail king's heathen enemy and so on.

Edward Edinger, another prominent first-generation writer, illuminates much of 'esoteric Jung' in his intense works. His treatment of Mercurius, however, is sparse. His *Mysterium Lectures* (1995) feature this figure most prominently. However, upon closer inspection, these prove to be mostly regurgitations of Jung.

Considering astrology and first-generation Jungians, I return to von Franz. Her voluminous writings reveal an interest in the 'transition of the Ages'. However, upon closer inspection, her scope is limited. Indeed, she admits that astrology is 'not to her taste'. Edinger, although fairly strong on alchemy and champion of the 'alchemical myth', is, however, even weaker than von Franz on astrology. For example, his commentary on *Aion* exhibits flaws on the basics, such as the historical timing during the Aeon of Pisces (see Edinger 1996: 70). Elsewhere, he boldly announces Jung as avatar of the Aquarian Age, yet neglects to credibly substantiate such a claim (ibid.: 192).

Concerning biographies on Jung, the most notable is von Franz's *C.G. Jung: His Myth in Our Time*, which includes two chapters on this theme ('Le Cri de Merlin' and 'Mercurius'). Curiously, her long-time companion Barbara Hannah gives it only one mention in her biography. Van der Post's *Jung and the Story of our Times* (1976/1985), which so elegantly captures cultural themes, inclusive of grail stories, omits mention of Mercurius (Merlin appears a couple of times). Brome's *Jung: Man and Myth* (1985) includes a couple of mentions. Noll, one of Jung's harshest critics, does not deal with this figure even though he probes into such esoteric areas as astrological aeons. Hayman's *A Life of Jung* (1999) has no references in the index (there is one in the text). The most recent biography by Bair, titled *Jung* (2004), is the most voluminous work to date. Here we do not come across a single reference in the index or in the text. This is a significant discrepancy, in contrast to von Franz's biography. In summary, apart from von Franz's work, this figure is almost non-existent in the biographies.

As a whole, I claim that post-Jungian writings reflect a similar (though less dramatic) trend of neglect. This claim is easily borne out by a perusal of the index section of books and journals in a typical library of Jungian materials. For example, performing a word search of the *Journal of Analytical Psychology* with the keyword *Mercurius* results in only eight hits (the word *Christ* yields thirty-five hits). Other Jungian journals do not contain a single article, so far as I have been able to find, in which the word Mercurius appears in the title. A brief excursion into post-Jungians on alchemy, astrology, mythology, synchronicity and shamanism corroborates such a view.

Beginning with post-Jungians on alchemy, Stanton Marlan's masterly overview chapter in *The Handbook of Jungian Psychology* (2006) identifies and contextualises the major trends. In following up on key texts we find some coverage in works such as Marlan's *The Black Sun* (2005), Jeffrey Raff's *Jung and the Alchemical Imagination* (2000), Nathan Schwartz-Salant's *The Mystery of Human Relationship: Alchemy and the Transformation of Self* (1998) and, more recently, Joseph Henderson and Dyane Sherwood's *Transformation of the Psyche* (2003/2005). An observation, however, is that when these authors do mention Mercurius it is often embedded within a quote from Jung, or as part of an image illustration. More specifically, concerning post-Jungians on alchemy, I note that nowhere do we get a full chapter or even a number of pages that deal exclusively with this character. In addition, their treatments of alchemy are mostly oriented toward clinical applications and conceptual developments rather than the cultural, religious or esoteric. Furthermore, although they often allude to such conceptions as a 'transforming god-image' and the contemporary relevance of the alchemical myth, they have not chosen to place such a theme centre stage or to engage in any significant way with astrology. Such an emphasis has resonance, perhaps, with James Hillman's approach. His various articles on alchemy steer clear from what he calls 'Jung's noble metaphysics', his concerns being 'clinically immediate and less spiritually progressivist' (Hillman 2010: 7).

Moving to mythology is interesting. If we exchange the word Mercurius for Hermes or use the word 'trickster', then we are flooded with material. Academics such as Ricki Tannen, writing in *Trickster* (2007), sometimes mention Mercurius, yet fail to follow its tracks deeply into Jung's primary texts. Concerning Hermes, a notable example would be Raphael Lopez Pedraza's *Hermes and his Children* (1977/2003). Indeed, it might be said that Hermes and the more generic 'trickster' in many ways have become paradigmatic of Jung and many of his followers. However, as we shall see in chapter 1, there is a problem in equating Hermes with the alchemical Mercurius. In a nutshell, the latter is a much more sophisticated figure that combines the ancient Egyptian Thoth with the Greek Hermes, as Hermes Trismegistus.

Furthermore, notable post-Jungians on astrology, such as Liz Greene and Karen Hamaker-Zondag, have also not engaged significantly with this theme. Their interests have gravitated more toward a synthesis of modern western astrology with analytical psychology rather than with precessional astrology, alchemy and the theme of Jung's 'life myth'. Another notable author, Richard Tarnas, performed a Herculean labour in *Cosmos and Psyche* (2007) by correlating the outer planets' angular relationships to historical data, based on a theoretical premise of 'archetypal astrology'. His critique of western culture, use of mythic themes and Renaissance-style spirit was both useful and informative. However, he too did not choose to apply his staggering knowledge and experience to the theme of Jung's life myth, let alone to a focus on Mercurius. He often intones that we are in a 'transitioning of the Ages' yet does not develop this theme. In contrast, the Jungian analyst Alice Howell shows great interest in the Aquarian Age, such as in her *The Heavens Declare* (1990/2006). The feminine Sophia as a divine immanence (Holy Ghost) was a key theme in Howell's personal narrative *The Dove in the Stone* (1988). However, her works do not engage intensely with a wide range of Jung's primary texts and are thin on alchemical references.

Jungians on Christianity would appear to have also neglected this figure. For instance, James Heisig's scholarly and rigorous *Imago Dei* (1998) does not mention this figure (apart from two appearances in the notes). Similarly, the theme is not covered in Michael Palmer's *Freud and Jung on Religion* (1997).

The spirit-matter theme and synchronicity also strongly relates to Mercurius. Post-Jungians on synchronicity such as Aziz (1990), Combs and Holland (1994), Peat (1988), Mansfield (2001), Main (2004), Sparks (2007) and Cambray (2009), however, have not chosen to explore this theme in any detail. Of these, Sparks gives most coverage, especially in relation to the Jung–Pauli relationship.

Jung's depiction of Mercurius also places it, arguably, as quintessential shaman within the context of a disenchanted and ailing Christianity. Indeed, the idea of Mercurius as culture-specific shaman for the west can be argued for, based on renditions from specialists in this area such as Mircea Eliade (1951) and, more recently, Halifax (1979), Hutton (1993) and Kottler, Carlson and Keeney (2004). However, post-Jungians on shamanism, such as Sandner and Wong and their colleagues (1997), Ryan (2002) and Smith (2007) have not explored this specific topic.

Jungian scholars tracing the historical and philosophical influences of analytical psychology, such as Clarke (1992) and Paul Bishop (2007a, b), fail to adequately explore such key areas as Hermeticism and astrology. A notable exception here is Wolfgang Giegerich (1999) whose discourse, in some ways, is imbued with the flavour of Hermeticism. Indeed, he even equates *The Logical Life* with Mercurius. However, in failing to engage with precessional astrology and the grail legend he falls short, in my opinion, of comprehensively locating this figure within Jung's life myth.

Apart from Jungian materials, further key directions pursued have included research into Hermeticism, alchemy, precessional astrology and the grail legend. Texts on these topics are introduced, as appropriate, in the forthcoming chapters.

The above literature overview, by no means exhaustive, hopefully captures the gist of my point: that the alchemical Mercurius, although found scattered in first-generation and post-Jungian literature in many contexts, has not been dealt with sufficiently. To reiterate: as far as I am aware (and apart from von Franz and Emma Jung's work) we do not see a single book, article or even chapter dedicated to this theme, despite the centrality of this figure in Jung's primary writings.

* * *

The structure of the book consists of three parts. Part I establishes an overarching theoretical orientation and historical context, under the broad Hermetic theme of the *Aurea Catena* (Golden Chain). I effectively identify 'mercurial themes', illustrate how these can be understood in specific historical and biographical contexts and thereby set up a basis for a more detailed enquiry related specifically to the life of Jung (Part II) and to his works (Part III).

Chapter 1 considers the origins of Hermeticism and its mythical founder, the 'faceless prophet' as Hermes Trismegistus. It explores the theory and practice of Hermeticism and touches on the tenuous relationship between Hermeticism and Christianity, with emphasis on the Renaissance. A range of 'mercurial themes' are then distilled out, as a means of establishing a foundational basis.

Chapter 2 focuses on the alchemical aspect of Hermeticism and traces the development of key alchemical ideas (biased toward the literal substance mercury) from antiquity through to Jung. Within this development, notable historical personalities such as Newton and Goethe (as notable 'links' of the *aurea catena*) are considered. This serves to deepen the context for Jung's specific interest in the alchemical Mercurius.

Chapter 3 is a case study of the sixteenth-century English Renaissance Magus John Dee. I view his life as an 'alchemical parable'; as Hermetic theory and practice played out on the stage of sixteenth-century Europe. In then comparing Dee with Jung, I propose a similar archetypal resonance.

Chapter 4 deals more explicitly with Jung and his alchemical project by tracing its genesis from childhood through to old age. I then assemble his 'alchemical myth' and his portrayal of Mercurius. After this, his views on precessional astrology are clarified. I then identify alchemy and precessional astrology as two of my three 'threads' in a life-myth construction.

Part II looks at four thematic (and roughly chronological) biographical moments of Jung's life: 1914 up to 1928, based on his 'confrontation with the unconscious' and its processing; the 1930s up to the early 1940s, portrayed as a 'warring of Christian and Pagan spirits'; his 1944 near-death visions as an alchemical transformation mystery; and on toward Merlinesque sagacity in old age.

Chapter 5 traces the development of key childhood memories through his 'confrontation with the unconscious' and into old age. I illustrate how a disparate numinosum experienced in childhood evolved in mid-life and then found its greatest level of integration in old age through his study of alchemy. The interrelationship of astrological and alchemical themes evident in such a development is also used as a preliminary corroboration of my claim that he believed his life-myth was integrally yoked to the dawning of a new Platonic month (an emphasis of chapter 5 is *The Red Book*).

Chapter 6 looks at Jung's (1936) fish–snake incident, at a time during which he was writing 'Wotan'. I interpret this as a synchronicity, as a political augur and as an image that captured, prospectively, a resurgent pagan spirit (serpent) on the European political stage that threatened to devour the Christian spirit (fish). I locate this event esoterically in terms of Jung's belief that a turbulent and chaotic end of the Aeon of the Fishes (Pisces) was imminent, and that the birth of a new Aeon (Aquarius) would follow. I argue that the association of serpent with Mercurius gives a sophisticated nuance to the effect that the warlike Wotanic spirit could be alchemically transformed. Jung's alleged anti-semitism, from this esoteric perspective, is also considered.

Chapter 7 considers Jung's (1944) near-death visions using alchemical amplifications. I build an argument to the effect that he may well have considered this experience to have been a profound alchemical transformation mystery (apotheosis) synchronistic with the dawn of a new astrological Aeon. I also identify 1944 as a pivotal year, after which a 'new Jung' more firmly correlated with his so-called No. 2 personality can be discerned.

In chapter 8 the relationship between Mercurius and Merlin is clarified. The 'thorny problem' of a Jung–Merlin affinity is investigated and a range of Merlinesque symmetries are identified. Based on such observations I make the claim that his life project embodied a neglected holistic worldview characterised by strong resonances to the grail legend and, more particularly, to the figure of Merlin. This constitutes my 'third thread' in a life-myth construction.

These perspectives are then used, in Part III, to inform a close textual study of key works from Jung's magnum opus. A major common theme concerns the idea of the alchemical coniunctio in light of the precessed equinox entering a new Platonic month.

Chapter 9 focuses on the Jung–Pauli quest for a big-picture model of a unified spiritual and physical universe (as coniunctio theme). Mercurius is identified as 'problematic fourth' in both the physics and religious quaternio models. Exposition of Pauli's 'confrontation with the unconscious' is used to add depth and context from which to view his self-acclaimed life-myth as the 'redemption of Merlin'.

Chapter 10 brings to light Jung's views on Christ, Antichrist and Mercurius across the centuries of the Aeon of Pisces, and in terms of a genesis of the self. Using this as a basis, I then assemble the view of Mercurius as 'transcendent function' for Christianity in crisis.

I go on to argue that *Mysterium Coniunctionis* (chapter 11) can be understood as embodying a new myth as a continuation of *Aion*, and in terms of a 'historical nexus' as the gradual ending of the Age of Pisces and the dawning of the Age of

Aquarius. Mercurius, featuring as *the* most prominent figure in this work, is shown as embodying a compensatory and complementary 'myth' relative to the 'Christian myth' and as a figure that 'stitches the opposites'; effectively as a *quintessential symbol* and *agency* capable of both healing and renewing an ailing Christianity.

In chapter 12 the grail legend is used, in combination with the preceding developments, to construct a life-myth. I assemble the idea of a meta-narrative in which the grail legend, an alchemical transformation mystery and the astrological precession of the equinoxes all converge at a momentous time in history synchronistic with Jung's life.

I then end with a brief critique, identification of further directions and a final conclusion.

Notes

1 Concerning clinical aspects and the fairytale 'Spirit in the Bottle', Hillman writes: 'Psychotherapy has made this tale a root parable' (Hillman (2010): 294).

2 I highlight the example of his 'hallucinations' (shared with an acquaintance) in Ravenna in 1933. Jung's description of this incident was not well received in the makings of *MDR*: 'There was one point, however, on which all those who meddled with Jung's text were united: that he must delete a long, rambling account of his two visits to Ravenna because they were factually incorrect. Jung could not be persuaded even by Cary, who told him that to include it would make him look 'crazy'. 'That settles it,' Jung shouted. 'The chapter stays in. I *want* the book to look crazy!' (Bair (2004): 613).

3 This might explain why the word 'Mercurius' only appears three times in *MDR*.

4 This word was jointly coined by Shamdasani and Mikkel Borch-Jacobsen (Shamdasani 2005: 4).

Part I

Aurea catena

> Mercurius, as 'quicksilver', as the *aqua permanens*, is a living and liquid concept. This is why 'The highest mystery of the whole Work is the Physical Dissolution into Mercury'.
>
> (Figulus, cited in Giegerich 1999: 137)

Chapter 1

Hermeticism

> ... rich initiatic symbolism, whose aim can best be described as *gnosis*, does in fact produce an invisible fraternity among those who have glimpsed the mysteries. In this sense a secret Fraternity does exist – and anyone can enter in who sees and seizes the point.
>
> (Churton 2005: 137)

In this statement we can discern three overarching features that are said to characterise Hermeticism: revelation, secrecy and initiation. For Jan Assman, the most important of these is revelation of a supra-mundane knowledge comparable to that in the Bible. Allied to such revelation is the need for secrecy as, unlike those in the Bible, such mysteries are considered only suitable for an elect and worthy few, as their initiates (Assman, foreword, in Ebeling 2007: ix–xii). Thus, the tradition of Hermeticism is coloured by the notion of an inspired lineage of sages imagined as an *aurea catena* (golden chain) originating with the legendary Hermes Trismegistus whose mysteries can be revealed to initiates by the sage himself, as a spiritual presence, in any given time.

Jung wrote of the *aurea catena* in terms of an *opus magnum* or *divinum*, with he himself taking up the thread from the likes of Goethe and Nietzsche. He considered Goethe to be 'in the grip of that process of archetypal transformation which has gone on through the centuries ... what was alive and active within him was a living substance, a suprapersonal process, the great dream of the *mundus archetypus*' (Jung 1963/1995: 232). In a letter dated 1944, we read:

> Nowadays, certainly, the number of hermetics has grown increasingly small. But it was never particularly large, because the *aurea catena* they write about does not run through schools and conscious tradition but through the unconscious. Hermeticism is not something you choose, it is a destiny, just as the *ecclesia spiritualis* is not an organization but an *electio*.
>
> (Jung 1973–75: 351)

This makes clear that Jung considered the *aurea catena* at a specific historical period to be a process refracted in a number of creative individuals in the grip of the unconscious (not restricted to a single individual). It is also clear he considered himself a member of such an *electio*, in contrast to his more open persona as an 'objective scientist of the psyche'. Consequently, the task of better understanding his esoteric identity requires an investigative style that largely brackets off such a scientific persona.

As a basis for such an investigation I begin with a largely non-Jungian enquiry as a means of establishing a broad context. More specifically, the four chapters in Part I respond to the following questions:

1 What do we understand by the term *Hermeticism* in terms of origins, theory, practice, historical influence? From this, can we discern 'mercurial themes' as a lens through which to better evaluate Jung's 'esoteric identity'?
2 What role does Mercurius play in the history of western alchemy and what specific qualities and themes does this figure constellate?
3 As a case study, are there useful symmetries between the English Renaissance Magus John Dee and Carl Jung that enhance an interpretation of 'esoteric Jung'?
4 What were Jung's alchemical and astrological 'myths'? Is it possible to discern a convergence of these myths pivoted around the figure of the alchemical Mercurius?

These questions are addressed in chapters 1–4, respectively. As will become apparent, the three most prominent figures that emerge are Hermes Trismegistus, John Dee and Carl Jung. From the perspective of precessional astrology, these personalities (together with their historical eras) can be viewed as significant 'links' in the *aurea catena*. Hermes Trismegistus anticipates the first (vertical) Fish of the Age of the Fishes (Pisces). John Dee's life coincides with the precessed equinox 'touching' the tail of the second Fish in this Aeon. Jung's life is then synchronous with it, reaching the head of the second Fish and touching the first 'waters' of the new Platonic month of Aquarius.[1] I now proceed, in this chapter, to address the first of the above questions.

* * *

As a basis on which to work toward unravelling 'esoteric Jung' I develop here a broad portrayal of Hermeticism, with an especial emphasis on the following: Hermes Trismegistus; Hermeticism's theory and practice; Hermeticism and Christianity; and the Renaissance.

Hermes Trismegistus

> At first glance the contours of Hermes Trismegistus seem sharp, but on closer inspection they dissolve. Was he a god, like Hermes and Thoth? Many viewed him as such, but for others he was a prophet. It seems to have been in the

> nature, in the very essence of this fictive figure to be shimmering, iridescent, without form, for many ancient writers were unclear regarding his identity.
>
> (Ebeling 2007: 7)

Hermes Trismegistus, according to the German scholar Florian Ebeling, was a 'fruitful fiction' born from two diverse cultures; an amalgam of the Egyptian Thoth and the Greek Hermes. Thus, according to one ancient source, the ibis-headed Thoth as a Moon god was identified with the 'first Hermes' who inscribed sacred hieroglyphic writings. The 'second Hermes', identified as Greek, is said to have transferred the sacred writings to books after the Flood (Copenhaver 1992/2000: xiv–xvi). Antoine Faivre, who includes Arabic–Islamicist conceptions, offers a third 'Idris/Hermes' as the teacher of alchemy (Faivre 1995: 20). Such a threefold depiction affords a chronological perspective to Hermes' 'thrice-great' epithet. This epithet, however, more usually refers to him as the greatest philosopher, the greatest priest and the greatest king; possibly alluding to an earlier Egyptian custom (Ebeling 2007: 62).[2] Other instances in which the 'thrice-great' epithet applies regard his ubiquity within the three worlds, as subterranean, earthly and celestial; the three-sided stones where three roads meet; his three-pronged golden wand, and so on (Faivre 1995: 80).

The synthesis of Hermes Trismegistus from Egyptian and Greek culture saw him, in the first few centuries CE, also breaking the mould of his familiar mythological forms. In Garth Fowden's words:

> The new syncretistic Hermes as a cosmic power, creator of heaven and earth and almighty world-ruler . . . Presiding over fate and justice, he is also lord of the night, and of death and its mysterious aftermath . . . He knows 'all that is hidden under the heavenly vault, and beneath the earth', and is accordingly much revered as a sender of oracles.
>
> (Fowden, cited in Linden 2003: 9–10)

According to Faivre, there are also numerous examples of 'shifting or transition between the figure of the sage Trismegistus, who is a mortal, and the god of Olympus' (Faivre 1995: 16–17). His role in the *Corpus Hermeticum*, for example, shifts from that of god, to sage, to disciple of the *Nous* or Divine Intellect. As Faivre further points out: 'according to the Arab tradition, his life is simultaneously physical and transtemporal, after the example of Elijah's, and even in his body he manifests a state of eternity' (ibid.: 20). Another perspective highlights mortal beginnings and the subsequent transmutation of the human sage Thoth into a god, by means of his wisdom (Freke and Gandy 1999: xiii). Either way, legend has it that this god took on human form, functioning variously as prophet, sage and teacher. Thus, as emissary from the divine, he is said to introduce humanity not only to theology and the arcane arts but also to the more secular disciplines of language, writing, music, medicine, astronomy and architecture. The particular nature of this knowledge has also been described in holistic terms as 'a means of attaining to a knowledge that may be Gnostic, eclectic, or transdisciplinary – or all of these at once' (Faivre 1995: 11).

Concerning the transcription of such revelatory knowledge, the original number of these sacred texts was said to be 'twenty thousand' and, elsewhere, 'thirty-six thousand and fifty-five'. The surviving texts – considerably fewer – consist in a few works collectively known as 'the Hermetica'. These form the basis of the Hermetic tradition, which includes not only a revelatory theology, as found in the *Corpus Hermeticum*, but also more utilitarian subjects such as astrology, alchemy, talismans and magic (Copenhaver 2000: xvi).

As Ebeling points out, the mystique of the Hermetic texts derives from the notion of them as being divinely inspired and originating from an ancient Egyptian past, earlier even than the biblical prophets (Ebeling 2007: 8). However, revised dating of such seminal works as the *Corpus Hermeticum* has largely collapsed such assumptions. Specifically, in 1614, Isaac Casaubon provided a convincing case that the *Corpus Hermeticum* was more likely to have been compiled between the first and third centuries CE, in the cosmopolitan city of Alexandria (ibid.: 95). Indeed, Casaubon's demystification is generally considered to have been a significant catalyst in the rapid decline of Renaissance Hermeticism. Based on such observations, scholars such as Ebeling are of the opinion that the literary origins of the writings ascribed to Hermes Trismegistus are rather 'the product of the syncretic, Hellenistic philosophy of nature, which itself was a conglomeration of Aristotelian, Platonic, Stoic and Pythagorean doctrines, interspersed with motifs from Egyptian mythology and themes of Jewish and Iranian origin' (ibid.: 9).

Others emphasise that the Egyptian hieroglyphs were only translated a couple of centuries after Casaubon's critique. Timothy Freke and Peter Gandy, for example, consider these hieroglyphic writings, over 5,000 years old, as 'identical to those expounded in the Hermetica' (Freke and Gandy 1999: xxvii). In light of this they consider the *Corpus Hermeticum* to be a second-century reworking of ancient Egyptian wisdom to accommodate a contemporary Greek-speaking readership. In such debates a key issue at stake, at least for some, is the contention that they are a cultural construction (more human-centric) as opposed to an age-old divinely inspired revelation, the *prisca theologia*. In the words of Assman, 'greater age meant higher truth. The best knowledge was the oldest knowledge. As a result, Hermetic knowledge came to be viewed as rescued primeval knowledge, the wisdom of Adam, that had in some way survived the Flood' (Assman, foreword, in Ebeling 2007: ix).

Hermeticism: theory and practice

The *Hermetica* consists of two distinct forms as theory and practice, underpinned by the notion of an original divine revelation transmitted by Hermes Trismegistus to a circle of adepts. The theory aspect includes a religious doctrine in which man's place and purpose is revealed in relation to world, cosmos and the divine. The practical aspect, on the other hand, consists of a variety of technical methods said to facilitate such a realisation and to also catalyse man's spiritual destiny. These include theurgy, astrology, alchemy, magic and talismans. As such, Hermeticism is considered predominantly in doctrinal terms as a spiritual way rather than a philosophical worldview (see Salaman, Van Oyen and Wharton 1999/2004: 126).

However, in the purist sense, there are problems. For example, we can recall how the important *Corpus Hermeticum* was shown to date from the first to third centuries CE, instead of a primeval past. A further difficulty concerns inconsistencies in this text:

> The *Corpus* . . . presents two incompatible doctrines that entail two precisely opposed attitudes. In one . . . the world is penetrated by divinity, therefore beautiful and good. In the other the world is essentially evil, not the work of God' and further that these represent 'notions so diverse . . . [they] cannot lead to the same mode of action but must result in two antagonistic moralities.
>
> (Festugiere, cited in Copenhaver 2000: lv)

Such a theological–philosophical inconsistency runs through much of the *Hermetica*, leading scholars to divide the texts into monist–optimistic and dualist–pessimistic categories (Ebeling 2007: 32). Another 'third position' has also been posed. Brian Copenhaver, citing Fowden, restores a level of conceptual integrity by suggesting that specific philosophical biases would suit different stages of the initiate's spiritual progress:

> a positive view of the cosmos as good and worth understanding would suit an earlier stage of the initiate's labours . . . when the body's needs were still great, while a negative treatment of the world as evil and unworthy of thought might befit a farther station in the spirit's journey . . . which entailed liberation from the body.
>
> (ibid.: xxxix)

A further difficulty, in Copenhaver's opinion, includes a disjunct in the *Hermetica* between theory and some of the praxis, such as the role of magic (ibid.: xxxvii). Indeed, such problems undermine the notion of a single coherent and unambiguous doctrine, leading commentators such as Heinrich Dorrie (cited in Ebeling 2007: 11) to describe Hermeticism as a 'thing without corners and edges'.

However, despite such problems, a definite 'orienting myth' and technical methods can be discerned. In light of this, and in the context of this limited study, it is deemed sufficient to progress by distilling out key 'mercurial themes' of the theory and practice that characterises the *Hermetica*.

Concerning theory, an overarching theology is to be found in the *Oracles* in which the divine is composed of three parts: a first paternal transcendent Intellect, a second world-creating Demiurgic Intellect and a third animating female Power as the World Soul. In this conception, the human soul's redemption lies in escaping the 'foul tomb' of matter and ascending to the deity (Copenhaver 2000: xxv).

In this sense, a Hermetic notion is that all of existence can be considered as thoughts in the 'Big Mind' of God, resulting in a monist-style theology: 'Because he unites every thing, his nature is paradoxical. He is the creator who creates himself. He is always hidden from us, yet he is also the world around us. He has no particular name, because all names refer to him' (Freke and Gandy 1999: 17; see also xxxi).

The material cosmos, as described in the *Corpus Hermeticum*, is also animated with a continual influx of energy by the divine Life-Force. This is described, in cosmogonic terms, as an erotic divine coupling. The cosmos is thus considered living and dynamic, with every being composed of both matter and *Nous* in a continual play of growth, dissolution and rebirth (Salaman, Van Oyen and Wharton 1999/2004: 16–17, 53, 59). Tobias Churton develops this conception by describing the Hermeticist deity as a 'Great Conjuror' in a situation in which 'the cosmos is revealed as a continual miracle' and 'there is no end; it is an eternal life – the life of the aeons – which springs from the source of "the All" ' (Churton 2005: 7; 155).

Intrinsic to such a 'Hermetic myth' is the notion of apocalypse, revelation and the return of a golden age inaugurated by a divine child. According to the myth this can only be effected by access to the original lost primeval knowledge captured in the Hermetic texts, or if the ancient knowledge was again revealed, such as through theurgy (Ebeling 2007: 46; Copenhaver 2000: xxx).

The *Hermetica* also makes clear that the human soul, in particular, is unique and holds a special place in creation in that it is composed of both earthly and divine parts. Most importantly, the human soul has the potential of awaking to its divine nature and thus coming to know God, who appears as a 'friend' on the spiritual path (Freke and Gandy 1999: 70, 72–33, 106). Such a realisation of *Gnosis* can lead to a sudden awakening, conceived as a second birth (Salaman, Van Oyen and Wharton 1999/2004: 15).

Furthermore, the earthly part of human nature consists of the four material elements (earth, water, air and fire) and is inscribed by celestial revolutions. This part, subject to the compulsion of an astrologically pre-ordained fate, is susceptible to corruption, illness and death. Indeed, it is only the heavenly part of the soul that can find salvation and release by knowing God and entering, ultimately, a purely spiritual existence.

Ultimately, in this conception, the pious have the possibility of returning to their divine origin, whereas the unawakened and less pious are reborn, after death, into another body. With this the adept is also reminded, in texts such as the *Asclepius*, of the divine in nature, knowledge of which leads to theology and knowing God. In this model the human is reminded of a dual destiny. The earthly side of his/her nature, expressed as reverence and knowledge of body and world, must be developed alongside a spiritual side on a path leading to a knowledge of both God and nature. Indeed, such a reverence for material reality extends to a valuation and encouragement of the sexual act as reflection of the divine creation. In essence we could say that such tenets of Hermeticism integrate cosmos, human and God in a holistic and meaningful model (Freke and Gandy 1999: 72–3; Ebeling 2007: 14–16).

A key theme here is the possibility of human salvation and restitution to a state of grace, before the Fall. Humanity can thus choose between the path of the body or the path of the spirit. A progression toward spirit implies greater closeness to God and, eventually, to a final state of redemption (Faivre 1995: 59–60):

> If he recognizes that he owes his essence, his spiritual nature, to his transcendent creator, he can shed his physical drives. He can leave the corporeal behind, ascend through the celestial harmonies and return the lower parts of his soul to the seven planetary spheres and enter the eighth, where he will sing the praises of God and finally merge with God himself. It is 'the blessed goal for those who have attained enlightenment to become divine'.
>
> (Ebeling 2007: 13)

An example of such a salvation is the 'Discourse on the Eighth and Ninth', a Hermetic Codex discovered at *Nag Hammadi* in 1945. The text describes the final steps of the initiate as recognising an authenticity of being in relation to God, and of thus attaining godhood (Copenhaver 2000: xxxix; see also chapter 7). Elsewhere we read that such a state of godhood, if achieved in life, requires the adept in a 'missionary call' to extol such a vision of God in an 'imperishable book' (Ebeling 2007: 17).

In Book 4 of the *Corpus Hermeticum*, Hermes informs his son Tat of a further way of achieving godhood. He explains that God sent down a bowl filled with *Nous* and intended it as a prize for worthy souls. The worthy are instructed to plunge into it, and thus to be reborn in spirit and raised up to God. The bowl itself is said to be of God.[3]

Another method of experiencing divinity is then suggested in Book 11. Here the adept is instructed to overcome body and time, to grow immeasurably in size and thereby to understand eternity and God. A similar theme appears in *The Definitions of Hermes Trismegistus to Asclepius.* Here initiates are encouraged to experience their threefold nature – intelligible, animated and material – which allows for an expansive mobility – a cosmic ubiquity – in the spheres of heaven, sea and earth (Salaman, Van Oyen and Wharton 1999/2004: 30, 39, 71, 128–9).[4]

Such methods veer toward the practical side of the *Hermetica* dependent on a contemplation, knowledge and manipulation of the natural world, viewed as a manifestation of the divine: 'The universe, conceived as a system of analogical and dynamic relationships, like a text to be read, decoded' (Faivre 1995: 57). Thus the observation of birds in flight, a study of animal entrails or listening to the whisperings of the sacred oak are akin to reading the mind of God, and act as methods of divining the past, present and future and thereby of comprehending a mysterious and deep truth only expressible in enigmatic symbols (Salaman, Van Oyen and Wharton 1999/2004: 79; Ebeling 2007: 140).

A particularly important divination method in which nature is 'decoded like a text' is astrology. This is viewed as a technology, according to the *Hermetica*, that affords a heightened knowledge of self and God. Accordingly, one's bodily nature is said to be determined by the periodic movements of celestial bodies: the 'as above, so below' of the *Tabula Smaragdina*. One's spiritual nature, however, affords the possibility of overcoming such a celestially determined fate, enshrined as the 'Hermetic way' (Ebeling 2007: 21–3).

Elaborating this astrological worldview; Book 16 of the *Corpus Hermeticum* details a cosmology based on a heliocentric universe, surrounded by eight spheres: one earthly and six planetary spheres, and an outermost eighth orb as the fixed stars. A ninth sphere is described as the realm of the divine.[5] In this model the soul descends from a heavenly realm and down through the planetary spheres into a womb, in a process through which it 'clothes itself' with attributes and a fate. The planets are conceived of as animated, spiritual powers and the Sun, as God's physical correlate, as a conduit for divine creative energy (Salaman, Van Oyen and Wharton 1999/2004: 96–7). Within this cosmology the sage Hermes Trismegistus, after his death, is said to have ascended to the heavens, where he became the planet Mercury (Ebeling 2007: 27).

A related practical aspect of the *Hermetica* is theurgy. This refers to the ritual invocation and communication with God or a spiritual power via a human medium or a statue (Copenhaver 2000: xxv). For example, planetary powers can be 'drawn down' and harnessed for magical purposes such as love charms, healing, talismans: 'the Magical Papyri promised . . . a way to manipulate the divine and natural worlds for more or less concrete and immediate purposes' (ibid.: xxxvi). The temptation here is to view the technical *Hermetica* as being in the service of ego-oriented self-interest. We are reminded though that both theory and practice are interrelated and lead toward the singular goal of salvation and knowledge of God (ibid.: xxxvii). Alchemy, in particular, is a good example of a synergy between the theoretical and practical aspects of the *Hermetica* (see chapter 2).

Hermeticism and Christianity[6]

Ebeling notes that many understood Hermeticism in terms of 'a primeval knowledge that bore all that followed in embryonic form, a divine revelation imparted even to pagans and one that was nearly identical to Christianity, an all-embracing doctrine of reconciliation' (Ebeling 2007: 2). Furthermore, although nowhere included in the Bible, Hermes Trismegistus (styled as an Old Testament prophet) is said to have prophesied the coming of Christ and the birth of a new religion (ibid.: 38, 63). Indeed, in early Christianity Hermes-logos was even compared to Christus-logos. As the Good Shepherd, Hermes was often depicted as carrying a ram or ewe. Like Christ, he also functioned as a psychopomp, as a guide for the souls of the dead.

Faivre further points out that such attributes led to later representations of Hermes as an *angelus bonus* (good angel), sometimes conflated in Christian iconography with Archangel Michael or Gabriel. The name Trismegistus was also interpreted by sympathetic Christian theologians in terms of the sage's reverence for a Trinitarian yet monotheistic God. The appearance of numerous pieties in the *Hermetica* afforded yet further acceptance by many Christian theologians of the 'Egyptian Hermes' and his teachings. However, despite this benevolent reception, an alternative view of considerable impact condemned him as a devil (Faivre 1995: 20–2; Copenhaver 2000: xlii).

An example of a sympathetic reception was that of Lactantius, a theologian of the late third and early fourth centuries and advisor to Constantine I, the first Christian Roman Emperor: 'For Lactantius, Hermeticism and Christianity do not contradict each other . . . the transcendence and unknowability of God and his uniqueness as creator of all being are taught by both' (Ebeling 2007: 41). An influential counter-opinion can then be found in Augustine the Bishop of Hippo (late fourth to early fifth century CE), who chose rather to see Hermeticism as pagan idolatry and theurgic magic (ibid.: 42). Thus, according to Ebeling, the fifth-century Christian 'could understand Hermes as a prophet of Christ and his concept of God as an overture to Christianity; or, with Augustine, he could view the demonology of Hermeticism as superstition and idolatory' (ibid.: 43).

In this vein an interesting development, fertile for the integration of Christian and Hermetic doctrines, was catalysed in the late twelfth century by Joachim of Fiore and his idea of God's successive revelations to humankind as Father, Son and Holy Ghost. The 'age of the Holy Ghost' was considered the final revelation, equated with a golden age of divine immanence amongst humankind. As Churton points out, such a notion played a significant role in apocalyptic expectation not only in the thirteenth century, but also in the sixteenth century and beyond (Churton 2005: 102). Being 'filled with the Holy Ghost' and being healed or prophesying has, of course, resonances with Hermeticist theurgy.

Notably, Hermeticism as 'archetype of a third position between Christianity and paganism' is said to have had its 'finest hour' in the Renaissance and to have 'shaped the intellectual history of the early modern period into the seventeenth century' (Ebeling 2007: 59). In this era the 'Egyptian Hermes' was considered to have pre-dated Moses, and thus to have been the original prophet and founding father of the Judaeo-Christian religion (Salaman, Van Oyen and Wharton 1999/2004: 102; Churton 2005: 60).

By the sixteenth century evangelists such as Giordano Bruno were espousing the dawning of a New Age in which the 'Egyptian' religion of Hermes Trismegistus was 'now poised to become the unifying religion in which Jews, all denominations of Christians, Platonic humanists, and even Muslims could meet and resolve their differences'[7] (Freke and Gandy 1999: xxiv). In Johannes Andreae's *Chymical Wedding*, for example, we see the equating of Greek pagan deities with Christian figures: 'Hermes = S. John the Baptist; Pegasus = the dove of the Holy Spirit' (Churton 2005: 137).

This same century saw the likes of Hermeticist John Dee active in a project to reunite the split Protestant–Catholic Church and prophesying an astrologically pre-ordained New Age (see chapter 3).[8] Indeed, it has been noted by various authors that 'wherever the Hermetica was studied, religious toleration and cosmic understanding grew' (Churton 2005: 60–1). Furthermore, Hermeticism in the Renaissance might be said to have inspired a grand holistic vision in which areas such as science, art, religion and literature were studied as parts of a united whole.

Unfortunately, the dream was to end. Ebeling describes the seventeenth century as a '*saeculum horribile*' for Hermeticism, catalysed by Casaubon's critical analysis of the *Corpus Hermeticum* in 1614. His analysis questioned both its authorship and its ancient origins. Scholarship of the day also swung from sympathy with an 'ontology of the hidden and its semiotics of symbolism' in an epistemological reorientation toward surface and scientific rationality. Before long, the *Hermetica* as a whole fell irrevocably out of fashion (Ebeling 2007: 95, 114–5).

> Hermeticism, with its hermeneutic, remained committed to a traditional belief in authority. Its adherents held that the doctrinal content of the authoritative texts of the *Ars Hermetica* could never be falsified but only verified – which is the opposite of a fundamental postulate of the philosophy of science.
>
> (Ebeling 2007: 109)

In the new zeitgeist of what was to become modern science, with its ethos of hard-won ontological truth (as opposed to backward affirmation of revelation), nature lost both its mystique and its dignity: 'without necessary recourse to the Bible, the Book of Nature was read according to its own laws, lending encouragement to the secularization of the sciences. The two worlds were uncoupled: religion and science were no longer united' (ibid.: 107). Consequently, the following centuries would see the dominance of an Aristotelian-oriented scientific epistemology.

Jung and Hermeticism

Faivre identifies Jung as one of three major figures to have transposed Hermeticism into the twentieth century (Faivre 1995: 63).[9] Roderick Main has, to an extent, clarified this in his questioning of whether Jung's primary identity should be viewed as that of psychotherapist or esotericist (Main 2010). Such orientations form a basis and context for the present research that seeks to bring Jung's esoteric identity more fully to light.

For the purposes of this research I narrow the definition of 'esotericist' by restricting it to key 'mercurial themes' distilled out in this chapter. For the practical side of Hermeticism this includes alchemy, astrology, theurgy, magic and talismans. The theoretical side includes revelation, initiation, secrecy, apotheosis, apocalypse, a golden age, a holistic worldview and a universal religious doctrine. These practical and theoretical facets of Hermeticism are used, loosely, as a frame of reference in the forthcoming chapters. Furthermore, although a focus will be on the alchemical, my choice is to retain a relatively 'wide net' that includes the broader Hermeticist perspective. Later, I also introduce the grail legend.

As a preliminary example I consider 'Jung and theurgy'. This feature is starkly apparent as his 'ghostly psychagogue' Philemon, with whom he 'walked up and down the garden', and whose image he so powerfully captured in *The Red Book* and in his Bollingen tower. The final chapter of *Liber Secundus* especially gives a sense of the enigmatic depth of his communication with this figure. In *The Red Book* he is represented as an *angelus bonus*, winged and with a golden halo.[10] His prior form, as Elijah, casts him as one with prophetic authority.

Seen as a whole, Jung's literary and imagistic depictions of Philemon (which further evolved throughout the course of his life) can be shown to strongly conflate with the legendary Hermes Trismegistus, especially during his alchemical period (see chapter 5).

Another example, to conclude this chapter, reveals perhaps a 'synchronistic' relation between Jung and Hermeticism. The story, to be found in Bair's recent biography, relates that shortly after Jung's death his daughter Marianne organised the making of a death mask for the purpose of a bust. Stoiber, the local specialist commissioned for the task, remarked that Jung's corpse was 'so impressive' and that 'on his forehead were three lines, "like a triton," a pattern similar to some she had seen in India on the faces of worshippers of Ra, the sun god' (Bair 2004: 623). Stoiber's unique ritualistic method, after taking a plaster cast, was to then infuse it with a combination of beeswax, resins and incense 'for symbolic reasons'. She chose beeswax because of its 'certain meaning, immortality for example' and the bee as 'a symbol of the pharaoh'. For the cast, although not knowing much about Jung, she selected 'brown with lots of red', sensing that 'he was a very earthy man besides his spirituality and he had a good relationship to stone' (ibid.: 623–4).

The description is evocative of an ancient Egyptian funerary rite. In particular, the triton on Jung's forehead might be interpreted as his being touched by the three-pronged golden wand of the thrice-great 'Egyptian Hermes', as the 'lord of the night' and 'sender of oracles' whose wand can bestow both life and death.[11]

Notes

1 See chapter 4 for a description of precessional astrology.

2 The epithet was apparently more generally applied to Hermes–Thoth from the second century CE (Ebeling 2007: 6).

3 Of related interest is that modern research has linked the Greek krater (bowl) to the word 'Graal', suggesting a basis for the chymical branch of the Grail legend (Faivre 1995: 19).

4 The first image in *The Red Book* portrays a cross-section of heaven, earth and sea.

5 The *Nag Hammadi* Codex 'Discourse on the Eighth and Ninth' refers to such a cosmology.

6 Hermes Trismegistus also had a powerful influence on non-Christians: 'Moslems and other non-Europeans of late antiquity and the early middle ages outdid their Western contemporaries in preserving and extending the Hermetic tradition' (Copenhaver 2000: xlv). The Arabic texts, however, emphasised his magical above his theological–philosophical attributes (Ebeling 2007: 48).

7 In 1600 he was ceremonially burnt alive by the Roman Catholic Church, having refused to recant after eight years of torture (Freke and Gandy 1999: xxiv).

8 Churton cites a further example: 'Tommaso Campanella had been incarcerated in a Naples dungeon. In 1598 he also had seen signs. His interpretation of the signs convinced him that a universal Hermetic-Christian Republic was imminent, and that he should assist things along by participating in a rebellion against the Spanish Hapsburgs' (Churton 2005: 102).

9 The other two being Martin Buber and Franz von Baader.

10 The front of his gown also includes a patterned sequence of thirteen squares. Hermes Trismegistus' associations with this number are found, for example, as the thirteen axioms in the *Tabula Smaragdina*.

11 An excerpt from *Aion*: 'Hermes is equipped with the golden wand. With it he "drops sleep on the eyes of the dead and wakes up the sleepers"' (Jung 1951a: 208).

Chapter 2

Alchemy

A good example of how both theory and practice in Hermeticism dovetail toward the goal of spiritual transformation is that of alchemy.[1] For instance, the bowl filled with *nous*, as already mentioned, takes centre stage in the alchemical imagination as early, at least, as Zosimos in about the third century CE, and possibly even earlier than 200 BCE (Ebeling 2007: 11, 26; Copenhaver 1992/2000: xxxiv). However, as Stanton Linden has pointed out, the cornerstone of western alchemy is not the *Corpus Hermeticum* but the *Tabula Smaragdina* (Emerald Tablet), a book also characterised by elusive and ancient origins, purportedly discovered by Alexander the Great in Hermes' tomb or, in an alternative origin tale, being taken from the dead Hermes in a cave after the Flood (Linden 2003: 11).

Despite the supposed primeval origins of the *Tabula Smaragdina*, we do not find ancient alchemical texts characterised by such a mystique. Thus, according to Linden, the inclusion of a mysterious Hermetic dimension is clearly visible only in the third or fourth century CE as appearing, for example, in the works of the alchemist Zosimos (ibid.: 9).[2] More broadly though, the heritage of western alchemical texts might be summarised as follows:

> . . . from the legendary Hermes Trismegistus, contemporary of Moses, down to those of the present and recent past; the originating cultures from which these treatises derived would have included the ancient Graeco-Egyptian era (roughly the first seven centuries AD), the Islamic period expanding from the mid-seventh to the thirteenth century, followed by the Latin culture of medieval and Renaissance Europe.
>
> (Linden 2003: 3)

Using this as a basic historical and cultural guide, I now chronicle a few highlights of western alchemy centred predominantly on the broad range of meanings constellated around the substance mercury. Here we should remember that just as Hermes Trismegistus is said to have become a planetary power, so his earthly correlate finds expression in the metallic mercury as well as in the whole process of alchemical transformation.

We should also remember that Hermes Trismegistus is generally considered not only the founding father of alchemy but also a presence, guide and psychopomp in the work of the pious alchemist. Indeed, the alchemical treatises in which he appears (often as a wise old sage) might be used as an indication of the author's inclusion of an overtly spiritual dimension.[3] He is often shown together with a younger initiate (the adept) in a *senex-puer* constellation, or together with the alchemist and his *soror mystica*.[4]

The spiritual dimension in alchemy, in the Hermeticist sense, is also often evident in the use of religious imagery and motifs. Thus, by the sixteenth and seventeenth centuries, a number of alchemical treatises displayed a rich variety of religious symbolism.

> The successive stages in the preparation of the philosopher's stone are likened to Christ's nativity, crucifixion, and resurrection, and, by a curious extension of the analogy, the two major events in the world's past and future, the Creation and the Last Judgement, are often described in terms of alchemical process. Following this identification of the philosopher's stone with Christ, the alchemical imagination quickly discovered many other ingenious links between biblical themes, characters, and events and the search for the alchemical opus.
>
> (Linden 2003: 23)

Amidst the various contemporary perspectives on alchemy, it is the Hermeticist viewpoint that I choose to emphasise. This serves the purpose of better understanding the role of alchemy for Jung as a basis for constructing a life myth. Subsequently, it is this consideration that has largely informed the choices of material for inclusion.

Specific alchemical notions I now develop include: primal substance, world soul, a transformation mystery, a mystical wedding, transmutation of base metals and the philosopher's stone. The roughly chronological development of ideas is also placed, more or less, into thematic schema as follows: transformation of the dragon; Red Man and White Wife; Newton – star regulus; Goethe – *urpflanze*; the return of Hermes.

The development can also be read in relation to Jung's second essay of 'The Spirit Mercurius'. A criticism of this essay is that the material, arranged thematically, takes little account of chronology and is also uprooted from its various socio-cultural, religious, scientific, esoteric, etc. contexts. What follows thus motions, in a limited way, toward a redress of such shortcomings. In the spirit of James Hillman and Edward Whitmont, I have also tried to imbue the material with a stronger sense dimension, by including reference to ontological properties of the substance mercury. This compensates for such neglect in Jung's treatment of alchemy (perhaps due to his supposed 'inferior sensation function').

Transformation of the dragon

Classical Greek philosophy is said to have shaped much of the theoretical side of western alchemy. A key contribution, for example, is the theoretical reduction of the physical world to four elements – earth, water, air and fire – and the notion of their mutual interconvertibility, as derived from Empedocles, Plato and Aristotle.[5] Furthermore, from the Greek philosophers, 'alchemy derived its *hylozoistic* conception of the universe, the idea that external nature is alive and sentient. It also relied on a close and harmonious relationship between macrocosm and microcosm' (Linden 2003: 7–8; also 29).

It is within such a rudimentary theoretical context (and within the broader Hermetic worldview) that we can consider a basic chemical transformation, as described by Cathy Cobb and Harold Goldwhite, evident in those times.

> Heating cinnabar drove something off and left a puddle of silvery metal behind. If this was not sufficient proof for transmutation, then they only had to show that heated again, the puddle reformed as a red solid. It was not the return of cinnabar, as they thought – it was an oxide of mercury that also happened to be red.
>
> (Cobb and Goldwhite 1995: 30)

Such a spectacle no doubt served as a magnet for a plethora of projections: a mysterious substance hidden in a soft reddish rock; an elusive and mirror-like quicksilver; a return of the quicksilver to its original solid form yet with a crystalline luminosity. In short, the spectacle had the aura of a transformation mystery. Indeed, this basic chemical process exemplifies a number of alchemical notions derived from classical Greek philosophy and key texts such as the *Tabula Smaragdina*, as I now briefly illustrate.

The 'watery metal' known as quicksilver (mercury) is found in high concentrations in a soft, red-coloured ore known as cinnabar (blood of the dragon). By crushing and heating this ore, a metallic vapour 'escapes'. If this vapour is then contained and distilled, it yields the familiar quicksilver. If we then re-heat this quicksilver, it solidifies into a pinkish crystal with a resemblance to the original cinnabar ore. In addition, shaken quicksilver illuminates in the dark.

Note that in these transformations there are *phase changes*. The substance undergoes conversions from solid to gas to fluid and back to solid in its progression from cinnabar to metallic vapour to quicksilver to luminosity to crystal. It also traverses the four traditional elements of Greek philosophy, earth–air–water–fire, and thereby hints at what might have inspired such notions as the 'interconvertibility of the elements'. Furthermore, in each of these forms, one can also discern a level of *paradox*. The soft-stone as cinnabar is the alchemist's 'stone that is no stone'. The metallic vapour is *heavy yet light*, as the alchemist's 'stone uplifted by the wind'. The quicksilver is the 'water that is no water' that can be agitated into forming a luminescence as 'cold yet hot'.[6]

The soft and reddish cinnabar ore that 'bleeds' when it is 'hit' also affords an appropriate projective hook for such hylozoistic notions as the earth as a living being (World Soul, Earth Dragon, etc.) that undergoes an alchemical transformation.[7] Thus the initial stone is crushed (dismembered) and heated (tortured). An 'indwelling being' is sublimated out of the rock as 'vaporous spirit' and re-formed as distillate in the form of a mysterious, volatile, shining metallic liquid.[8] Re-heating this quicksilver then produces a pink crystal, with a luminosity. In effect, there has been a journey of a 'chthonic spirit' being released from the earth, reconstituted in a purified form and then returning to earth as luminous 'living rock' reminiscent of the alchemical *lumen novum*. This journey corresponds to the alchemical process as a torturous mystical rite for the 'living substance' reflective, perhaps, of a similar psycho-spiritual process in the alchemist and his *soror mystica*. It also adds an insight into the notion already mentioned of alchemy assisting nature toward spiritualisation. Here we see how a basic chemical operation may have inspired a convergence of Hermetic theory and practice.

* * *

However, not all alchemical ideas are so easily mapped to such visible displays. For example, an axiom in the *Tabula Smaragdina* concerns the ubiquity in the natural world of a subtle mercurial spirit (as a unitary physical and spiritual presence). Greek philosophy then considered this 'mercurial spirit' in terms of an irreducible 'primal substance' characterised by the fire–earth–air–water quaternary. Plato elaborated by suggesting the four primal elements could change or *transmute* into each other. Aristotle added the notion of a teleological principle: that the universe was unfolding according to a purpose (Cobb and Goldwhite 1995: 24–5).

Such philosophical notions seeded a number of more florid alchemical beliefs: all metals could be reduced to a 'primal mercurial substance'; the primal substance could transmute such as from quicksilver to gold; this transmutation was dependent on a spiritual attitude (the piety of Hermeticism); the transformed substance as a spirit–matter amalgam possessed a number of magical properties (long life, health, etc.); the 'mercurial spirit' as world soul is evolving (accelerated by alchemical efforts) toward becoming the philosopher's stone (transformation of the dragon). Indeed, these more elusive theoretical concepts and practical goals would not only greatly inspire but also vex and disillusion alchemists in the forthcoming centuries.

Sulphur and mercury – red man and white wife

A complementary conception to the 'transformation mystery' of ascent and descent (vertical) described above is the idea of a 'mystical wedding' (horizontal) and the subsequent birth of an enigmatic being as the philosopher's stone. Such ideas are intrinsic to the *Tabula Smaragdina* and also find a theoretical basis in classical Greek philosophy.

Concerning Greek philosophy, I highlight Empedocles' four-element system animated by the unifying force of love and the separating force of hate. Later, Aristotle added to this by proposing that metals were formed by the combination of a moist, vaporous exhalation and a dry, smoky one (Cobb and Goldwhite 1995: 20–5). Here we see a philosophical basis for the alchemical sexualisation of substances, and an added dimension (sexual) concerning the transmutation of base metals. Related notions are found in the *Tabula Smaragdina* as the Sun and Moon conceiving a child that is then carried by the wind into the womb of the earth to gestate, to become the philosopher's stone.

This collection of ideas was further developed by a number of female alchemists. For example, in the first or second century CE, the alchemist Cleopatra[9] (purported to have known the secret of the philosopher's stone) observed 'the analogy between ... human birth and the formation of the philosopher's stone, or the death-resurrection motif, as applied to materials within the alchemical vas' (Linden 2003: 44).

During this time there was also optimism about the more ambitious goals of alchemy. Metals could be treated with a mercury amalgam to create the illusion of having created silver. In a similar way, 'gold' was created by treating an amalgam with sulphur. 'Magical powders' also seemed evidence of alchemical transmutation: 'when our first chemical forebears made a yellow or gold-coloured powder, they had no reason to believe that it was not gold, so it was reported as such. When assay techniques became better, they realized that the product was not gold' (Cobb and Goldwhite 1995: 30). Not surprisingly, these wondrous substances – mercury as liquid metal and sulphur as the stone that burns – became central to alchemy in Alexandria (ibid.: 36).

However, the following couple of centuries (approximately 100 CE to 330 CE) saw disappointments in literal transmutation and a consequent shift away from practical alchemy: 'the objective ... shifted from solid gold to a golden soul: Spiritual transmutation of the alchemist became the new goal' (Cobb and Goldwhite 1995: 39). This was followed by a more dramatic turn. In 330 CE, the Roman Emperor Constantine instated Christianity as the official religion, ushering in the violent banishment of alternative spiritual orientations such as alchemy and mystery cults (ibid.: 40). Western alchemy went largely underground for the next few centuries. During this period alchemy found greater prominence in Islamic countries. Thus, for example, by the late eighth or early ninth century CE, ideas such as gendered substances had been taken up by the Arabian scholar Jabir ibn Hayyan (Geber) and developed into the popular sulphur–mercury system.

> 'Sulphur' is identified with fire and possesses the qualities of hotness and dryness; 'Mercury,' identified with water, possesses coldness and moistness. These two 'principles,' which are not to be confused with common sulphur and mercury or quicksilver, interact in the form of subterranean exhalations or vapors (the former 'male,' the latter 'female'), and if the conjunction occurs under proper conditions – the degree of heat within the earth is especially important – metals are formed.
>
> (Linden 2003: 14)

Here we see a sexualisation in which sulphur and mercury conjoin to create the metals.[10] This enduring idea in alchemy was not only represented theoretically, but also took personified form in the *vas*: 'Red Man and White Wife are common designations for the opposing "principles" of sulphur and mercury that are conjoined in the chemical wedding to produce the philosopher's stone' (ibid.: 115, footnote 7). I also highlight here the ambiguous boundary in alchemy between literal substance (in the *vas*) and 'philosophical substance' as a metaphysical concept.[11]

In the eleventh century we then see Avicenna accepting Jabir's sulphur–mercury theory yet rejecting the notion of transmutation. He believed transmutation would only be possible if metals could be reduced into their constituent parts and reassembled (ibid.: 67). Such scepticism also became evident in England through such notables as Bartholomew the Englishman (1000–1200 CE), who believed transmutation was possible, just very hard to achieve (ibid.: 78).

It was within such a disillusioned climate that the discovery of acids, in the period 1000–1200 CE, gave the alchemists renewed hope. For example, a particular acid (*Aqua Regia*) proved to dissolve even the supposedly incorruptible gold (Cobb and Goldwhite 1995: 88). The possibility of transmutation due to the dissolution of metals into their seeming constituent parts thus reinvigorated the alchemical imagination, giving 'ideas to some Europeans . . . how, with the right ingredients and the right combination, one could cook up a fortune in a backroom vat. The stage was set for the European alchemist' (ibid.: 88).

Such renewed vitality was still evident some centuries later, as in the life and work of the irascible and impassioned Paracelsus (1493–1541). His wide-ranging interests included 'the making of the homunculus, the generation of metals, the doctrine of signatures, and the role of magic and astrology in his practice of the "Spagyrical Art" ' (Linden 2003: 151). He also modified Geber's sulphur–mercury theory to include a third element, becoming his popular sulphur–mercury–salt theory (ibid.: 151).

Concerning this theory we read: 'For Mercury is the Spirit, Sulphur the Soule, and Salt the Body' (Paracelsus, in Linden 2003: 154). Indeed, 'all things created by nature' are explained by Paracelsus as being composed of these three substances (ibid.: 165). Furthermore, we read that 'living Mercury is the Mother of all the seven Metalls . . . and as it contains all colours, which it manifests in the Fire, so also occultly it contains all Metalls in it selfe' (ibid.: 154). Mercury is also described as a non-reducible primal substance, key to the transformation of metals:

> . . . generation and renovation of Metalls is made thus: As a man may return into the womb of his Mother, i.e. into the earth, out of which hee was first made a man, and shall again bee raised at the last day: so also all Metalls may returne into living (mercury) againe, and become mercury, and by Fire bee regenerated and purified, if for the space of forty weeks they bee kept in a continuall heat, as an infant is in his Mothers wombe.
>
> (Paracelsus, cited in Linden 2003: 154)

Paracelsus thus eschews the idea of a transformation mystery involving a death and rebirth. I also emphasise that 'planetary colours' in the heated mercury resonate with the Hermetic notion of a mystical ascent through the planetary spheres.[12]

Moving to the seventeenth century, we then see a further refinement of the original sulphur–mercury system. In George Starkey's epistle to King Edward IV, we read:[13]

> ... he who understands these two *Sulphur's & Mercuries* aright, shall find that the one is the most pure red *Sulphur of Gold*, which is *Sulphur in manifesto*, and *Mercurius in occulto*, and that other is most pure white *Mercury*, which is indeed true *Quicksilver in manifesto*, and *Sulphur in occulto*, these are our two Principles.
>
> (Starkey, cited in Linden 2003: 215)

Here we see a more complex representation of 'opposites' reminiscent of the Chinese yin–yang.

However, in this same century even the acids, in the final analysis, had not helped to realise the dream of transmutation. Consequently, by the early 1600s, European alchemy had largely separated from chemistry. Whereas chemistry dealt with acids, medicines and salts, the word 'alchemist' became associated with gold-making swindlers (Cobb and Goldwhite 1995: 111). Of course, there were exceptions. Robert Boyle, described as the 'father of modern chemistry', still believed in transmutation: 'When he died he left Newton a sample of red earth that he believed would turn mercury into gold' (ibid.: 119).

Isaac Newton (1642–1727) – star regulus

In contrast to his secular education, as described by Betty Jo Teeter Dobbs, Newton grew up in a worldview influenced by natural philosophy in which 'alchemy was not mysterious and was no longer treated as closely guarded esoterica but as an honourable branch of natural philosophy which would someday reveal its secrets to rational and chemical investigations' (Dobbs 1992: 89).

Newton's scientific career was coloured by such a mix of both technical rigour and an immersion in the arcane: 'In fact most of his great powers were poured out upon church history, theology, "the chronology of ancient kingdoms", prophecy and alchemy' (Dobbs 1992: 6). His particular style of alchemy was 'rigorous and quantitative', yet he also 'took certain myths to be the bearers of alchemical secrets and on occasion allowed the story line of the myth to determine his experimental procedure' (ibid.: 111).

Such methods that combined precision and rigour with 'Renaissance Hermeticism' were an efficacious mix, resulting in such watershed works as his *Principia*. Critics' views concerning his theory of gravity, for instance, were that 'Newton's forces were very much like the sympathies and antipathies found in much of the occult literature of the Renaissance period' (Dobbs 1992: 211). His theory of seven primary colours in *Optics* received similar criticisms, as this number was steeped in Hermetic associations.

Such astonishing successes as his *Principia*, as proof of the efficacy of his methods, no doubt reinforced his faith in the notion of 'original wisdom', the *Prisca Sapientia*, lost and only partially recovered (Dobbs 1992: 90). His life purpose, from this perspective, might be viewed as being in service of the divine to recover the mostly lost wisdom of God.

Inspired by Comenius, the founder of pansophy, Newton also believed that an inner light within the human mind complemented the outer light. According to Comenius: 'When man opened his eyes to both, then he would see the ultimate truth of the universe' (Dobbs 1992: 60). Effectively what Comenius was seeking, through such illumination, was nothing less than a 'simplifying key, the ultimate reduction, which would unlock the complexities and allow the essences to shine through and be readily comprehensible' (ibid.: 61). Comenius' followers, including Newton, turned their gaze toward natural science, wherein they 'came to seek a universal chemical key to unravel the incomprehensible tangle of natural phenomena' (ibid.: 62).

Indeed, turning from the celestial heights to the alchemical *vas*, we can only ponder what Newton's 'inner light' might have revealed as he contemplated, in the twilight of old age, such marvels as the extraordinary transformations of mercury.

> Mercury appears ... sometimes in the form of a tasteless, pellucid white Earth, call'd Mercurius dulcis, or in that of a red opake volatile Earth, call'd Cinnabar; or in that of a red or white Precipitate ... and in distillation it turns into a Vapour, and being agitated in vacuo, it shines like Fire. And after all these Changes it returns again into its first form of Mercury.
>
> (Newton, *Opticks*, Query 30)

In this chemical spectacle a red and a white substance differentiate out from a single material (*separatio*) and then recombine (*coniunctio*) into the 'original' unified form. Viewed as a symbol and from the perspectives developed in this chapter, we see the combination of a transformation mystery with a mystical marriage.[14]

Not surprisingly, mercury was of great interest to Newton. During his so-called 'early alchemy' from 1668 to 1675, a primary concern was that of the 'mercury of the metals' (Dobbs 1992: 128). From this viewpoint any metal in its liquid form is 'mercury'.[15] The idea was that metals could be melted or dissolved down into their 'first mercurial matter' and their 'metallic seeds' could then be extracted. For example, gold seeds fed with quicksilver would grow into gold (the transmutation of mercury into gold).[16] In this way the natural conflict and imperfections of base metals are said to be resolved in their transmutation into the incorruptible gold.

However, the mercury in which Newton was primarily interested was different to the common one, or even melted metals. Rather, he was looking for the more elusive 'philosophick mercury', which would appear to derive from the common quicksilver by its being 'philosophically opened' (Dobbs 1992: 84, 145). As a highly sought-after substance it was said to be 'all things to all men', created by 'ordinary or extraordinary chemical means' (ibid.: 136). Physically, this 'pure liquor' was described as 'the "water that does not wet one's hands," or, simply "our mercury" ' (ibid.: 84). Newton even claimed to have achieved some success in preparing philosophical mercury, which he used for 'ye Regimen of ye work in common gold' (ibid.: 2). He claimed his 'activated mercury' could reduce all metals, including gold, which was 'notoriously difficult to dissolve' (ibid.: 184).

Such extraordinary chemical means to extract a 'philosophick mercury' from the common mercury was apparently made possible using the star regulus (Dobbs 1992: 152, 176).[17] Apart from its 'magical properties', this star had impressive visual appeal: 'the crystalline 'branches' may be arranged around a central point and so take on the appearance of a star. The star of antinomy fascinated the alchemists, and especially Newton' (ibid.: 146, 192). For him, it was a very special phenomenon: ' "signed" as it was with the star, it seemed ... to have the power to attract celestial virtues' (ibid.: 183).[18] However his main use, apart from philosophic mercury, would seem to have been to utilise the star's 'magnetick qualities' which, he believed, could be used to draw out the seeds of the metals (ibid.: 158).

However, the usefulness of such a 'philosophick mercury' was doubted by critical alchemists of the day. The alchemist Wilson reported that 'after many trials, we found it of no more virtue than the common water ... the more experiments we made, the more we were convinced that our mighty expectations were vainly founded' (Dobbs 1992: 84). Careful empirical methods and scrupulous documentation of procedures resulted in 'the accumulation of negative evidence that finally caused a significant decline in the popularity of the concept of transmutability' (ibid.: 46). Consequently during Newton's lifetime the dream of alchemy, at least in its literal form, once again eluded realisation.

Overall, his contribution has been considered in terms of a link between 'Renaissance Hermeticism and the rational chemistry and mechanics of the 18th century' (Dobbs 1992: xii). The ensuing enlightenment, which produced a 'century of genius' (ibid.: xi), shed the more esoteric worldviews as it moved into the so-called age of reason. From such a perspective it has been suggested that Newton was 'not the first of the age of reason ... he was the last of the magicians' (ibid.: 13).

The 1700s thus emerged with a new passion: to throw off tradition and embrace scientific progress, in what became known as the Enlightenment (Cobb and Goldwhite 1995: 128). Amazing scientific achievements, such as Newton's physics, catalysed a shift away from the arcane. For instance, a number of discoveries about gases landed a final death blow to the much-loved and stubbornly adhered-to theory of phlogiston (ibid.: 147). In such a zeitgeist of demystification, it is easier to comprehend how cherished notions of alchemy also became discredited. A plethora of scientific discoveries led to rapid advances in engineering and technology and the auguring in of the Industrial Revolution.

Wolfgang Goethe (1749–1832) – *Urpflanze*

During the Industrial Revolution, the 'age of the machine', the naturalist Wolfgang Goethe was born. As a German Romantic he was part of a movement that was 'in some ways a reaction to the Industrial Revolution and the Enlightenment with its steel-edged rational approach. The Romantic thinker was able to accept some truths not necessarily proved by rational or scientific examination' (Cobb and Goldwhite 1995: 186).

Goethe also grew up in an age in which alchemy, in discrete circles, was all the rage, as the shift from the Renaissance to modern science was still in its infancy. At the tender age of 19, whilst in convalescence from university, he embarked on intensive studies (and some practice) of alchemy that included a desire to create a panacea for himself. However, as recounted by Ronald Gray, all he admitted achieving was 'a fine powder in which he was quite unable to perceive any magical properties' (Gray 1952/2002: 4). In the following year, upon returning to university, he abandoned the practical side of alchemy, but retained an enduring and passionate interest in the subject.

Goethe's disillusionment with literal alchemy gave way to a more symbolic alchemy in which the natural world was conceived of as a *vas*. 'God in nature' as immanence of the divine took on alchemical meanings. The philosopher's stone, for instance, was considered by him in spiritual terms as a union with God, the *unio mystica* (Gray 1952/2002: 21). It also had its literal correlates in the natural world.

In this respect, Goethe recounts an epiphany upon reaching the summit of a mountain. Here, in a state of 'complete detachment' and at a 'point where earth and heaven meet', he came across a red granite rock. He described the rock as 'more than a rock, it [is] an experience, a symbol of chthonic splendour' (Gray 1952/2002: 138). Gray further recounts:

> Red symbolized for him that which was represented to the alchemists by the Philosopher's Stone. The reasons for his high esteem for granite are of a kindred nature: here again he felt himself awe-struck at the apparent union of opposites, the highest and the lowest, heaven and earth, the impulse toward the ground and the impulse toward the sky. It was a happy coincidence, and, as he felt, perhaps more than a coincidence, that granite was also red.
>
> (Gray 1952/2002: 139)

Goethe's granite as red stone amplifies his mountain epiphany in that 'red too was a symbol of majesty, a beginning and an end, a meeting place of heaven and earth, an object of awe and reverence, almost beyond time and space' (Gray 1952/2002: 138). Furthermore the three main constituents of granite as quartz, feldspar and mica (reminiscent of the Paracelsian sulphur–salt–mercury system), represented for him the triune nature of the Godhead of the Christian trinity; once again, indicating God's immanence in nature.

Interest in the philosopher's stone involved yet further adventure. His ambitious project was nothing less than to discover, through scientific study, the fundamental unity of nature. He was 'looking for analogies which would lead to some all-embracing law, not deducing separate laws for each sphere of operations' (Gray 1952/2002: 61).

He was particularly concerned with such a task in 1786, whilst immersed in botanical studies: 'by this time Goethe was already on the track of a complete theory which would explain the development of plants, and although many details were still not clear to him, he felt himself in possession of the basic ideas' (Gray 1952/2002: 62). One gets the impression he experienced something of a revelation.

> I am beginning to grow aware of the essential form with which, as it were, Nature always plays, and from which she produces her great variety. Had I the time in this brief span of life I am confident I could extend it to all the realms of Nature – the whole realm.
>
> (Goethe, cited in Gray 1952/2002: 63)

Concerning this, 'Goethe felt that he had stumbled upon a secret of the greatest possible importance', whose 'unravelling was to occupy him for the remaining half century of his life' (ibid.: 63).

In such a spirit of anticipation he travelled to Italy in search of an enigmatic plant that would confirm his botanical theories. At this time, he had a profound dream that provided further impetus for his optimism. In what he called his 'pheasant dream', he recounts being in a large boat which moored on an island lush with vegetation. On this island were a large number of pheasants, which impressed him greatly. He bought as many as he could afford from the local inhabitants, and loaded them onto his boat. Sailing back from the island, the pheasants formed on the periphery of his boat with their tail feathers splayed into a circular, or elliptical, formation. The dream had also morphed the pheasant tails into a brilliant display of peacock feathers as a shimmering iridescence (Gray 1952/2002: 65).

As Gray points out, the significance of this dream is deeply alchemical. 'The "peacock's feathers" were a widespread symbol in all alchemical literature, representing either the philosopher's stone itself, or the stage in the *Magnum Opus* immediately preceding it' (Gray 1952/2002: 65). The philosopher's stone, for Goethe, was also a 'secret of greatest importance'. In light of this, according to Gray, Goethe's dream was symbolic of a hope that in Italy he would discover the 'key to the universe'. An intrinsic aspect of this key was that in the microscopic detail would be found the nature of the Whole (ibid.: 66).

A year later and upon return from his field trip, Goethe's botanical work began to converge into his concept of the *urpflanze*: 'a primal plant, which was to represent in itself the whole nature of the vegetable kingdom' (Gray 1952/2002: 71). His confidence in this concept was overwhelming: 'nature herself will envy him his "model," with which he will be able to invent as it were an infinite number of plants, all based on the same law of development' (ibid.: 71). Indeed, 'the urpflanze was ... one manifestation of this omnipresent, immanent divinity. Goethe came across a "One and All" in botany, which fills him with wonder ... the urpflanze demonstrated the universality of the divine being, even in the smallest manifestations' (ibid.: 73).

However, according to Gray, Goethe is ambiguous concerning the *urpflanze*'s true nature. On the one hand, it would seem he considered such a plant a literal reality that he hoped to discover on a field trip. On the other, it represented for him something akin to a Platonic Idea (71). Once again, however, a tangible alchemical goal that seemed within grasp, in the literal sense, proved to be yet another illusion.

The return of Hermes

Dizzying scientific and technological progress in the nineteenth and twentieth centuries was paralleled by an increasing spiritual disenchantment. The Renaissance Hermeticist dream in which science, religion and art were considered part of a grand whole had now shattered.

Yet science itself would turn, in the twentieth century, from a predominantly reductionist–linear toward a unitary–organic worldview. Such a shift became evident especially in relativity theory, quantum theory and chaos and complexity theory. On the macro scale, Einstein's relativity theory favoured a unitary space–time universe. On the micro scale, quantum theory championed not only the interrelated universe but also a curious psyche–matter entanglement. Chaos and complexity theory allowed for a return of the 'as above, so below' adage by means of its self-similarity concept in which parts of a system are seen in relation to the whole.

Uncannily, such a return is also evident if we restrict our gaze to the substance mercury. The retired chemist Leonard Goldwater, for example, informs us that modern science has discovered that the metal mercury is found throughout the natural world (this is unique to mercury and arsenic); in the lithosphere, hydrosphere, biosphere, and atmosphere of the Earth (Goldwater 1972: 2). Such pervasiveness matches the ubiquity of the spirit mercury, as recounted in the *Tabula Smaragdina*. Goldwater also notes that mercury's presence in the natural world has been observed as being *dynamic,* in that it is considered part of a cycle in nature that traverses the lithosphere, hydrosphere, and so on (ibid.: 149). To an extent, this correlates to the notion of the 'interconvertibility of the elements', in that mercury literally moves from air to earth to water, and so on. Furthermore, Goldwater also reveals how the substance is intrinsic to organic chemistry, and might therefore be considered a 'living metal' (ibid.: 103). Amongst a staggering amount of other intriguing features and uses (much of which corroborates alchemical intuition), I single out the finding that the element mercury (eighty protons), 'bombarded with electrons undergoes a process known as electron capture, and in the process mercury ... is transmuted into element number 79, gold: The alchemists would have cheered' (Cobb and Goldwhite 1995: 428).

In many ways all these twentieth-century developments corroborate the Hermetic worldview. This said, the scientific picture under construction in the twentieth century was, however, still predominantly decoupled from psyche, spirituality and religion. It was within such a zeitgeist that Jung's contribution to the scientific worldview might be characterised, quintessentially, by the inclusion of psyche and meaning – a remythologisation.

More specifically however, concerning alchemy, we see a further abstraction in Jung's theory relative to his forebears. Whereas Goethe had inflected the alchemical mystery from *vas* to natural world, Jung relocated it into the invisible world of psyche. In his Kantian epistemology in which only the 'psychic image' is considered for empirical investigation, he effectively excluded ontological reality: the 'spirit' was drawn off from matter. Indeed it was only during old age, in the form of his synchronicity concept, that 'spirit' was, cautiously, returned to matter.

Notes

1 The origins of the word 'alchemy' have been traced to the Islamic 'al Khem', translated as 'art of the dark country', which refers to Egypt and its apparent 'dark soil' (Linden 2003: 4).
2 According to Churton, the name 'Mercurius' from the fourth century onwards 'would be inseparably linked to Hermes or Mercurius Trismegistus' (Churton 2005: 21).
3 Here 'spiritual alchemy' might be compared to alchemies predominantly concerned with technical methods, such as the making of dyes, metallic compounds, etc.
4 This might also be interpreted as a combination of the 'Egyptian Hermes' (Thoth) and the Greek Hermes.
5 Pythagoras, on the other hand, differentiated *five* elements (air, water, fire, earth and ether) of which all matter was comprised (Cobb and Goldwhite 1995: 19).
6 Consider also the 'watery metal' known as quicksilver that easily dissociates into multiple beads, each one similar to the original whole yet reflecting a unique perspective of the surrounding environment – an effective image of the 'as above, so below' axiom found in the *Tabula Smaragdina*.
7 Red cinnabar ore and its mercury derivatives (white and red) have been associated, anatomically, with the heart, blood, semen and milk of the 'Earth-Mother' (Eliade 1956/1978: 120–1). Eliade also notes that in ancient Greece, the three oracles (including the Delphic oracle) were located in caves where red earth is found. He connects this with menstrual blood: '. . . in the three sites where the Sybils were located there was red earth . . . the red earth symbolized the blood of the Goddess' (ibid.: 41).
8 For an amusing dialogue between an Alchymist, Nature and Mercurius, see the account by the Polish Sendivogius. An excerpt – Mercurius to the Alchymist: 'O my noble Master, I beseech thee pardon mee, wretch that I am, I did not know that thou wast so great a Philosopher' (see Linden 2003: 183–90).
9 This is not the famous Egyptian Queen Cleopatra.
10 Such a sexualisation was portrayed in divine terms such as King and Queen, and also in profane terms. For example, 'Ruland notes that Hermetic philosophers have given the names, bitch and dog, respectively, to 'their Mercury, or Feminine Seed of their Stone' and 'their Sulphur, or to the Masculine Sperm of their Stone' (footnote 11, in Linden 2003: 77).
11 Consciousness of the alchemist changes (ennobles) the substances: 'Our Mercury is in substance one with common Argent Vive, but far different in Form; for it hath a Form Coelestial, Fiery, and of excellent Virtue: and this is the Nature which it receives by our Artificial Preparation' (Linden 2003: 218).
12 In the theory of correspondences, each metal is associated to a planet as well as to a colour.
13 Starkey sometimes wrote under the pseudonym Eirenaeus Philalethes (Linden 2003: 211).
14 Consider also Newton's writing on sulphur and mercury: 'Sulfur is mature quicksilver, and quicksilver is immature sulphur; and on account of this affinity they unite like male

and female, and they act on each other, and through that action they are mutually transmuted into each other and procreate a more noble offspring to accomplish the miracles of this one thing' (Newton, in Linden 2003: 246–7).

15 Hence we have the 'mercury of lead', the 'mercury of gold', and so on.

16 Boerhaave, summarising an alchemical view of the times, wrote that 'In the earth . . . "metallic seeds" are nurtured by suitable warmth and aliment until they mature; that the aliment is probably quicksilver... "the common Matter of all Metals" which requires to be "concocted" by a "Metallific Power" called "Sulphur". Quicksilver has in it "an original Flaw or Blemish", but if that could be removed...' (Dobbs 1992: 86).

17 Such a star could be created in the laboratory by a compound from antinomy ore and the 'sulfur' of the iron (Dobbs 1992: 183). Star Regulus is also the brightest star on the ecliptic in the constellation of Leo, known as the 'heart of the lion'.

18 Antinomy, as the basis of the star, was therefore often used to make cups (emetics) to harness such 'celestial virtues' (Dobbs 1992: 189).

Chapter 3

John Dee

The colourful life of John Dee, the so-called Renaissance Magus, embodied many elements that might be described as *mercurial.*

My choice to use Dee in particular (compared, say, to Paracelsus, Fludd, Agrippa, etc.) was based on a number of factors. First, the times in which he lived shared notable characteristics with those of Jung, such as the radical shift of scientific worldview that combined with the astrological notion of a 'transition of the Ages'. Second, based on the sparsity of references, it would appear that Jung did not study him in any great depth (Dee can thus be viewed in both a contrasting and a complementary light to Jung). Third, his life story embodies many components that can be described as *mercurial* in the broader Hermeticist sense of this term, including talismanic magic, theurgy, etc. (see chapter 1). A further consideration is the resurgent popularity and reframing of this figure's role in contemporary British culture.[1]

In what follows I begin by providing a fair amount of biographical exposition on Dee as a means of bringing out textural depth, contextualised within both an exoteric and an esoteric milieu. Biographies consulted include the 1909 work by Charlotte Fell-Smith (of which Jung was aware), Peter French's *John Dee: The World of an Elizabethan Magus* (1972/2002) and a more recent work by Benjamin Woolley, *The Queen's Conjuror* (2002). This forms a context for a more specific commentary on Dee's *Monas Hieroglyphica*. I then identify resonances with Jung's life and provide further rationale for my inclusion of this topic.

Biographical excerpts – omens and angels

Dee was born in England on 13 July 1527. It is unknown exactly where his birth took place, as the only evidence is apparently based on his astrological chart. This suggests he was born either in or close to London (Woolley 2002: 3).

His father, a textile merchant and 'gentleman sewer' to King Henry VIII, had the means to ensure a good education for his prodigy son. Accordingly, after undergraduate studies at St John's College, John Dee progressed to Cambridge University. He had an especial affinity for mathematics (not part of the curricula).

This subject was associated, in those days, with magic, conjuration and 'calculing', and studied in conjunction with both astronomy and astrology (Woolley 2002: 12). Against the grain of the new humanism, Dee's extracurricular activities also included passionate studies of Hermeticism and neo-Platonic philosophy (French 1972/2002: 22).

After graduating in 1546, he progressed to a position at Trinity College. It was here that he awed the audience in a production of Aristophanes' play *Peace*, by devising a special effect in which a character mounted on a mechanical scarab proceeded to fly into the air. Such incredible spectacles clearly demonstrated his skills in mathematics, mechanics and perhaps beyond: as a conjuror (Woolley 2002: 13). Indeed, by the age of 26 he was to become one of England's foremost intellects, famed for his skill in mathematics as well as the arcane arts; conjuror, magician, alchemist and astrologer (Sumner 2001:1).

Dee's arcane interests, however, were matched by an intense Christian piety. In an England characterised by religious upheavals, such a mix would prove both dangerous and useful: dangerous in that he was under almost constant suspicion for such dubious enterprises as conjuration and magic; useful in that his Hermetically inspired belief in a universal religion afforded him the versatility to shape-shift, opportunistically, between religious divides.

This was no trifle, as deep and painful divisions had polarised the Protestant and Catholic religions in Britain (and much of the continent) since the Reformation in 1517. Thus, at the age of 21, Dee was forced to convert to Protestantism when King Henry VIII broke away from the Catholic Church in 1534.

A few years later, with the accession of Queen Mary in 1553, Catholicism was once again instated as the prevailing religion. By 1555, Protestants refusing to convert were imprisoned, interrogated, tortured and, in some cases, burnt at the stake (Woolley 2002: 30–1). In this same year Dee was arrested under suspicion of being a secret member of a Protestant cell clustered around Mary's sister Elizabeth. However, the accusations levelled at him gravitated more around conjuration, magic, witchcraft, the illegal casting of astrological charts, and also that he 'endeavoured by enchantments to destroy Queen Mary' (ibid.: 38). He was subsequently deprived of his professional post and handed over for further investigation on suspicion of religious heresy.

However a few months later, during his cross-examination, something unusual happened: 'no record remains of Dee's interrogation ... nor of his subsequent treatment. He disappeared into St Paul's a suspected heretic, and now emerged an obedient Chaplain' (Woolley 2002: 44). How he achieved such a transition from suspected Protestant heretic to Catholic chaplain and interrogator is apparently unclear.

With the subsequent coronation of Elizabeth I, in 1559, the religious tide once again turned; this time from Catholicism back to Protestantism.[2] In this ambience, Dee happened to be in good favour with Elizabeth from the beginning. Specifically he was consulted, in his capacity as astrologer, to determine a propitious date for her coronation. This progressed to his occasional role as Queen's advisor and, apparently, also her spy:[3]

> Thus it was not as a shamed member of a failed regime that Dee emerged into the limelight in late 1558, but as the loyal ally of a glorious new one, as an 'intelligencer', in all the possible meanings of that peculiar Elizabethan term: a seeker of hidden knowledge, philosophical and scientific, as well as a spy.
>
> (Woolley 2002: 62)

As an example, we see Dee in 1563 following the lead of 'a most precious jewel' rumoured to have surfaced in Antwerp as the deceased Trithemius's *Steganographia* (written in 1499–1500). In a letter Trithemius claimed this text, once finished, would be 'a great work . . . that, if it should ever be published (which God forbid), the whole world will wonder at' (in Woolley 2002: 73). The author also claimed it included such marvels as hidden writing systems, the transmission of messages over long distances using fire, a method of teaching Latin in two hours and so on (ibid.: 74).

Dee, lodging at The Golden Angel, managed to get a brief loan of the elusive work; long enough to work day and night to transcribe it by hand. For him this text, inspired by Cabala, also included a mysterious aspect: 'Since language was tied into the formation of the universe, words had the potential to change it. Cabalism provided a technology for engineering incantations that could summon spirits and influence events' (Woolley 2002: 71). Accordingly, for Dee, such 'a most precious jewel' had enigmatic occult potential. It might also be used for espionage purposes, giving England the advantage amidst a Reformation Europe hungry for secret codes and ciphers (ibid.: 71).

In the following year, at the age of 37, Dee himself was to experience a 'eureka moment' of the calibre that inspired Trithemius. Specifically, in a 'mystical rapture' lasting twelve days he wrote *Monas Hieroglyphica*, having been 'pregnant' with the concept for about seven years. This short and unusual book, spurned by the academy that 'dispraised it, because they understood it not', was dense with meaning: 'it considered pagan matters, combining numerology, the Cabala, astrology, cosmology and mathematics' (Woolley 2002: 83–5). Although he dedicated this enigmatic work to the broad-minded and newly crowned Holy Emperor Maximillian II, he wasted no time in presenting it to Elizabeth who, Dee later proclaimed, became a 'sacred witness' to its secrets (ibid.: 84).

Commenting on this work, Woolley writes: 'The monad was an astrological sign Dee invented. He regarded it as the key to a true understanding of the unity of the cosmos' (2002: 55). Woolley further comments:

> Dee thought that the 'astronomical' symbols were relics of a lost universal language that transcended national and, by implication, religious barriers. What Dee claimed to have discovered, the 'very rarest thing of all,' was that all the symbols could be combined into one, a variant on the sign for Mercury. This

> symbol formed the central motif of the *Monas*, exemplifying the unity of the universe...
>
> (Woolley 2002: 84)

Dee's influence on Elizabeth, however, extended beyond the secrets of his *Monas*. A few years later a number of numinous celestial events captivated imaginations across Europe and beyond. The first of these occurred in 1572 when a nova appeared in the constellation of Cassiopeia (an M-shaped group of stars located in the Milky Way, known as the 'queen of heaven'). This 'new star', clearly not a comet, challenged the contemporary worldview of an unchanging and immutable 'starry realm' created and perfected by God and the notion that the stars were but holes through which the light of heaven shone.

> When all the implications were worked through, the new star threatened to undermine the entire basis for contemporary cosmology. This created the perfect environment for alternative theories to be considered seriously. One in particular ... was Copernicus' theory of the heliocentric universe.
>
> (Woolley 2002: 153)

This daring worldview of a heliocentric universe – with similarities to the Hermetic view – and of the stars extending into a depth of space represented stirrings of a radical paradigm shift in which the earth and humanity no longer featured at the centre of the universe. These tectonic shifts in conception of the physical cosmos were accompanied by a vivification of existential questions.

Not surprisingly, the new star attracted speculations of a spiritual–religious nature. Opinions included the idea that a previous appearance of such a new star had occurred long ago, as the star of Bethlehem itself. Now, centuries later, another new star 'appearing miraculously' next to the constellation of the queen of heaven was surely portentous.

The skies provided further corroborating omens. In 1577, three years after the disappearance of the nova, a large comet appeared in the west – coinciding, apparently, with Dee and Elizabeth's discussions about expansion into the New World. Dee, optimistic about this 'blazing star', assured Elizabeth that 'it was a portent not of her destruction but of her elevation, and the fulfilment of a destiny greater than even she might have imagined' (Woolley 2002: 161–2). In this same year Dee published what he considered his magnum opus, in four volumes. In the first of these we see an interesting image as frontispiece. Perhaps concentrated with talismanic magic, the image (see Figure 3.1) portrays Elizabeth inaugurating a new world of expansion, trade and riches.

> *Memorials* was a typical Dee production: practical, political, scholarly and mystical. Its title page combined all these elements in an elaborate allegory that has been called a 'British hieroglyphic'. Elizabeth sits at the helm of the ship of imperial monarchy, watched over by St Michael, and is drawn by the figure of 'Lady Occasion' ... to a fortified citadel overlooking conquered lands.

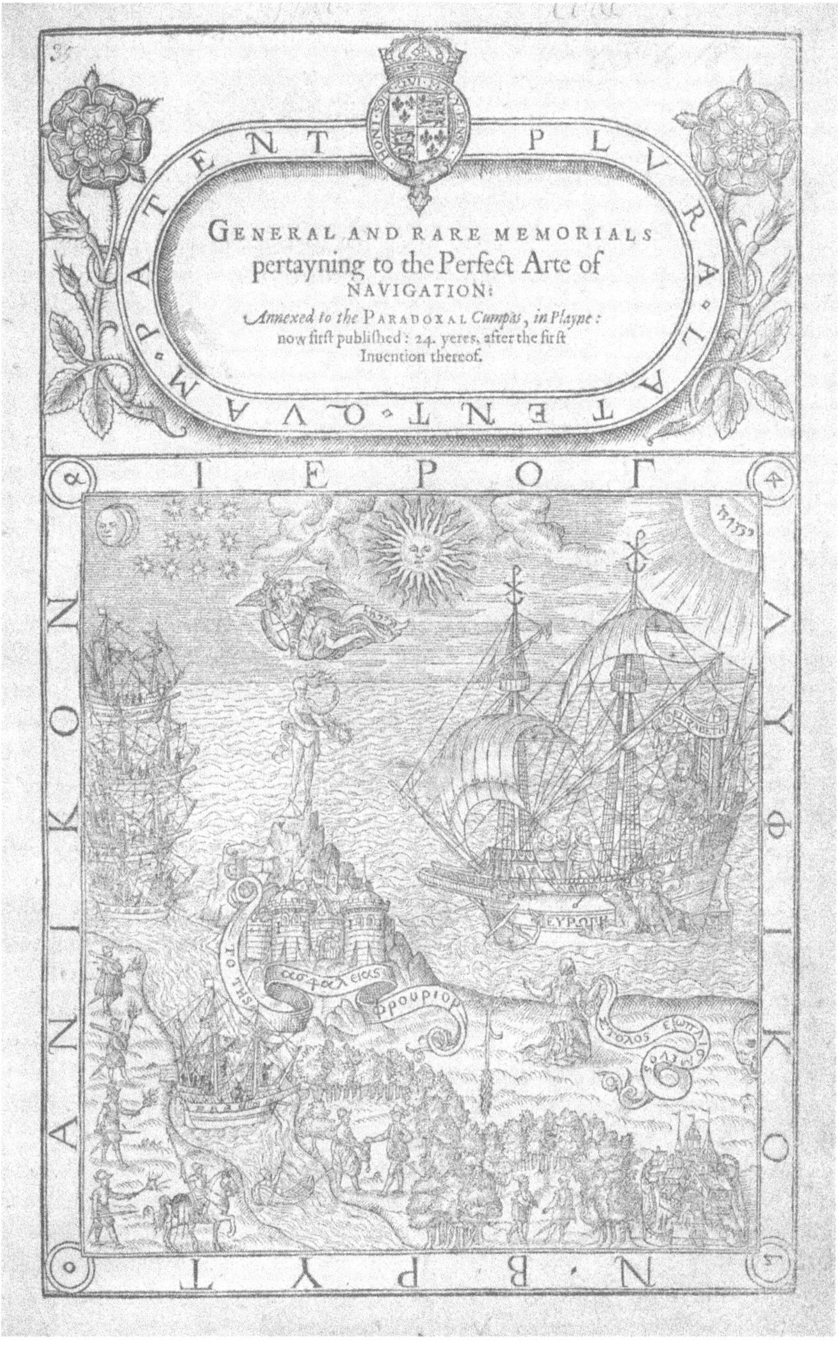

Figure 3.1 Frontispiece of Dee's *General and Rare Memorials*, 1577.

> Above Elizabeth hang the Sun, Moon, stars and a glowing sphere bearing the tetragrammaton, a potent Cabalistic formula, all of which shine down their blessings on the enterprise.
>
> (Woolley 2002: 132)

As Woolley (2002: 132) further points out, 'it was one of the earliest authoritative statements of the idea of a British Empire, and was delivered to the Queen during the period when that Empire was about to make its first appearance on the geopolitical scene'. Dee's various skills in celestial navigation, cartography and mineralogy were also put to practical use in the form of instructional manuals and training, thereby facilitating this new era of exploration.

In this context we should also include 'Dee as Antiquarian', considering his desire to salvage the rich English heritage from the aftermath of the English Reformation. In particular, it was the grail legend of 'the return of Arthur' that fed his expansionistic ideals (French 1972/2002: 189).[4] According to French (ibid.: 194): 'Elizabeth was metaphorically and commonly seen as the living Arthur, and John Dee consequently conceived it her sacred duty to build a British Empire'.[5] Here we see Dee's Merlinesque role in nurturing and paving the way for a 'return of the king'.

Returning to the sky, we see that such unexpected appearances as a new star and a comet were accompanied by yet another heavenly phenomenon. This time, however, the spectacle accorded with the security of known celestial events. Specifically, the cyclical bright Saturn–Jupiter conjunction would be occurring in Pisces, in 1583, at the end of an approximately 960-year 'watery trigon' cycle. A new cycle starting in the 'fiery trigon' would begin roughly twenty years later with a Saturn–Jupiter conjunction in the first astrological sign of Aries. Indeed, astrologers had noted the momentous nature of such prior transitions, in eras associated with Enoch, Noah, Moses and Jesus Christ (Woolley 2002: 159). The astrologer Richard Harvey, commenting on this specific transition, captured the apocalyptic mood: 'we are most like to have a new world, by some sudden, violent, & wonderful strange alteration' (Harvey, cited in Woolley 2002: 160).

About a year before the fateful conjunction in Pisces, Dee was introduced to the skryer Edward Kelley. On the evening prior to their meeting, the skies over Mortlake apparently lit up with 'flashings of fire' (Woolley 2002: 162–4). Such supernatural activity was to characterise their long and tenuous relationship, characterised by Dee's passion to communicate with the spirit world.

Such communications took place by means of 'actions' in which the skryer, using tools such as a shewstone and a crystal ball, entered mediumistic states. Dee's predominant interest was in the contacting of angels such as Uriel, Michael and Anael for the purposes of an extraordinary enterprise. This was nothing less than a reconstruction of the 'lost book of Enoch' containing the Adamic language given to Adam in paradise; effectively, a key to divine knowledge.

In 1583, the year of the fateful Saturn–Jupiter conjunction, this enterprise intensified. In an action a new 'merry spirit', dressed like a fool, made its appearance.

The angel opened its body to reveal the inscription 'El' on its heart. El proceeded by promising Dee that the holy alphabet would be his within forty days. However, the demands of this angel and the flood of a continuing and remorseless dictation of the Adamic language became overwhelming. By this time tensions between Dee and Kelley had also escalated.

Amidst such tensions, the angelic mission progressed. Over the course of the next few days, lists of strange words and letters flowed out. This culminated in an action, on 5 May 1583, 'when a new alphabet of 'holy letters,' the alphabet of Enoch's divine revelation, was communicated' (Woolley 2002: 201). This was only the beginning of the angelic mission that would continue as an integral part of their travels on the continent.

In June of the same year a Prince Laski from Poland arrived at Mortlake, by boat, to visit Dee in person. This was the beginning of an intrigue that would see Dee and Kelley leave England surreptitiously, with the ambition of reaching Laski's home village, Lasko, in Poland.[6]

Upon eventually arriving in Lasko the actions intensified, with a flood of revelations. The angelic mission had resumed. The 'Cabala of Nature' came streaming through. After each action Dee laboriously integrated the new divine data, already begun earlier in England, into the holy book of Enoch. After one such action of assembling this 'language of Adam' he professed: 'It is so terrible, I tremble to gather it' (Woolley 2002: 234–5).

Shortly after, Dee moved to the Polish capital, Krakow. A few days later, on Easter Friday, he was followed by Kelley. The actions resumed. Finally, on 19 April 1584, in the fire sign of Aries, Dee showed Kelley the completed books, admonishing that 'he had some understanding of those holy words their significations' (Woolley 2002: 236).

Kelley, however, was suspicious and discredited his visions and communications. He did not doubt their validity as messages from a spiritual beyond, but rather considered them a 'spiritual mischief'. Dee, however, dismissed such doubts, preferring to believe in a meaningful purpose and authenticity of the angelic mission (Woolley 2002: 237).

About three months later, on Dee's 57th birthday, the angel Gabriel announced that Dee now possessed the keys to God's storehouses, 'wherein you shall find (if you enter wisely, humbly and patiently) treasures more worth than the frames of the heavens' (Woolley 2002: 238). Thus, amidst the precarious transitus from the Age of the 'watery trigon' to the Age of the 'fiery trigon', the 'lost book of Enoch' had finally been retrieved.

Despite such an achievement, Dee would have little rest. Commanded by angels and spirits, they continued to travel. From Krakow they moved to Prague, capital of Bohemia. Here the spirit Madimi, in apocalyptic mood, instructed him to seek an audience with the powerful emperor Rudolph, supporter of the arcane arts, to deliver both a reprimand and a revelation. Upon their acquaintance Rudolph commended Dee on his *Monas*, though admitted it was 'beyond his capacity' (Woolley 2002: 253). Dee, after elaborating on his travels and quest, then revealed the reprimanding message:

> The Angel of the Lord hath appeared to me, and rebuketh you for your sins. If you will hear me, and believe me, you shall triumph. If you will not hear me, the Lord, the God . . . putteth his foot against your breast, and will throw you headlong down from your seat.
>
> (Woolley 2002: 253)

According to Dee, the emperor 'said he did believe me' and subsequently granted the attentions of the 'magnificent' Jacob Kurz (who was to become imperial vice chancellor) for 'the business' (Woolley 2002: 255–6).

However, it was not long before the political atmosphere in Prague swung against Dee and his spiritual mission. Being married, for example, undermined his credibility (in a Catholic sense) as a mediator between God and humanity. Accordingly, his inspiring spirits were deemed to emanate not from God but from the devil. Tensions intensified over the following months, leading to accusations of necromancy and 'other prohibited arts', eventually culminating in his banishment by Rudolph.

After further travels and adventures, including patronage from the wealthy Rozmberk to set up alchemical laboratories in Trebon, Dee eventually arrived back in his home village at Mortlake in December 1589. By this time he had fallen out, irreversibly, with his skryer, Kelley. Nevertheless, back in England, the actions would continue with Bartholomew Hickman, his initial skryer, in a continued quest to transcribe and complete the angelic revelations. This continued project, however, never equalled the passion and zeal that characterised Dee's relationship with Kelley. In addition, Elizabeth's successor James I, after her death in 1603, was less sympathetic to the great enchanter and his arcane arts. Dee's magical life began to wane.

On an uncertain date three years later, at the age of 81 the 'Merlin of Mortlake' died and was buried at the local church. Both his gravestone and his cottage are long gone. Only a bench remains, overlooking the Thames. The uncertain place of his birth is thus matched by vagueness as to the time of his death – a fitting image that marks the elusive role in history of this 'great conjuror'.

Commentary on *Monas Hieroglyphica*

Monas Hieroglyphica emerged during a period in history characterised by intense religious conflict between Catholicism and Protestantism, yet also amidst more liberal views that encouraged a tolerance of religious differences. This included not only Dee but also royalty such as Queen Elizabeth and the Holy Roman Emperor Maximilian II.

This more liberal position reflected Dee's Hermetically inspired belief in a universal spiritual worldview, capable of uniting diverse beliefs: 'Dee's grand design for a universal religion even encompassed the widely despised Jews' (French 1972/2002: 124). In particular, the mercurial capacity to traverse either side of a conflicted situation, such as the Catholic–Protestant split, is apparent in Dee's shape-shifting appearances on either side of this divide. We can also discern an esoteric substrate to such religious turbulence.

Specifically, according to Alex Sumner, astrologers of the day considered the end of the sixteenth century to have celestial resonances with the birth of Christ. Such an omen heralded not only the Second Coming, but also the coming of the Antichrist. In this schema the prior split of the Christian church into Catholicism and Protestantism was considered the work of the Devil.

In such a climate, according to Sumner, Dee had sought reconciliation of the religious divides by recourse to Hermeticism: '... the Enochian material received by Dee is full of apocalyptic comments. For Dee did not see himself merely as an intellectual and a mathematician, but even as a magus commissioned by God to bring healing to the Western European civilisation' (Sumner 2001: 13–14).

Dee's choice to dedicate his *Monas* to the Holy Roman Emperor Maximilian II, champion of religious tolerance, hints at a purpose and hope that it might influence an empire. We see here intimations of the alchemical 'secret transformation of the king' typically ascribed to the transformative qualities of the 'philosophic mercury'. This same theme re-emerges a few years later when Dee boldly appears in front of Maximilian's son, Rudolph, to espouse his angelic mission.

These motifs of mediation, healing and peacemaking are represented in the staff of Mercury as caduceus, portraying two serpents in harmonious relationship (also abstracted into the astrological glyph of Mercury). Indeed, a variation of this glyph appears on the front and final pages of Dee's *Monas*, as illustrated in Figure 3.2.[7]

Monas Hieroglyphica, considered by Dee himself as a 'magical parable' with the central Monad as his 'London Seal of Hermes', has been described as 'possibly the most obscure work ever written by an Englishman' (Foreshaw 2005: 247; Burns and Moore 2007: 8). Despite this, it has also been described as the second most influential of Dee's works, in terms of modern occultism, falling just short of his *Enochian Magic* (Sumner 2001: 5). The poet William Yeats of the Golden Dawn, for example, was apparently of the opinion that it embodied a summation of the secret philosophy of the Rosicrucian manifestos (Burns and Moore 2007: 1).

Unfortunately, there are difficulties with its modern reception. These include problems with its translation, the belief it was accompanied by an oral tradition (now most probably lost) and the lack of contextual nuance in light of the not insignificant differences between the Renaissance and contemporary minds.

Difficulties with translation include not only the fact that Dee invented words, but also other subtleties: 'One soon finds that much of Dee's word play in Latin loses its resonance when translated, and by taking its most logical English equivalent – say, *circle* for *Circulus* – many of the multiple levels of meaning start to fade' (Burnes and Turner 2007: 1). Teresa Burns and Alan Moore go further. They cite the example of Dee's use of the genitive form, *veneris*, when writing 'Venus'. They note it puns with the Latin *veneror* (I venorate), and with the *mons veneris* (mound of Venus) which connects *mons* to *monad*. They interpret such associative clusters to allusions intended by Dee to emphasise ideas such as wisdom achieved through sexuality, as

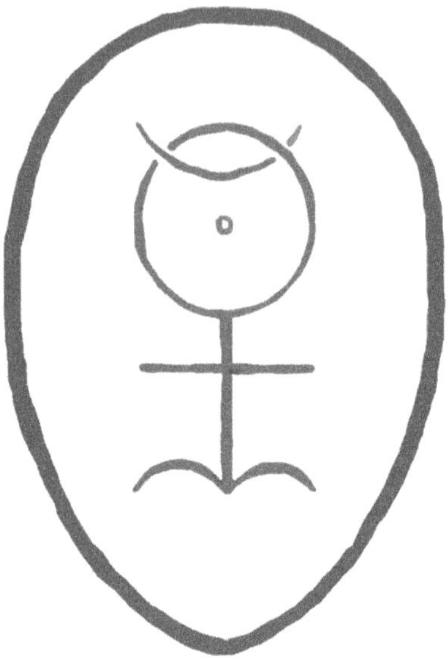

Figure 3.2 Dee's *Hieroglyphic Monad.*

a Sun and Moon *hieros gamos*. As another example, they point out that the Lunar glyph, reminiscent of the various horned Gods of the Old Religion, intersects the Solar glyph 'which is drawn with the circles slightly overlapping and so suggests one of the most sacred symbols to the Pythagoreans, the *vesica piscis*' (Burns and Moore 2007: 16).

In an attempt to further unpack some of its purported meanings, I highlight the scholar French's opinion that Dee's magical parable concerns the 'Gnostic ascent to the One ... The process of man's spiritual transformation is therefore the deepest subject of this work' (French 1972/2002: 76–7). He clarifies that '[t]he magical in Hermeticism cannot be separated from the mystical and religious since the Gnostic existed in an astro-magical universe. Magic enabled man to become *Aion*' (ibid.: 82) and further opines that 'Dee wrote within an oral and secretive alchemical tradition that has probably been permanently lost' (ibid.: 80).

Despite such limitations, Burns and Moore believe it possible to reconstruct much of the work's intended purpose and meaning, based on related texts. In this endeavour they identify two core oral teachings as precessional astronomy and tantric gnosis, as well as the theme of initiation into a mystery (2007: 2). Thus, for example, they highlight allusions to the *hieros gamos* as being central to one of Dee's theorems: that the marriage of Lucifer/Hermes/Mercury to his sister Diana/Venus/the Moon was necessary for the transformation to occur (ibid.).[8] Furthermore, they contemplate even more profound implications: 'we start to see the ... alchemical transformation of Hermes as the subject of the Inner Mystery: a cosmological unfolding of time and space, individual transformation and gnosis, and the ability . . . to aid in the perfecting of the consciousness of humanity' (ibid.: 22).

Other commentators have identified a mathematical layer of meaning, based on 'Mathesis' as 'a kind of mystical approach to Mathematics. Numbers were seen as the basic language in the mind of God. Therefore Mathesis involved understanding the equations which governed the universe' (Sumner 2001: 3). In particular, as Peter Foreshaw has pointed out, Dee considered the Cabalist's *tetragrammaton* – the four sacred syllables that supposedly comprise the name of God – to be nothing less than a correlate to his *Hieroglyphic Monad* (Foreshaw 2005: 252). In this schema, the four glyphs of the monad are viewed as an ultimate reduction with a unitary spirit–matter character. Such an ultimate reduction is also viewed by Dee as embodying the essence of the other planets: their glyphs can be reconstructed from these key shapes, corresponding to the alchemical idea that metals can be dissolved and transformed into 'higher metals' (Burnes and Turner 2007: 4).

It is of note that to achieve such a quaternary Dee had to add a fourth glyph to the ternary symbol of mercury. Here we should remember Dee's preoccupation with a three–four ambiguity.[9] Another observation is that this fourth glyph is the astrological sign for Aries, the spring equinoctial point, considered the alchemical heat necessary for transformation (Burnes and Turner 2007: 4). An important astrological connotation of this fourth glyph is thus the allusion to the dawning of a new era, characterised by the 'fiery trigon' beginning with a Saturn–Jupiter conjunction in Aries.

The above few comments reveal the dense symbolic character and multi-layered nature of this short work, steeped in Dee's great learning, and hence the many difficulties and challenges scholars face should they wish to adequately 'decode' it. For the present purposes, it is sufficient to have identified a few of the themes constellated: the relics of a lost universal language; a key to the unity of the cosmos; a sexual transformation mystery; a unitary matter–spirit worldview; the possibility of healing religious divisions; the awakening of humanity's spiritual purpose. Furthermore, and perhaps most importantly, we should also be vigilant of the appearance of this 'fertilised egg' on the cultural landscape at the dawning of a new astrological cycle and on the cusp of radical shifts of worldview, such as the adoption of the Hermeticist-like idea of a heliocentric universe.

* * *

It is also tempting to surmise that this same 'fertilised egg,' emerging from Dee's inner world, had something to do with Elizabeth, the virgin Queen with the divine touch. Dee, of course, wasted no time in inducting her into its 'sacred mysteries'. At this time England's economic weakness and political inertia perhaps called for a generative magic. Indeed, a few years later a seeming miracle did occur as perhaps another 'fertilised egg' – the unexpected appearance in 1572 of a 'new star' in the constellation of Cassiopeia, the queen of heaven centred in the Milky Way. Dee may well have interpreted such an omen as auguring Elizabeth's ascension, spurring him to a zealous championing of an expansionist policy in hopes of transforming Britain from a poverty of base matter to a wealth of the philosopher's stone, aided by his magical technology as the 'Adamic language' capable of reconfiguring spiritual and material realities.

The appearance of the nova in this specific location also allows for an astro–alchemical interpretation. Alchemically the substance quicksilver, easily fragmenting into a multitude of silvery globules, is associated with virgin's milk. This earthly 'below' has a stellar correlate to an 'above' in the form of the breast-like M-shaped constellation Cassiopeia, near the top of the celestial dome, which 'spews out' the Milky Way. In light of this one can appreciate how Dee may well have associated the appearance of a 'new star' in Cassiopeia with a corresponding alchemical transmutation, as the production of the philosopher's stone from a 'metallic seed' derived from the base matter quicksilver. Dee wrote: 'I did conjecture the . . . star in Cassiopeia . . . to signify the finding of some great treasure of the philosopher's stone' (Dee, cited in Woolley 2002: 164). In effect, for Dee, this was an unexpected and early heraldic omen of the beginning of a new astrological Age.[10]

Importantly, we should also remember that such celestial omens and 'fertilised eggs' were coupled with the angelic mission to transcribe, via séance, the 'lost book of Enoch' that would allow humankind, once again, to communicate directly with God. The angels as intermediaries can thus be seen to also represent the shape-shifting Hermes Trismegistus in his role of bringing skills such as writing to humanity. Indeed, Enoch has been associated with Hermes Trismegistus in a number of magical traditions (Burns and Moore 2010: 8).

* * *

To summarise: Dee's life spanned a period in history characterised by much cultural upheaval. Within such a context we see Dee grappling to restore humankind's spiritual purpose amidst a discordant social, religious, political and scientific atmosphere and in a much expanded and increasingly disenchanted universe. Woolley captures its essence:

> [Dee's] collection of books and scientific instruments, his contacts with Europe's most powerful monarchs and courts, his philosophical, geographical, political and mystical works, his imprisonment, his religious struggles, his involvement with ciphers and spies – all of these meant that he could see as well as anyone, perhaps better, that the entire world was in a state of transformation, and the angels captured this perfectly.
>
> (Woolley 2002: 327)

In overview, Dee's biography and life project might also be viewed, in a number of respects, as a living embodiment (an alchemical parable) of the phenomenon under scrutiny – the alchemical Mercurius – a figure exhibiting, to be sure, an elusive conceptual contour.

Woolley (2002: 329) further comments: 'with the onset of the modern, mechanistic age his own work helped to inaugurate – unity would become irrecoverable, and the magic would go out of the window forever'. It might be said that western culture was on a trajectory of increasing mechanisation, spiritual alienation and fragmentation; a phenomenon the twentieth-century sociologist Max Weber described as 'the disenchantment of the world'. This characterised much of the zeitgeist in which Jung lived.

Dee and Jung

Similarities between the lives of Dee and Jung include a Christian/Pagan ambiguity, communication with 'spirits', creation of a precious book, fascination with apocalypse, belief in a transition of astrological Ages, and interest in a unitary material–spiritual worldview. A more specific example would be Jung's interest in the monad glyph, as I now briefly clarify.

In Jung's handwritten notes on Rosenkreutz's *Chymical Wedding* we see an image of Dee's monad.[11] We also know that Rosenkreutz's *Chymical Wedding* was part of the original inspiration behind his important *Mysterium Coniunctionis* (Jung 1955/1956: xiii). Furthermore, based on a letter to the physicist Pauli, we also know that Jung read *Monas Hieroglyphica*, though he complained it was "simply unbearable" (Jung 1973–75: 23).

Another instance of this image occurs on Jung's Bollingen Stone. Here we are unsure if he intended merely the glyph of Mercury, or the extended form as Dee's monad. If we include the end of the manikin's gown, then one can discern the monad (Figure 3.3). It appears in the centre with glyphs of the remaining visible luminaries arranged in pairs (Sun–Moon, Mars–Venus, Jupiter–Saturn). Had Dee made such an image it would no doubt have involved an invocation of planetary powers in a gesture of talismanic magic, perhaps as a *hieros gamos* of heaven and earth. Of course, we can never be sure if Jung shared such an intention. Interestingly, though, it appears centrally on what we might consider his philosopher's stone, and was inscribed during the time he was working on *Mysterium Coniunctionis*. As a speculation, it is thus tempting to view it as a quintessential symbol embodying the 'riddle' of his life myth.

Jung also communicated with 'spirits', though without the assistance of a skryer. Such an encounter is colourfully portrayed in his *Red Book*. However, his relationship to these figures, although characterised by the numinous, is also that of critical dialogue. In contrast, Dee's relationship is predominantly that of a one-way reception of 'divine knowledge' and invocations for magical, healing or extra-sensory purposes.

Dee's primary intention with the actions was to salvage the 'lost book of Enoch' and to reconstruct the angelic alphabet, thereby re-establishing humanity's communion with the divine. Similarly, *The Red Book* includes a mystery in which identity with a divine figure is experienced, as, for example, in the final scene in *Liber Primus*.

Figure 3.3 Jung's Bollingen Stone (personal photograph).

The Red Book also includes unique glyphs and unusual letters in a number of the images, as intimations of a 'holy script' (see Shamdasani's footnote 155, in Jung 2009: 291–2). This specific motif, however, is a more peripheral than central theme in *The Red Book*.

It is also possible to consider Dee's shape-shifting angels from the perspective of Jung's phenomenology of the unconscious, as devised in his mature thinking.[12] Each of these figures would perhaps represent various stages and experiences of the individuation process. More broadly, we might highlight Jung's portrayal of Mercurius as a personification of the unconscious that shape-shifts into such a range of figures and forms, including the bedevilling and mischievous, in its psychopomp role as a *principium individuationis*.

In this context Jung's 'spirits', not unlike Dee's, not only functioned to re-establish communion with the divine, but were also integral to the forging of his theoretical framework. Here, for example, we can think of similarities between the 'states of possession' during which Dee 'transcribed' *Monas Hieroglyphica* (at age 37) and during which Jung 'transcribed' his *Septem Sermones ad Mortuos* (at age 41).[13] Similarly, the physicist Pauli's engagement with imaginal figures would appear to have assisted in his quest toward formulating a big-picture model of the universe (see chapter 9).

* * *

Both Dee and Jung were also enmeshed in a radical shift of scientific worldview. The Copernican revolution brewing in Dee's life was matched by the impact of relativity and quantum physics during Jung's life.[14] Interestingly, the shift to a heliocentric worldview during Dee's life corroborated ancient Hermetic views. Similarly, Einstein's space–time model and the consideration of a psyche/matter entanglement in the Jung–Pauli model resonate with Hermeticism's unitary and living universe. In particular, Jung's sophisticated portrayal of Mercurius accommodates such a re-enchantment on a grand scale as a motion toward a re-assertion of the world soul, in stark contrast to the prevailing twentieth-century scientific view of a largely dead 'clockwork universe'.

Apart from such scientific paradigm shifts, their lives were also characterised by momentous religious and political instability. Indeed, in 1942, Jung compared the mid-twentieth century to the tumultuous sixteenth century. This was a time, according to him, when 'a storm bird did indeed escape from a spiritual vessel' (1943/1948: 203). Given such apocalyptic changes, it is therefore not surprising that both men invoked the notion of astrological Ages as a soothsaying meta-narrative in which rebirth follows apocalypse. However, unlike Dee's astrological Ages based on Jupiter–Saturn cycles, Jung's theoretical assumptions were derived from precessional astrology.

Framed within this model, Dee's life coincided with the precessed equinox approaching the second (horizontal) fish of the Piscean Age. This was a time Jung identified as an age of 'horizontal values' as exploration, appearance of the Antichrist and an infatuation with matter, compared to the first 'vertical fish' as Christ, characterised by 'upward and spiritual' values (1951a: 94–5). As Jung further noted, the twentieth century coincided with the precessed equinox reaching the head of the second fish and overlapping with the beginnings of the first waters from the Aquarian vessel – that is, the culmination of the Antichrist in a figure such as Hitler – yet also the ushering in of a new and hopeful Age (ibid.: 102; see chapter 6 and Part III).

* * *

In overview: in considering the lives of Dee and Jung we undoubtedly witness a broad archetypal resonance in their respective lives that constellates around mercurial themes. In Dee's case we witness the notion of a Renaissance Magus, as god-man, invoking magic, theurgy, talismans, astrology and alchemy in the pious Hermeticist task of guiding humankind through a difficult transitus and toward its next stage of spiritual evolution. In the chapters that follow I shall be constructing a life myth for Jung informed by a similar 'Hermeticist' template.

Notes

1 Nicholas Goodrich-Clarke writes that 'Dee's reputation as a key intellectual figure of his age [has] been restored' (preface, in Suster 2003: 5). Consider also, for example, the London opera's performance on Dee in 2012.
2 Queen Elizabeth apparently displayed more of a tolerance for religious differences, such as Protestantism and Catholicism, compared to her predecessor (Woolley 2002: 49).
3 As Elizabeth's spy he used the Cabalistic symbol 007, later popularised in a spy thriller (see Campion 2009: 121).
4 He named his first son Arthur. He also believed he shared a common Welsh ancestry with Elizabeth, and that he was descended from the Welsh Prince Roderick the Great (Suster 2003: 17).
5 French points out that '[a] spectacular recrudescence of interest in Arthur developed in the late 1570s and early 1580s, during the same time Dee was adamantly pushing his imperialist schemes based on Arthur's conquests' (French 1972/2002: 198).
6 According to Fell-Smith, Dee's support of Laski had a political intent: 'dreams of Laski as King of Poland, dispensing wealth and favour to his two helpers' (Fell-Smith 1909: 81).
7 The symbolism of mercury is central to this work. The frontispiece enshrines the glyph within two pillars – a clear allusion to Gemini, the astrological ruler of mercury. The final page features the virgin (Virgo), the other astrological ruler of mercury.
8 In this context it is of interest that Dee inserted Mercury conjunct Venus glyphs in his diary on the days he had sexual relations with his wife (Woolley 2002: 283).
9 Dee adopted the equilateral triangle (*three*) as his personal insignia based on the shape of the letter D. The letter D is also the *fourth* letter of the Greek, Roman and Hebrew alphabets (Woolley 2002: 249, 322).
10 At any rate, for him, this celestial appearance in 'the above' refracted into the appearance of literal gold in 'the below' manifested as the subsequent discovery of a goldmine (see Woolley 2002: 164).
11 The Monad appears on the wedding invitation in Rosenkreutz's *Chymical Wedding*.
12 Consider Edinger's summary: 'With the symbolism of the spirit Mercurius, we're dealing with the autonomous psyche in all its manifestations' (Edinger 1995: 299).
13 In a letter dated 1960, Jung wrote of *Septem Sermones ad Mortuos* as 'a poetic paraphrase of the psychology of the unconscious' (Jung 1973–75: 571).
14 Einstein was a dinner guest of the Jungs. Pauli and Jung had a long-standing friendship (see chapter 9).

Chapter 4

Carl Jung

Chapter 1 laid a foundation stone in which mercurial themes were identified, as a combination of theoretical and practical Hermeticism. Chapter 2 focused on the *alchemical* side of Hermeticism by means of a few historical snapshots, biased toward the evolution of key notions. Chapter 3 then viewed a period in the Renaissance through the personality of John Dee, as a means of illustrating how the 'Hermeticist project' played out on the sixteenth-century European stage. In each chapter I also referred to Jung, thereby intimating a few contexts of relevance toward understanding his esoteric identity. The remaining chapters are now oriented more specifically toward Jung.

In this chapter I give a biographical overview of Jung's alchemical interests from childhood up to 1928 (after which his more serious interest in alchemy began). I then give a brief description of his alchemical myth, and also elaborate what might be considered his 'astrological myth'.

Alchemical intimations

In the chapter 'School Years' in *Memories, Dreams, Reflections* (*MDR*), Jung recounts an increasing disenchantment with Christianity. Excursions into his father's library were driven by burning questions that revolved around the natural world, the devil and the reasons for the suffering and apparent imperfections in the world. However, he was not to find satisfaction in his father's books. Searching for answers regarding the role of the devil in Biederman's *Christian Dogmatics*, for example, proved to be gravely disappointing. Disillusioned, he pitied his father for succumbing to such 'drivel' and 'mumbo jumbo' (Jung 1963/1995: 77).

Jung recounts that it was around this time that his mother, 'in her No. 2 personality', suggested he read Goethe's *Faust*. He subsequently described *Faust* as a 'miraculous balm' that 'poured into my soul'. Here, finally, he found a work that grappled with such compelling questions as the role of the devil and the imperfection of creation, as well as the 'realm of the mothers' and 'the mysteries'. However, although deeply satisfying, this work was also problematic for him: the portrayal of Mephistopheles as being duped by 'little angels' such as Faust, for example, was unconvincing (Jung 1963/1995: 77–8). Later in *MDR* he writes that his work on alchemy reflected his inner relationship to Goethe. He considered himself on a similar path and as being 'in the grip' of an *opus magnum* or *divinum* as a drama unfolding through the centuries (ibid.: 232).

We witness here a spiritual tension from his early childhood, finding a mythic context as a continuation of the Faustian drama in the form of an alchemical *magnum opus*. We also see here how his mother's influence, in suggesting he read Faust, was catalytic. This is especially important as Jung points out that the feminine principle, in philosophical alchemy, plays an equal role to that of the masculine (Jung 1963/1995: 228). As we shall also see, this theme played a central role in his alchemical project as the coniunctio: an idea that not only involves the union of male and female, but also an above and a below.

This brings us to the next childhood memory of interest. In 'School Years' we read of his long school walks to and from the Gymnasium, along the river Seine. In this setting he recounts his first elaborate and systematic fantasy of a little medieval city on an island in the river. Apart from battlements, a library, cannons, schooners and a daily life in which he played a role as justice of the peace and arbitrator, there also existed a secret, an Arcanum, of which only he was aware. The secret consisted of a mysterious copper tree, inside the tower in the city. Its crown, at the top of the tower, consisted of a taproot with tiny rootlets in the air. The rootlets drew an 'inconceivable something' from the air into the copper trunk of the tree and down into a vaulted cellar. Here was an inexplicable apparatus that made gold coins from the 'spiritual essence' drawn from the air (Jung 1963/1995: 100–1).

This 'Arcanum' included a process in which the subtle (spirit) is transformed into the gross (material). The inverted metal tree also corresponds to the alchemical notion of the *contra naturum* (against nature). Importantly, it also affords unlimited material wealth, signifying a valuing of worldly pleasures and influence. Such ideas contrast with the Gnostic myth (and much of Hermeticism) that concerns an opposite movement as the release of spirit from matter. Of further significance is that it represents a process in which 'the above' and 'the below' are brought into relationship (the other facet of the *coniunctio*). Once again, as we shall see, these are all key motifs that feature in Jung's alchemical worldview.

A further alchemical influence came later, after his break with Freud. Silberer's *Problems of Mysticism and its Symbolism*, published in 1914, stimulated this interest.[1] Despite this, Jung professes that at the time he still considered alchemy as 'off the beaten track' and 'silly' (Jung 1963/1995: 230). Here I point out that the years 1914–28 included the creation of his *Red Book*, in which there is a dearth of alchemical references. It would thus appear that alchemy was still firmly in the background during those years. Retrospectively, though, he acknowledged the importance of alchemy as an invaluable conceptual framework: 'the process through which I had passed at that time [1913–1917] corresponded to the process of alchemical transformation' (Jung 1963/1995: 236; see also chapter 5).

In 'The Work', we then read that his alchemical fascination was further anticipated by a series of dreams dealing with the theme of a mysterious annex to his home. Eventually, he dreamt of finally entering the new annex. Here he discovered a 'wonderful library' predominantly composed of sixteenth- and seventeenth-century works, some of which were embellished with strange copper engravings and curious symbols (Jung 1963/1995: 228). Later, he was to recognise these as alchemical symbols. Accordingly, he interpreted the dream prospectively as an anticipation of the further growth of his personality by means of alchemical research.

He then recalls 'a crucial dream' from around 1926 that also anticipated his alchemical interests. In the dream he found himself in the back of a horse-drawn wagon being driven by a small peasant man in retreat from the frontline of a war. After passing over a bridge and through a tunnel they eventually reached a lovely springtime countryside which led to the courtyard of a country manor. Whilst in the courtyard, they heard the sudden clang of falling gates. The coachman hopped off and announced they were now trapped in the seventeenth century. Despite lengthy excursions into 'ponderous tomes' on history, religion and philosophy, Jung could find nothing that shed significant light on this dream. He stressed it was only much later that he realised it referred to the alchemy of that historical epoch.

Apart from such intimations, alchemy only really came to grip him when he was 53 years old. The catalyst came when his friend and sinologist Richard Wilhelm sent him a Taoist–alchemical treatise titled *The Secret of the Golden Flower* with a request the he write a foreword. Shortly before receiving the book, he had drawn a mandala that seemed to him 'so Chinese'. The apparent synchronicity of then receiving this ancient manuscript, illustrated with a similar image, was transformative (Jung 1963/1995: 223).

From around this time onwards, Jung shifted his interests from Gnosticism to Alchemy. Such research, which would occupy him for the remainder of his life, was to become a significant feature of his developing theories: 'Grounded in the natural philosophy of the Middle Ages, alchemy formed the bridge on the one hand into the past, to Gnosticism, and on the other into the future, to the modern psychology of the unconscious' (Jung 1963/1995: 227).

An alchemical myth

Apart from having a momentous personal impact, alchemy also contributed significantly to the further refinement of Jung's analytical psychology.

> Only after I had familiarised myself with alchemy did I realise that the unconscious is a process, and that the psyche is transformed or developed by the relationship of the ego to the contents of the unconscious. In individual cases that transformation can be read from dreams and fantasies. In collective life it has left its deposit principally in the various religious systems and their changing symbols. Through the study of these collective transformation processes and through understanding of alchemical symbolism I arrived at the central concept of my psychology: the process of individuation.
>
> (Jung 1963/1995: 235)

Accordingly, in his worldview, there is a personal individuation as well as a cultural individuation. Whereas personal individuation is embodied in the creative process of the individual's 'confrontation with the unconscious', collective individuation is embodied in the spiritual history of a particular society. For him, cultural individuation has also left its evolutionary traces in the undercurrents of history, such as in Gnosticism, followed by medieval alchemy, then culminating in its latest formulation as analytical psychology.

It is clear that Jung disbelieved any literal claims of the alchemists, such as the transmutation of lead or mercury into gold. According to him, the unconscious psyche got autonomously projected into their laboratory work: the concretisation of inner images into alchemical texts and pictures thus resulted in a rich yield of symbolic material, important in that it represents a historic correlate to his concept of individuation and gives valuable insight into the structure and dynamics of the collective unconscious (Jung 1945/1954: 299; also 1937: 475). Alchemy, for him, also functioned like dreams in the sense of being compensatory to consciousness.

> Alchemy is rather like an undercurrent to the Christianity that ruled on the surface. It is to this surface as the dream is to consciousness, and just as the dream compensates the conflicts of the conscious mind, so alchemy endeavours to fill in the gaps left open by the Christian tension of opposites.
>
> (Jung 1944: 23)

Further studies of his alchemical works not only disclose its integration within the conceptual framework of analytical psychology (and its expansion), but also reveal a concern with a broader cultural dimension. In particular, for him, the unique value of alchemy (as opposed, for example, to eastern religions and wisdom traditions) was especially important for 'western man' as it 'grew out of the soil' of Christian tradition: 'Any renewal not deeply rooted in the best spiritual tradition is ephemeral; but the dominant that grows from historical roots act like a living being within the ego-bound man' (Jung 1955/1956: 370).

Furthermore, as an example to clarify the relation between the 'Christian myth' and Jung's 'alchemical myth' we can consider the notion of the coniunctio, an idea he considered as being central to alchemy (1963/1995: 457). Concerning this notion, Jung stated that 'the [alchemical coniunctio] ... usually consists in the union of two pairs of opposites, a lower (water, blackness, animal, snake) with an upper (bird, light, head, etc.) and a left (feminine) with a right (masculine)' (1945/1954: 341). A comparison of two more or less contemporaneous images from the Renaissance can be used to briefly illustrate this specific idea.

In the alchemical image (see Figure 4.2) are two sets of opposites: a left and a right (king and queen) as well as an above and a below (bird of Hermes and a mercurial bath). These two sets of opposites are brought into a relationship of engagement. In the Christian image (see Figure 4.1) we see a similar quaternio, yet in a different relationship. There is a left (St. George) and a right (fleeing woman),

Figure 4.1 Saint George and the Dragon; Sodoma; 1518.

Figure 4.2 Rosarium Philosophorum; woodcut four; Frankfurt; 1550.

as well as a spiritual above (transcendent deity manifesting in the clouds) and a chthonic below (dragon).

We witness here a Christian worldview of a patriarchal deity, in sympathy with St George, in enmity with an earth-based religion (dragon) represented, possibly, as being in sympathy with the feminine. In contrast, the alchemical image brings the masculine and feminine in relation to each other, as well as the above (bird) and the below (mercurial water). Briefly, the former can be considered a 'separation of opposites' whereas the latter can be considered a 'synthesis of opposites'.

The above provides the gist of how Jung's alchemical myth can be considered in relation to the Christian myth. The role of the alchemical Mercurius in such a myth is also central, as will become increasingly apparent in the following chapters.

A further major and related theme, also more fully developed in coming chapters, concerns Jung's belief that religious history (and its undercurrents) constituted a 'transformation of the god-image' synchronistic with a meta-narrative scripted by the precession of the equinoxes through the astrological Great Year. Such a notion suggests a possible relation between his alchemical and astrological worldviews, and thus makes necessary a short excursion into clarification of what might be considered Jung's astrological myth.

An astrological myth

It is only in Jung's later works such as *Aion* that we come across explicit astrological references that appear to reveal his position as that of 'believer'. Such ideas only appeared in published works after his near-death experience in 1944, when he professed to having had the courage to write of his 'secret knowledge' (see chapter 10). Despite this, his later works are nevertheless minimalist and reticent in their astrological detail. Consequently, to read 'Jung as astrologer' is problematic, especially if we restrict ourselves to the originally published works, such as the *CW*s.

To discern a clearer picture of his astrological worldview therefore requires excursions into originally unpublished materials, with emphasis on the various seminar series and letters.[2] It is here that we find a number of excerpts which clearly reveal such a fascination, especially in the idea of Platonic months, the Great Year and the transition of the Ages. Accordingly, it is especially this aspect of his astrological perspective that requires further investigation. As a prelude, I first introduce the interrelated concepts of the Great Year, the Platonic month and the precession of the equinoxes.

* * *

In western astrology the Great Year is based on the time it takes our galaxy to complete one revolution: approximately 26,000 years. In this representation the spring equinox[3] precesses through the constellations along the ecliptic at a rate of approximately one degree every seventy-two years as the galaxy turns. The spring equinox therefore slowly moves through each of the twelve constellations along the ecliptic over the course of such a Great Year. The time it takes to move through an individual constellation is known as an astrological aeon, or a Platonic month. Each of the twelve aeons therefore takes about 2,143 years. In this view, each Age also has characteristics associated with its constellation.

Using this approach, many astrologers identify the Age of Pisces as being synchronous with the past 2,000 or so years of Christianity. Prior to Christianity was the Age of the Ram (Aries), and before this was the Age of the Bull (Taurus). In a sense, the astrological narrative flows 'backwards in time', in that the precessed equinox progresses in an opposite direction from the 'small year' (when the Sun moves from Aquarius to Pisces, etc.). Thus in the Great Year, considering the constellations of Pisces and Aquarius, the two fishes and the water, at least according to Jung, flow backwards into the jug of the water-bearer (Jung 1998: 111).[4]

Of especial relevance here is the shift from Pisces to Aquarius, popularly known as the 'New Age'. This term was apparently originally coined by Madame Blavatsky, the founder of theosophy, in her *The Secret Doctrine* (published in 1888).[5] More specifically, Blavatsky identified 1897 as the ushering in of the new era of a higher spiritual consciousness. Theosophist astrologers Bessie Leo and Dane Rhudyar went further by identifying this with the onset of the Age of Aquarius, 'letting loose a notion whose wingbeats still resound loudly in the astrological circles of the twenty-first century' (Spencer 2000: 116). However, specific timing as to when the so-called Age of Aquarius began (or still has to begin) is a matter of debate. For now, however, I brush such a question aside and progress to elucidate what might be considered Jung's astrological myth.

* * *

In the *Visions Seminars* (1930–1934), Jung notes that the astrological constellations are 'very intimately known by the unconscious mind', as they are effectively 'projections onto the skies' (Jung 1998: 109). He also states there is 'profound knowledge in our unconscious' based on the 'empirical knowledge stored up in our unconscious', and that 'certain things originating at a certain time of year have certain qualities' (ibid.: 109). Indeed, for him, 'nature is aristocratic . . . and, what is even more, *esoteric*' [italics mine] (Jung, cited in Heisig 1979: 44). More specifically, an understanding of his view on Platonic months can be found in the Dream Analysis Seminars:

> In the life of the individual the spring-point doesn't matter, but in the life of the tree of mankind, it matters very much. An ordinary year is to us what the Platonic year of 26000 of our years is to the race . . . The precession of the equinoxes might be said to be the clock-hand that marks the great spaces of time, the hand that measures time for the tree of mankind. On our clock, the hand moves forward, but with the clock of the race it moves in the other direction. Each zodiacal sign then becomes a [Platonic] month, and we call a certain period of 2150 years the [Platonic] month of the Fishes, for instance, which is of course again a projection. So for us, our whole historical life, the length of human consciousness, is only three months. But man has gone through those 26 000 years many times.
>
> (Jung 1984: 426)

His idea that human consciousness is 'only three months old' is derived from the idea that the zodiac itself was, as far as we know, only devised a few thousand years ago: 'at the time when the Zodiac was invented, man was in the springtime of consciousness, so the falling of the spring-point in Aries, a spring-sign, was appropriate; it is as if the horoscope of humanity had begun with the dawn of consciousness' (ibid.: 427). Of related interest, voicing the astrological opinion of the times, he also believed that a transition of the Ages from Pisces to Aquarius was contemporaneous with his lifetime. For Jung the specific images of the constellations also had profound symbolic meaning. The 'clock-hand' as the gradual precession of the equinoxes through these images mirrored a cultural individuation. His main ideas in such a schema can be summarised as follows.

The precession through the first vertical fish of Pisces represented an intense development of consciousness by means of a one-sided and masculine spiritual ascension (the age of Christ), and a corresponding devaluation of the feminine, chthonic and nature-based religions. Some centuries later, a shift to the second 'horizontal fish' corresponded to a swing from spiritual heights to a valuation of matter (the age of the Antichrist). The precessed spring equinox then reaching the head of the second fish as a culmination of the age of the Antichrist also corresponds, approximately, to the approach of the first waters from the jug of the forthcoming Aquarian Age (1998: 548–9). Further images of the Aquarian Age include a water-bearing vessel being held by a human figure of cosmic proportions, sometimes represented as angel-like, with wings.

Jung interprets such images in his own unique way, commensurate with his psychology. For example, the jug is interpreted as the psyche functioning as a feminine containing vessel which can 'hold the opposites', such as the spirit-matter Piscean fishes. The anthropos-like Aquarian figure, in command of the containing vessel, embodies the principle of an 'angel-like' self-image.

Continuing through the *Visions Seminars* we read of an interest in two further constellations. These are the *triangulum* (the triangle) above the constellation of Aries, and a *quadrangulum* as the square of Pegasus, above Pisces and Aquarius. Jung interprets the precessing spring equinox during its longitudinal alignment to *triangulum* starting 'in about the year 1000 B.C.', with the epoch in history 'when the intellect began to stir' resulting in the appearance of abstract ideas, philosophy and the trinitarian gods (Jung 1998: 730–1). Clarifying, he states that 'it is no longer Perseus, the mystical hero, doing great deeds of liberating mankind from the leviathan in the sea; it is now philosophy, it is abstract human notions' (ibid.: 730).

He then points out that a good number of centuries later, starting shortly before 1900, the precessed equinox then touched the first star of the square-like constellation of Pegasus: 'And people are now tremendously busy with squares as they were busy with the trinity before; all the old gods of India and Egypt and Greece were trinities' (Jung 1998: 731). Clarifying the meaning of Pegasus, 'the ruling principle at this time', he further remarks:

> the horse was a libido symbol, representing the animal part of man, and by pulling himself up upon it, by riding it, it thus becomes winged and divine; it is not only an ordinary animal, it is a divine animal. So it would mean a time in which man discovers that the real guiding principle is the living libido, and that would be represented by a square.
>
> (ibid.)

An added layer of meaning to Jung's astrological narrative thus emerges. The principle of Pegasus anticipates the transition from Pisces to Aquarius, the first stirrings having begun shortly before 1900. This period is ruled by the square as a spiritual continuation from the trinity of earlier history, around 1000 BCE. For him the square as a progression from the trinity is also a 'most helpful symbol' in that it represents a more complete personality, with the potential of healing the one-sidedness of a (trinitarian) neurosis (Jung 1998: 732). Intrinsic to such a healing is the integration of the instinctual with the spiritual, represented by the winged horse. Indeed, here we see inklings of how his alchemical myth of the coniunctio might be correlated with an astrological image.[6]

* * *

The above development clearly illustrates that the various astrological images (fishes, cup, water-bearer, winged horse, triangle, square, etc.) represented, for Jung, enigmatic symbols in a grand meta-narrative synchronous with the precession of the equinoxes. By inference it also emerges not only that he believed in the notion of astrological Ages, but also that his life either anticipated or was contemporaneous with the transition from Pisces to Aquarius.

However, there is a problem in that Jung does not elaborate an explicit method or theoretical orientation to explain his dating of the supposed transition of the Ages. His timings are also vague and occasionally change during the course of his lifetime. For example, in the first image of *The Red Book* we see a star placed in the constellation Aquarius, as if to suggest the years of his working on this text (1914–28) were contemporaneous with this transition (see Figure 12.1). However, apart from this, there is no explicit mention or image in this work that points to a specific date.

A later date has more credibility. In a 1929 seminar we read: 'In about 1940 we shall be approaching the first stars of the next sign, Aquarius. Of course there are no definite lines in the sky . . . but in 1940/1950 we shall be in the vicinity of Aquarius' (1998: 548; also 1984: 423). Further, in a letter dated 12 August 1940, we read: '1940 is the year when we approach the meridian of the first star in Aquarius. It is the premonitory earthquake of the New Age' (1973–75: 285). Later, in a footnote in *Aion* (published in 1951), he cites the years 1997 and 2154 as contenders for the start of the Aquarian Age (1951a: 94; footnote). In a letter to Victor White in 1953, two years later, he writes: 'we are still in the Christian Aeon, threatened with a complete annihilation of our world' (2007: 222). In a 1958 publication we read: 'We are now nearing that great change which may be expected when the spring-point enters Aquarius' (1958: 311).

In dealing with such inconsistencies I reiterate my purpose of constructing a life myth viewed through the eyes of Jung, and therefore take the position that all these dates have validity, determined by context (clarified in the coming chapters).

Mythic threads

Apart from an overview of Jung's alchemical and astrological worldviews, I also alluded to a convergence of these myths. For example, the instinctual yet spiritual Pegasus was compared to the alchemical coniunctio, as a union of the chthonic and the spiritual. We also witnessed a historical *triangulum* in relation to a 'contemporary' *quadrangulum* (trinity and quaternity), which also affords an astrological nuance to Jung's renowned 'three–four problem' (considered a 'riddle of Mercurius').

As shall become apparent in forthcoming chapters, such symbols and themes are intrinsically interwoven into the various shape-shiftings of a central character of interest, the alchemical Mercurius. Indeed, as I shall try to reveal, Jung's portrayal of this figure contributes significantly toward a convergence of his alchemical and astrological worldviews and thus also toward a better understanding of his life myth. In chapters 7 and 12 I also include Merlin and the grail legend respectively, to both enrich and corroborate such a perspective.

Notes

1 Jung corresponded with Silberer in letters yet to be published.
2 We know from a letter to Freud that Jung was interested in astrology from as early as 1911. Furthermore, based on reports from family and close associates, it would also appear that this interest had intensified in his last decades (see Tarnas 2007: 62).
3 The point on the ecliptic coinciding with sunrise on the spring equinox.
4 We can think of the 'special effect' of water flowing reverse-wise into a glass, created by viewing a video-film backwards.
5 Jung's library contains *The Secret Doctrine* (see Jung 1984: 607, footnote 4).
6 I add that the square, for Jung, also represents the 'God who is manifest in his creation' in contrast to the *deus absconditus* of the trinitarian formulation (see Jung, cited in Heisig 1979: 52).

Part II

Daimonic encounter

> Who spoke to me then? Who talked of problems far beyond my knowledge? Who brought the Above and the Below together, and laid the foundation for everything that was to fill the second half of my life with the stormiest passion? Who but that alien guest who came from above and from below?
>
> (Jung 1963/1995: 30)

Chapter 5

Chthonic spirit

> The question of the daemonic is on the one hand simple and on the other exceedingly complicated . . . Generally speaking the daemonic is that moment when an unconscious content of seemingly overwhelming power appears on the threshold of consciousness. It can cross this threshold and seize hold of the personality. Then it is possession, which can naturally be personified in many forms.
>
> (Jung 1973–75: 344)

In *Memories, Dreams, Reflections* (*MDR*) Jung uses the terms 'mana', 'daimon' and 'god' in the same sentence to express the idea of a seemingly objective strangeness external to the psyche. He continues by explaining that these 'mythic words' are synonyms for the unconscious (Jung 1963/1995: 368).

The specific expression 'daimon', however, evokes nuanced meanings of a struggle and an encounter (used as a verb as opposed to a noun) of a numinous nature.[1] Thus Jung talks of grappling, like Jacob, with an angel as emissary of God. In such a fracas he admits to a wounding (Jacob's dislocated hip) but also mentions that the angel too can be transformed, as voiced in his writings on Job's encounter with Yahweh. In this context, he also writes more impersonally of the life instinct in terms of unconscious libido which only becomes personified in projected form as it approaches consciousness (Jung 1963/1995: 377–90).

In essence, Jung's descriptions reveal the daimonic as a shape-shifter of many forms and of great ambiguity: personal and impersonal, controlling yet being controlled, wounding yet healing. We also witness a kaleidoscopic variety of such forms in his corpus, as Philemon, Salome, Abraxas, Phanes, Telesphoros, Wotan and so on. Some of these depictions (such as Philemon and perhaps Wotan) have become iconic in the post-Jungian culture. Others such as Mercurius have, in my opinion, been neglected. Indeed, it is this oversight in the biographies that I shall now endeavour to address.

A study of the literature with such a concern in mind resulted in the emergence of four particularly strong themes, driven by the following questions:

1 Can we discern a genesis of the figure of Mercurius in Jung's life, starting with early childhood and ending in old age?

2 Can we interpret his 'fish–snake' synchronicity of 1936 as an augury presaging a 'battle of a Christian and Pagan spirit' during the transition of astrological ages?
3 Can his 1944 near-death experience be interpreted in terms of an enigmatic alchemical transformation mystery synchronous with the start of the Age of Aquarius?
4 Is there resonance of his life with that of the legendary Merlin and, if so, what light does this shed in terms of his post-1928 project?

I now proceed to address the first of these questions.

* * *

I here trace the genesis of a 'chthonic Other' during significant moments of Jung's life by looking at excerpts from early childhood, mid-life and then on to old age, with emphasis on mid-life. I shall argue that these experiences find their most sophisticated resolution in older age as Jung's 'alchemical myth', with Mercurius, in particular, featuring as the central character.

An evolving life myth in three dominant phases can be applied. Thus, in early life, we have the idea of a 'childhood secret' composed of a range of disparate numinous experiences in contrast and often heretical to Jung's Christian upbringing. In mid-life there is a Herculean attempt toward resolution, creatively worked into his *Red Book*. Finally, in old age and with the assistance of alchemy, we find a more holistic synthesis creatively embodied not only in his writings but also sculpturally, such as in his Bollingen stone. Thus his Christian beliefs will be shown to have accrued both a compensatory and complementary development integral to an evolving life myth.

A childhood secret

It can be argued that much of Jung's 'life myth' originated in a number of childhood experiences as recounted in *MDR*. Here, I shall look at three such memories: the Jesuit priest trauma; a dream of a subterranean phallus; and his manikin and stone.

He recounts having experienced his first conscious trauma at the age of three or four. Sitting alone one hot summer day outside the family's house, whilst playing in the sand, he looked up at the road which led up to a hilltop and disappeared into the woods. Coming down along this road, from the woods, he saw a person in a strangely broad hat and dressed in a kind of long black robe, like a man wearing women's clothes. As the figure drew closer he recognised it as a man and, more specifically, as a Jesuit. He responded by frantically running into the house and hiding in the attic (Jung 1963/1995: 26).

He had recently overheard his father and a colleague remarking about the dubious activities of the seemingly dangerous Jesuits. Such memories contributed toward his ambiguous conception of Lord Jesus as both helpful redeemer, yet also bloody and crucified cadaver (ibid.: 28).

At about the same age (three or four) he then had the earliest dream he could remember, as follows: In a meadow near his home he unexpectedly came upon a dark, rectangular, stone-lined hole in the ground with a stairway leading into the earth. Upon entering, he descended the staircase and then came upon a round arch, closed off by a sumptuous brocade-like green curtain. Pushing the curtain to one side he peered in to find a rectangular chamber with arched ceiling hewn from stone. On the floor of the chamber was a blood-red carpet that ran to a low platform on which was a wonderful, fairytale-like golden throne. Standing on the throne was a tree-trunk about fifteen feet high and about two feet thick, composed of naked human flesh. On the top was a rounded head with an eye gazing skyward, on top of which was a bright aura. Paralysed with terror at the fear it might move and creep toward him, he then heard his mother from outside say: 'Yes, just look at him. That is the man-eater!', upon which he awoke in a terrified sweat (Jung 1963/1995: 27).

In pondering the dream he mentioned an ambiguous aspect in which the 'dark Lord Jesus, the Jesuit and the phallus were identical' (ibid.: 26). For him the phallus was a subterranean god 'not to be named', an 'underground counterpart' to the Christian deity and a 'frightful revelation'. Such a god was in stark contrast to the Christian God of his upbringing, seated on a throne in heaven (ibid.: 29).

Moving now to his ninth year, he recounts having carved a small figurine about two inches long of a man dressed in top hat, black frock and much in the likeness of the clergymen in the family. He made a bed of wool for the figurine, and accompanied it with scrolls written in his own secret language. The figurine was also accompanied by a smooth oblong blackish stone which he painted in such a way as to create an upper and a lower half. He recalls how these objects emotionally comforted him in times of distress. Such activities lasted about a year and took place in the attic: a forbidden part of the house, as it was deemed dangerous.

He later considered that the manikin was, for him, a blasphemous 'graven image' that included a secret personal relation to God without the intervention of Jesus. The manikin's stone was also considered his supply of life force:[2] 'I had a vague sense of relationship between the "soul-stone" [manikin's stone] and the stone which was also myself' (Jung 1963/1995: 42).

Taken as a whole, the impact of these secret childhood memories was both momentous and formative. They embodied an intense dynamism that would help shape Jung's ever-evolving life myth, as I now attempt to illustrate.

* * *

Jung's description of the Jesuit places this figure ambiguously within his Christian worldview. Judging by his father's dubious impression of Jesuits, the character embodied perhaps his father's shadow and, by extension, also the 'shadow of Jesus'. He emerges not from heaven but from the woods and, indeed, appears to be life-threatening instead of redeeming. As Christian shadow, the Jesuit also has a number of similarities to Wotan of the Forests, who wears a large cloak and broad-rimmed hat and who, as psychopomp, functions to guide souls to the land of the dead (see Grimal 1969: 367; also Jung 1963/1995: 345). The cape and large hat also associates him with the wanderer, prevalent in Roman times, whose tutelary deity was Hermes.

Jung later realised the man wasn't a Jesuit after all, but merely a priest. The realisation that the figure must have arisen more or less spontaneously from his psyche must have vaguely dawned on him even at this tender age, as if there were a deeply heretical inner figure who was related, yet different, to Jesus and his Christian father, and who seemed to include the feminine (women's clothing). In particular, this figure shares a number of attributes similar to Jung's depiction of the alchemical Mercurius. The hermaphroditic 'Jesuit' wearing women's clothing has correspondences to Mercurius, who is often described as being both male and female (Jung 1944: 294–5). The Jesuit as a kind of shadow figure relative to his Christian father also has resonances with the notion of Mercurius as Christ's shadow (Jung 1943/1948: 245–6). The pagan, psychopompic and Wotan-like features add further symbolic layers.

Similarly, Jung's subterranean phallus dream can be shown to represent features of Mercurius. The phallus itself corresponds to the ithyphallic Hermes, representing the generative aspect of the earth. The yoni–lingam style images of dark earth womb with its virginal brocade, in which is found a phallus associated with light,[3] also relate to the idea of the alchemical coniunctio in its chthonic aspect. In the dream we could also say that Jung, as a little boy, finds himself on the subterranean 'royal path'. We can recall here the alchemical transformation of the blood-red cinnabar into gold, and of the quaternary foundation to such a completed goal. Indeed, von Franz has identified this 'God not to be named' as the alchemical Mercurius (von Franz 1998: 25).

Considering now his manikin and stone, we see the anthropomorphic and inanimate aspects of the numinosum brought into symbolic relationship and creatively translated into miniaturised effigies; the manikin resonates to the 'Jesuit trauma' and its stone to the 'subterranean phallus'. The stone also recalled childhood experiences of the divine in nature, in both living and dead matter (Jung 1963/1995: 86). The stone, divided into an upper and a lower, might also be considered a symbolic representation of a psychic split, yet also resolution, of an above (father–spirit) and a below (mother–matter). His scrolls have also been described as representing an early attempt at developing a symbolic language to engage with this Other as manikin (Papadopoulos and Saayman [eds.] 1984: 58).

Each of these three childhood experiences (Jesuit; subterranean phallus; manikin) also embody not only an uncanny Otherness, but also aspects of the Christian trinity. The 'Jesuit' is human-sized and associates with Christ, the son. The superhuman-sized phallus associates with God, the father. The manikin, as miniature, corresponds to the Holy Ghost as 'communicable link' between man and God.

In summary, Jung's manikin-stone conjures up not only the familiar Christian (clergymen) but also an unfamiliar and mysterious Other (Jesuit, phallus, paganism, etc.) in an ambiguous symbolic image with healing power.[4] A heretical communication with the numinosum has also begun through the scrolls to his manikin.

Together, these elements can be considered to be a relatively undifferentiated and disparate numinosum which develops, throughout Jung's life, into progressively more sophisticated forms. They prefigure the symbolic beginnings of a lifelong creative struggle involving a range of contrasting tensions – Christian–pagan, male–female, light–dark, matter–spirit, above–below, sacred–profane, animate–inanimate, transcendent–immanent, ego–self, etc. – which inform an evolving life myth. In particular, in later life, a key figure emerges as the paradoxical Mercurius; a figure I consider Jung's most sophisticated resolution of such contrasts.

I now leave Jung's childhood and progress to the turbulent and uncertain time after his break with Freud. The subsequent years, which included a mid-life crisis experienced amidst tempestuous historical times, resulted in not only apocalyptic visions and powerful dreams but also an experimental 'confrontation with the unconscious'. This was initially transcribed into his *Black Books* and then aesthetically reworked into *The Red Book*.[5]

In this work we witness an astonishing development of Jung's daimonic encounter. In particular, I here look at three excerpts with the common feature of an 'alchemical coniunctio' and birth of a god. The first of these is from the first part of *The Red Book*; namely, *Liber Primus*. The remaining two are from the second part, *Liber Secundus*.

Liber Primus

Liber Primus opens with Jung offering a Faust-like lament: all his worldly achievements and scholarly learning as success in 'the spirit of the times' had lost meaning, and a loss of soul ensued: 'I had cultivated my spirit, the spirit of this time in me, but not that spirit of the depths that turns to the things of the soul, the world of the soul' (Jung 2009: 236).

During this malaise, he is gripped by the spirit of the depths, who 'took my understanding and all my knowledge and placed them at the service of the inexplicable and the paradoxical' (ibid.: 229). Amidst intense psychic turmoil, the spirit of the depths then shape-shifts into a range of figures and embroils him in a mystery play of biblical proportions.

A central theme of this mystery gravitates around the conception and birth of an ambiguous god within his soul, who is 'born from a dark ambiguity and rises to a bright ambiguity' (Jung 2009: 244). The ambiguous god, born from a marriage of order and chaos, becomes a divine child which Jung is instructed, by the 'spirit of the depths', to serve. This god is difficult to bear as it includes the abject, the banal, the incapacitated, the horrific, the fearsome, etc., in a more complete picture compared to the Christian deity.

On the night of considering the essence of this god, Jung recounts entering an imaginal realm. In MDR he describes this as a feeling of being in the land of the dead. In this 'ancestral land' he met up with an old man with a white beard who identified himself as Elijah and his companion, a beautiful young girl who called herself Salome (and was blind). They were accompanied by a black serpent.

Elijah, Salome, the serpent and Jung then become entangled in a mystery drama in a space-time warp bridging two millennia. Salome reveals herself as Jung's brother, and also desires to be his lover. She also claims 'their' mother to be Mary, the mother of God. Jung is horrified as Salome was the murderer of John the Baptist, the 'Holy One'. He also has no wish to be the son of Mary (Jung 2009: 249). Despite such protestations, the mystery unfolds: 'Salome embraced me and I thus became a prophet, since I found pleasure in the primordial beginning, in the forest, and in the wild animals' (ibid.: 251).

A number of such exchanges take place over a couple of nights. On the third and final night there is resolution. It begins with a vision of Elijah on a steep ridge in a wasteland: to his right is dark night, and to his left is bright day separated by a rock. A large black serpent from the night side then engages in a battle with a large white serpent from the day side. After a struggle involving 'great billows of dust' there is no victor. Instead, a single serpent combining black and white emerges, in which the two have unified.

After a sequence of events, the drama then leads toward the place of Christ's crucifixion, where he also sees 'the divine child, with the white serpent in his right hand, and the black serpent in his left hand' (Jung 2009: 252). He then witnesses a green mountain upon which is the crucified Christ in his last hour, with blood streaming from the mountain's summit. Jung's identity suddenly changes. He becomes Christ:

> I am held fast and I spread my arms wide. Salome draws near. The serpent has wound itself around my whole body, and my countenance is that of a lion ... I see that a terrible and incomprehensible power forces me to imitate the Lord in his final torment ... the serpent squeezes my body in its terrible coils and the blood streams from my body, spilling down the mountainside.
>
> (Jung 2009: 252)

The ordeal then ends with Salome regaining her sight and the serpent dropping off Jung's body. He steps over the languid serpent and kneels in front of a shining Elijah. The drama ends: 'Tears fall from my eyes, and I hurry out into the night, like one who has no part in the glory of the mystery' (ibid.: 252).

In commenting on his ordeal, Jung states: 'the depths do not hesitate any longer and will force you into the mysteries of Christ. It belongs to this mystery that man is not redeemed through the hero, but becomes a Christ himself' (ibid.: 253). Further on, he sums up: 'I saw a new god, a child, who subdued daimons in his hand. The God holds the separate principles in his power, he unites them' (ibid.: 254).

* * *

In considering this central drama of *Liber Primus*, it is interesting to note that although Jung is tempted to reduce Elijah and Salome to Logos and Eros principles, he also insists they are who they are (1963/1995: 207). Here we can reflect on their most renowned features: Elijah as prophet of the coming of Christ, and Salome as lover (unrequited) and murderess of John the Baptist.

Salome's expression of love places Jung, in a sense, as a John the Baptist figure, as champion of the mysteries. Elijah, the prophet, is here a catalyst for an epiphany as the birth of a divine child which appears out of a great conflict between a black and a white serpent.[6] The divine child's ability to separate and unite the serpents corresponds to the emergence of a god-image that unites opposites, not unlike the caduceus of Hermes. To an extent this god-as-a-child born in his psyche follows the same trajectory as his childhood manikin to whom, in a sense, he gave birth.

Alchemically, this drama can be related to an early stage of the opus as a separation of the *serpens mercurialis* into white and black serpents and of their unification by means of a coniunctio. Von Franz writes of this as an awareness of the creative (white serpent) and destructive (black serpent) aspects of the unconscious itself (von Franz and Hannah 2004: 155–6). In analytical psychology the imaginative engagement of consciousness with such an ambiguous unconscious can result in the birth of the divine child as creative solution, the transcendent function.

The mystery then climaxes as an apotheosis in which Jung viscerally identifies with Christ's death agony. His form as a man with lion's head and entwined by a serpent finds amplification in the Leoencephalus, found in the Mithraic Zervan Akaruna, or *Aion*.[7] The leonine head and serpentine body also has similarities to the Gnostic Abraxas, as found in Jung's mandala *systema munditotius*, and as appearing in his *Scrutinies*. Both figures include the twelve astrological signs (or seven traditional planets): inscribed on Aion's wings, and as the star-like crown of Abraxas.

Joseph Campbell gives an imaginative account of how the typical initiate of the Mithraic mysteries would become identified with this deity (see Campbell 1964/1982: 262–9). He considers the lion to be a solar symbol of eternity and the serpent to be a lunar symbol of time. Accordingly, the name Zervan Akarana translates to 'Boundless Time' (ibid.: 266). For Campbell the lightning bolt on the chest represents 'ultimate illumination' achieved by means of such an apotheosis during identification with this deity (ibid.: 263). Alchemically, the Solar lion (eternity) and the Lunar serpent (time) unite in a coniunctio during an eclipse.[8] We might say that Jung is here being 'fixed in the mercury' as the binding agent of the coniunctio of Sol and Luna (see chapters 10 and 11).

Considering astrology, I point out that Elijah and Salome appear at the transition from the Age of Aries to the Age of Pisces. The reappearance of these figures, two millennia on, suggests the start of a new Great Month – this time as the transition from Pisces to Aquarius. This is of especial relevance considering Jung believed his lifetime coincided with this momentous transition. More specific to this event, however, is that his temporary identity with Aion has the stamp of a broader experience of 'all Ages', as this figure includes the images of all twelve constellations. We might say he experienced an initiatory 'deepest level of time' as all Ages within the 'rupture' between Platonic months.[9]

This experience also suggests a radical shift of his relation to the daimonic, compared to his early childhood. The Mithraic-like apotheosis has, perhaps, similarities to his childhood dream of a subterranean phallic deity which combined solar (eye, golden light) with lunar (phallus as 'serpent'). In *Liber Primus* he is inducted into a temporary transformation into this fearful childhood daimon; the 'God not to be named'.

In summary, we see in *Liber Primus* an apotheosis and the birth of an ambiguous god as a divine child within the psyche. A broader reading of Jung, expanding into his later works, makes clear such an epiphany is not meant for him alone, but rather comprises a new spiritual dispensation enshrined in his individuation concept as a 'Christification of the many' (Jung 1952a: 470). Here we can recall the opening title of *Liber Primus*, 'The Way of What is to Come', which reinforces such prophetic allusions. Indeed, much of *The Red Book* is comprised of sermon-like monologues that could be construed as a fleshing out of such a new spiritual dispensation.

Liber Secundus

Liber Secundus begins in an imaginal realm as an encounter with 'The Red One'. Jung is wearing green garments and is standing watch in a castle turret. He spots a red point coming nearer on a winding road that twists through forests. Eventually The Red One arrives, walks up the castle steps and approaches him. Jung fears he might be the devil. Fortunately though, he is not harmed. Instead, a lively dialogue ensues. Jung remarks: 'You're no real pagan, but the kind of pagan who runs alongside our Christian religion' (Jung 2009: 259). The Red One responds favourably that he is 'truly a good diviner of riddles' (ibid.).

A little later, after further discussion, The Red One talks of the advantage of dancing through life and philosophises on 'some third thing for which dancing would be a symbol' (ibid.: 260). At this moment, a change occurs. The Red One transforms into a reddish flesh colour and Jung's garments burst into leaf.

Later, after further adventures, Jung comes across an ascetic Christian anchorite called Ammonius[10] living alone in the Libyan desert, in contemplation of scriptures. Apart from philosophical discussions, Jung is left to contemplate and dream in the solitude of nature. Ammonius thereby opens him to a profound appreciation of not only Holy Scripture but also the desert, and its millennia-old solar cycles. However a climactic moment arises when Ammonius, induced by Jung's soliloquy on the Sun as a god, loses himself in reverie over 'glorious Helios'. He suddenly gathers himself and responds: 'no, that is pagan – what's wrong with me? I'm confused – you are Satan – I recognize you – give way, adversary!' (ibid.: 272). He aggressively lunges at Jung, who then recedes to safety by returning to the twentieth century.

A little later, whilst ruminating on darkness and evil, Jung dialogues as if with Ammonius on the relativity of good and evil. He ends with a reprimand: 'You locked Satan in the abyss for a millennium, and when the millennium had passed, you laughed at him, since he had become a children's fairy tale' (ibid.: 274).

Soon after, a development ensues when Jung comes across both The Red One and Ammonius whilst journeying in a meadow amidst hills and flowers and a green wood in the distance. Both have changed. The Red One is tall, gangly, shabby, worn out, and his red hair has become grey. Ammonius appears as an old monk with a paunch.

A number of exchanges ensue, after which Jung leaves. A powerful transformation then overcomes him. Upon reflecting on night and the solemnity of death, an angry life impulse emerges. Amidst drunkenness, dance, music, 'the giggling of luscious whores' and 'the reek of the human animal', he is delivered as a baby in swaddling clothes: 'I was born into life from below, and I grew up as heroes do, in hours rather than years. And after I had grown up, I found myself in the middle land, and saw that it was spring' (ibid.: 276). Shortly after, he recounts:

> . . . a strange being grew through me. This was a laughing being of the forest, a leaf green daimon, a forest goblin and prankster, who lived alone in the forest . . . neither disposed or indisposed toward men, full of mood and chance, obeying an invisible law . . . utterly inconstant and superficial, and yet reaching deep down, down to the kernel of the world . . . within myself I had become one as a natural being . . . I was a hobgoblin.
>
> (Jung 2009: 276–7)

* * *

This scene of The Red One, Ammonius and Jung's eventual transformation into a hobgoblin reflects a significant development on the theme of daimonic encounter. Specifically, the opening scene of The Red One winding through woods and slowly approaching is reminiscent of Jung's childhood memory of the 'Jesuit'[11] and perhaps embodies a processing of this trauma. Viewed alchemically, I draw attention to the idea that 'a "red man" appears as the personification of the *prima materia* of the philosopher's stone. It was said that he should be gently treated and not feared, since he was helpful in spite of his terrifying appearance' (Emma Jung and von Franz 1970/1998: 57).

The Red One in this case, neither Christian nor pagan, also corresponds to 'present times' which, astrologically, places him as a figure synchronous with the head of the second 'matter fish' in the Pisces Aeon. Glowing red, the colour of passion and instinct, he personifies the repressed instincts of 'below'. His encounter with Jung turns out to be mutually beneficial. The Red One becomes more humanised (flesh-coloured) and Jung has a burst of new growth, symbolised by his green garment sprouting leaves. Jung's engagement with The Red One has a life-enhancing nuance.

The subsequent figure of Ammonius can be viewed in a contrasting light. Dressed in a white garment and dedicated to many years of study of a single holy book, he personifies Christian ascetism and a spiritual 'above'. He initiates Jung into a profound appreciation of scripture, as well as a spiritual contemplation of nature's endless cycles. However, Jung catalyses in him a sudden shift toward a pagan-like recognition of his spiritual reverence for nature, and a return to the world and its 'sinful pleasures'. Astrologically Ammonius can be located in the first 'spiritual fish' of the Pisces Aeon as the dating is synchronous, historically, with this time (see Shamdasani's footnote 45, in Jung 2009: 267).

Later in his travels, after meeting up with both The Red One and Ammonius, a dramatic change occurs in which he undergoes a death-like experience and is magically reborn into a spritely nature hobgoblin. Alchemically, we might say that a coniunctio of a red and a white 'substance' has produced new life as the viriditas – the blessed greenness: the 'vertical spiritual fish' (Ammonius) and 'horizontal matter fish' (The Red One) have united in the *vas* of a womb and given birth. The 'divine child' in this case, predominantly as a nature spirit, could be said to compensate the civilised Ammonius and The Red One. Ammonius and The Red One might also be considered further differentiations of the ambiguous Jesuit figure from Jung's youth, already identified as a symbolic pre-figuration of Mercurius.[12]

The most prominent image to appear within this narrative appears on page 22 of *Liber Secundus*. On the left and right are upward and downward pointing crucifixes with serpents. These are symbols of the Christ and Antichrist dyad, with the serpent giving a Gnostic and alchemical colouration. The first 'Christ' cross is associated, in Jung's worldview, with the first Fish of Pisces. The second, 'Antichrist' cross is associated with the second Fish of Pisces (see chapter 10). In my interpretation I link Ammonius to the first of these symbols and The Red One to the second. The centre represents Jung's transformation as a greening (the colour of the Holy Ghost). The image as a whole might also be viewed alchemically, as a *circulatio*, animated by the scarabs in a motion that unites an above with a below. The scarabs might also be viewed as inaugurating a new sunrise (as the birthing of a new Aeon).

* * *

The next adventure takes Jung east, the direction in which the Sun rises daily. He travels through a narrow valley gorge in his bare feet amidst jagged rocks and alternating steps of hot, black iron and white ice through a rocky basin and up toward a mountain ridge. As he approaches the top, he hears the approach of a mighty giant Izdubar[13] with bull's horns, armour and carrying a double axe (Jung 2009: 278). Izdubar spares his life and a dialogue ensues in which Jung, representing modern man from the west, engages with this primitive giant from the east. Izdubar agonises upon hearing the scientific worldview of the west; a disenchantment that has destroyed the idea of an immortal soul and of a mythic world.

Jung's serpent-like modern knowledge further mortifies Izdubar. He reflects: 'I opened his eyes and lamed his powerful limbs with a poisoned stab. And he lay crying like a child ... a primordial grown child that required human Logos', and goes on: 'compassion seized me, since it was plain to me that I should not let him die ... He whom I sought I now possessed. The East could give me nothing other than him, the sick and fallen one' (Jung 2009: 281).

Returning to his western land, Jung magics the 'dead' Izdubar into an egg to retain the secrecy of his god. Back home, he places the egg on a sacred red rug and incubates it 'with the magical warmth of his gaze' (Jung 2009: 283–4). A series of incantations reminiscent of Vedic hymns[14] follow in which he identifies himself as 'the mother, the simple maiden, who gave birth and did not know how' (ibid.: 284). In the first incantation, for example, he recognises his god: 'He is the eternal emptiness and the eternal fullness. Nothing resembles him and he resembles everything. Eternal darkness and eternal brightness. Eternal below and eternal above. Double nature in one' (ibid.: 284).

On the evening of the third day he opens the egg. Smoke rises, and then Izdubar appears, transformed and whole, as if awoken from a deep sleep. Staying with the development, the opened egg and fiery smoke then results in the emergence of the divine child Phanes.[15] The legend reads: 'This is the image of the divine child. It means the completion of a long path ... I called him Phanes, because he is the newly appearing God' (see footnote 211).

Phanes then shape-shifts into a sequence of figures: he reappears as the cabiri Telesphoros, daimon of the Greek healer Asklepius; as slayer of the monster Atmavictu; as cosmic anthropos, etc. Of these various shape-shifts, I draw particular attention to the image appearing on page 123 of *Liber Secundus*, dated 4 January 1920. Later in this chapter, I shall amplify this specific image using astrological symbolism.

* * *

Commenting on this part of the drama, I begin by noting that the name Izdubar is a synonym for the Sumerian high priest Gilgamesh, the epic poem about whom is thought to have originated from around 2500 BCE, a time of Goddess worship. It thus constellates a deeper mythico-historical layer (compared to Elijah, Salome, Ammonius and The Red One) as the Age of the Bull, ruled by Venus, the Sumerian Ishtar.

Considered 'two thirds god, one third man', this solar hero was the dead and resurrected son and consort of the Goddess. In an effort to tame his 'unbridled arrogance' the creator Goddess made a twin, a lunar brother, as a challenger. Thus the wild man Enkidu emerged, who roamed with the wild animals, grazing like a gazelle. A disconcerted Gilgamesh lured Enkidu, using a temple harlot, into his precinct. After a gruelling fight Enkidu emerged as victor. Gilgamesh, impressed by such an adversary, reconciled with him and they became inseparable friends (see Campbell 1964/1982: 87–92).

In another adventure, catalysed by grief over Enkidu's death, Gilgamesh, questioning his mortality, ends up on a quest to find the plant of immortality. After an arduous adventure, he eventually discovers the magical plant in the depths of the ocean, only to lose it again to a serpent (Campbell 1964/1982: 91–2).

Jung's image of Izdubar/Gilgamesh includes bull's horns (see page 36 of *Liber Secundus*). This motif associates mythically with the crescent moon. The solar

Izdubar has here integrated his lunar brother Enkidu. We thus see a reappearance of the Sun and Moon coniunctio, at a more differentiated 'human' level, compared to the original lion and serpent 'animal' coniunctio. The learned priest as Gilgamesh and wild man as Enkidu are united. Here, again, is resonance with the ambiguous Jesuit that combined both priest and 'man from the woods'. The basis in the more remote past, compared to Ammonius and The Red One, means this figure can also be interpreted psychologically (in a Jungian way) as an eruption from a deeper stratum of the unconscious psyche. He brings with him a pre-Christian Goddess worldview.

Izdubar as 'consort of the Goddess' also unites the above and the below, symbolised in his clothes as a combination of blue and red (we can think here of the spiritual and chthonic polarities of the archetype, explained by Jung as 'ultra-violet' and 'infra-red' extremities of a single continuum).[16] Viewed alchemically, we see a reappearance of our *prima materia* as the 'red man of terrible countenance, not to be feared' now tempered by the inclusion of blue.

After a death and incubation as an egg, Izdubar re-emerges as the spiritual epiphany of Phanes of the Orphic mysteries; of great splendour, having four eyes, four wings, etc. Indeed, there has been a transformation from a 'dark ambiguity' as Izdubar to a 'bright ambiguity' as Phanes. Jung appears to have required a psychic digestion of this figure, which he represents as a series of mandalas, the first of which is titled Phanes[17] and subtitled 'metabolism in the individual' (2009: 361; see also mandalas 80 onward). Viewed alchemically, the hermaphrodite-like duality of Phanes could be interpreted as a coniunctio on a 'spiritual level'.[18] This can also, perhaps, be considered a further 'alchemical sublimation' of the Jesuit trauma from a giant, frightening Izdubar to a benign, spiritually luminous Phanes.

The subsequent transformation of Phanes into Telesphoros, one of the cabiri, also emphasises that this new god-image includes an aspect of a healing communication 'whispered to the physician', similar to Jung's childhood manikin memories.

Before discussing the last image I have chosen to look at (page 123 of *Liber Secundus*), I refer to the final part of *Liber Secundus*, titled *The Magician*. In this scene Jung encounters Philemon[19] and Baucis, the loving couple living close to the earth, who welcomed the gods into their humble home when the rest of the community had forgotten them.

* * *

After a long search in a quest to learn 'magical arts', Jung eventually finds Philemon and Baucis in their small country home, in front of which is a large bed of tulips. He ponders to himself: 'There goes old Philemon in the garden, bent, with a watering can in his shaking hand' (Jung 2009: 312).

Upon meeting, Jung coaxes the elusive Philemon to teach him 'the black arts', lest this knowledge die with the latter. Philemon replies: '... why should I tell you anything? It would be better if everything were buried with me ... It will never be lost to humanity, since magic is reborn with each and every one of us' (ibid.: 313). He is a little persuaded, however, and begins to discuss the irrational incomprehensibilities of magic. Jung, having partially understood, muses: 'The magical way arises by itself. If one opens up chaos, magic also arises' (ibid.: 314).

After a satisfying exchange, he expresses gratitude to Philemon: 'Now I know your final mystery: you are a lover. You have succeeded in uniting what has been sundered, that is, binding together the Above and the Below' (ibid.: 315). Continuing, he says: '*You lie in the sun*, Oh Philemon, like a serpent that coils around itself. Your wisdom is the wisdom of serpents' (ibid.: 315). A bit further on, he adds: 'Oh Philemon ... fructifying water flows into your garden from inexhaustible jugs . . . you pour out living water, from which the flowers of your garden bloom, a starry water, a dew of the night' (ibid.: 316).

* * *

Before discussing the relevance of Philemon, as portrayed here, a few preliminary observations of the image appearing on page 123 of *Liber Secundus* are in order.

This 'cosmic anthropos' is not directly referred to in the text. By inference, however, it can be shown to relate to the water-bearer constellation of Aquarius. The water in this picture undulates in the same manner as the Aquarian glyph, which is also composed of 'two waters'. In addition, prior to Aquarius (above the ecliptic and between Pisces and Aquarius) is a 'quadratus' constellation, often depicted as a celestial temple, as we see in this image (also often depicted as the winged horse Pegasus). Of further relevance is that Jung, in the *Visions Seminars*, considered this constellation in terms of Hermes–Mercurius: 'Aquarius represents the thing above as well as the thing below. Therefore in the semi-antique representations of Aquarius ... he is shown as an ithyphallic figure, like a very primitive god of fertility' (Jung 1998: 733).

In this image we also see that the *prima materia* as Izdubar has been transformed. His blue and red have undergone 'alchemical processes' and reappear in the *vas* of the cosmic anthropos as a fructifying liquid. For Jung, this perhaps corresponds to a successful unification of the instinctual and spiritual polarities of the archetype, in the form of an alchemical coniunctio of an above and a below.

Such observations allow for a satisfying juxtaposition of Philemon with the Aquarian water-bearer as 'cosmic anthropos'. We can think of Philemon 'watering his tulips' and of his 'starry and fructifying water' that flows from 'inexhaustible jugs'. Philemon is also described by Jung as a lover and as one who unites the above and the below. Described as a serpent, he is, in a sense, also ithyphallic. Furthermore, the building in the top left can be related to Philemon and Baucis' hut, which was transformed by the gods into a temple.

In this sense, Philemon represents a sophisticated celestial counterpart of Jung's 'underground god' from his childhood subterranean phallus dream. He can also be considered a celestial 'shadow counterpart' to the Christian God in heaven. His reflection below, as a human-like daimon with whom Jung dialogues, affords a further nuance condensed as both 'son of God' and Holy Ghost.[20]

To emphasise: Philemon as Jung's 'psychagogue and guru' is here revealed as a god-image commensurate with the angelic-like water-bearer of the approaching Aquarian Age. *The Red Book* as a whole also reveals his relation to the daimonic as having shifted from childhood 'scrolls to his manikin' to that of enigmatic dialogue.

The Red Book – a Gnostic or alchemical myth?

The Red Book has features of a personal experience of the numinosum, akin to a Gnostic myth. We should remember Philemon was described by Jung, in *MDR*, as a pagan with an 'Egypto-Hellenistic atmosphere' and a 'Gnostic colouration' (Jung 1963/1995: 207). We can also consider the transformation of the chthonic Izdubar (consider his bull's horns and his emergence from the depths of history) to the spiritually luminous Phanes. There is a development from a 'dark ambiguity' to a 'bright ambiguity'. This has intimations of the Gnostic myth of the fallen anthropos imprisoned in matter, and of its re-collection and redemption into a spiritual being of light. The most notable characters in *The Red Book* are also male, which is further reminiscent of a patriarchal Gnosticism.

However, it contrasts with Gnosticism in that it values the chthonic. The Red One's effect on Jung, for example, is to value instinctual joys. Philemon, as lover, also unites the instinctual below with a spiritual above. Indeed, *The Red Book* was begun after Jung's years of championing Freud's psychoanalysis, which sought to value and 'redeem' the repressed instincts.

This said, a full integration of the chthonic is not satisfyingly apparent in *The Red Book*. For example, the spiritual divine child Phanes (image 114) is immediately followed by a more disturbing human/animal headed image as the 'shadow of God' (page 115 of *Liber Secundus*). This image, not mentioned in the text, might be considered compensatory to the overly bright Phanes. Its absence in the narrative reveals a tension, in my opinion – Jung's difficulty in conceptually integrating this figure within his current (predominantly Gnostic-informed) myth.

We witness a similar theme in the evolution of the 'Gnostic' Philemon. Jung recounts that, later, Philemon was modified by the assimilation of a figure he called Ka, based on the Egyptian idea of the 'king's Ka' as his embodied soul in earthly form. He envisaged his Ka-soul as having come from below, from a 'deep shaft in the earth' (Jung: 1963/1995: 209). Thus, in one of Jung's paintings, Philemon with a kingfisher wing is combined with Ka in such a way as to also include a stone herm-like base with a bronze upper. He points out the demonic Mephistophelian expression of Ka, surrounded by a celestial halo (ibid.: 209).[21]

The earthly Ka figure could be seen as compensating for the more spiritual, winged Philemon's suffering a lame foot (symbolic of a wounded relation to materiality and the earth). Indeed, in *Black Book* 7 Ka is described as Philemon's shadow (Jung 2009; see footnote 232). The herm, with base of stone and upper bronze and crowned by a 'celestial halo', also has elements of his childhood phallus dream, modified to include a 'spiritual above' as Philemon's wing. The inclusion of stone and bronze also anticipates his alchemical fascination with the inorganic and seeking toward a spirit–matter synthesis. This image also points toward a sacralisation of the inanimate (stone, bronze) and therefore suggests a further stage of integration of his childhood manikin and stone into his evolving myth.

Ka, like the 'shadow of God', features in *The Red Book* (his image appearing on page 115 in *Liber Secundus*), but not in the text. Again this reflects, in my opinion, the difficulty of integrating such a figure at this stage of his life. Indeed, we read of further developments in which he contrasts the spiritual meaning aspect of Philemon with the nature-spirit and alchemical Anthroparion 'with which at the time I was still unfamiliar'[22] (Jung 2009: 209–10). We then read that 'in time I was able to integrate both figures [Philemon and Ka] through the study of alchemy' (Jung 1963/1995: 209–10).

In light of the above, *The Red Book* can be considered a stage in his evolving life myth from what can be considered a predominantly pre-1929 *Gnostic* phase to a later post-1929 *alchemical* phase. The appearance of alchemical motifs in *The Red Book*, such as the various coniunctios, might be considered illustrative of how a psychic process can be amplified using alchemy, especially considering that it was completed prior to the start of his serious interest in this area, in 1929. Indeed, this is what Jung believed. In the final paragraph of *The Red Book* he reiterates that 'in time I was able to integrate the figures through my study of alchemy' (2009: 360).

In particular, specific features of his alchemical worldview that contributed toward the further development of his myth revolve around a stronger inclusion of the feminine, the chthonic and the inanimate. This model strives for an ultimate 'unification of opposites' that includes the male with the female (artifex and *soror mystica*), as well as the spiritual with the chthonic, to the depth of inorganic matter.

Thus, although the feminine appears prominently in *The Red Book*, there is still an under-representation. For example, a solar Philemon and a lunar Priestess appear together, on consecutive pages (see images 154 and 155 in *Liber Secundus*). However, the lunar Priestess is absent in the narrative. Philemon's partner Baucis also hardly gets a mention. Overall, there is a dearth of sexual imagery in *The Red Book*, compared to typical alchemical images.[23] In alchemy, for example, we need only consider the following: 'Mercurius represents the 'continuous cohabitation' which is found in unalloyed form in the Tantric Shiva-Shakti concept' (Jung: 1943/1948: 231). A personal example of such a 'sexual coniunctio' is found in his 1944 near-death visions which culminated in the *heiros gamos* (see chapter 7).

The inanimate, neglected in his Gnostic phase, also finds fuller expression in his alchemical model. Indeed, he admits to having 'overlooked' an aspect of the self that included the inorganic. For example, in 1939, whilst working on *Psychology and Alchemy*, he recounted a hypnagogic-like vision of a not quite life-sized, greenish-gold crucified Christ at the foot of his bed. He realised this pointed to an alchemical vision of Christ; an analogy to the alchemists' *aurum non vulgi* and *viriditas* as a facet of the self-image which he had overlooked. This vision, for him, was 'a union of the Christ-image with his analogue in matter, the *filius macrocosmi*' (1963/1995: 237). For him, the green-gold alluded to the living quality not only in the human but also in the inorganic realm, as the *anima mundi* or world-animating and cosmic anthropos.

I now consider Jung's old age, by means of a brief commentary on his medieval-style retreat beside the lake, his Bollingen tower, and his now iconic Bollingen stone. This allows for a beginning, as his early childhood memories, to be viewed in light of an ending, embodied in stone, in old age.[24]

Old age – Bollingen

A reading of the chapter 'Bollingen' in *MDR* reveals a figure-ground shift in which Jung's No. 2 personality, as the ancient and timeless 'age-old son of the mother', takes prominence. Here we see a dramatic shift in his relation to Other, compared to his early 'childhood secret'. It would even appear that he has here *become* this Other, and that his life myth has now been 'immortalised' in stone.

The tower itself, emerging from the earth and pointing into the sky, shares features with the phallic-god of his childhood dream, now transformed into a Holy Sanctum. Erect into the sky, it can be interpreted as a coniunctio of earth and heaven. Indeed it is possible that Jung considered himself to be imbuing it with 'magical efficacy' as a talisman, in the Hermetic sense, to help facilitate, amongst other things, a healing coniunctio in the broader culture as a major theme of the coming Aquarian Age.

His Bollingen stone also shares such features. On the front face is an arrangement of the traditional planets paired as oppositions in coniunctio relationship: Sun–Moon; Mars–Venus; Jupiter–Saturn. One can further amplify this stone with his numerous alchemical references to the *lapis*, such as his descriptions of it as the *lumen novum* (new light). In addition, of particular relevance is that we see on the front face and in the centre an engraved manikin Jung identified as Telesphoros. In the centre of this manikin we see the astrological glyph for Mercury, as if to suggest this figure embodies the core 'riddle' of the stone's meaning.

Essential features of the Bollingen stone also resonate with Jung's childhood memories. His childhood manikin appears as the central Telesphoros figure, now fused with the stone. Thus the ambiguous Christian–pagan manikin and an animistic-like reverence for fire and stone are brought into a harmonious relationship (the engraved Telesphoros 'glows like a star'). The inscriptions in the stone are reminiscent of the scrolls he gave his manikin. The divided stone of his childhood (an upper and a lower half) is also reflected in the astrological glyphs separated into opposing pairs arranged as a coniunctio. We might further consider this stone as the 'head' of his childhood subterranean phallus dream. The 'eye' of the phallus from this dream relates to the first image he noticed in the stone, a 'sort of an eye, which looked at me', from which he chiselled the homunculus Telesphoros (Jung 1963/1995: 254–5).

In summary, contemplating his Bollingen tower and stone, we see a beginning meeting an ending. A cluster of disparate numinous phenomena, awakened in early childhood and loaded with the charge of western culture's unresolved psycho-spiritual problems, finds a level of resolution as his life myth embodied in the images of his old age as the alchemist's *lapis philosophorum*. Furthermore, this seemingly incongruent collection of symbols, as I have tried to illustrate, coalesces around the paradoxical alchemical Mercurius – a figure whose glyph features centrally on this stone.

Notes

1 Jung uses the spellings 'daimon' and 'daemon' interchangeably (Jung 1973–75: 465). For more detail on the idea of the daimon, see von Franz 1980/1995: 143–59.
2 Later, around age 35, he recognised in this figure 'a little cloaked god of the ancient world, a Telesphoros such as stands on the monuments of Asklepios and reads to him from a scroll' (Jung 1963/1995: 38).
3 Jung believed that 'phallus' is etymologically linked to the word 'phalos', meaning 'shining', 'bright' (see Jung 1963/1995: 28).
4 In contrast, consider Hayman, who states that 'Unlike the fire and stones, it [the manikin] did not represent his secret self. If it had, he would not have made it look like a clergyman' (Hayman 1999: 15). Hayman neglected to mention that Jung himself, at least later, associated the manikin with both the familiar clergymen and the Jesuit priest (Jung 1963/1995: 42).
5 *The Red Book* is made up of *Liber Primus*, *Liber Secundus* and *Scrutinies*.
6 von Franz has likened the image of black and white serpents to two 'paradoxical' aspects of the unconscious (*serpens mercurialis*) that can be either healing or destructive, or both. Its mastery (as achieved by the divine child) signifies for her the achievement of a 'right relationship' to the unconscious (see Hannah and von Franz 2004: 154–8).
7 This image appears on the frontispiece of Jung's *Aion*.
8 Christ's crucifixion occurred during an eclipse.
9 Here, Taylor's concept of 'higher times' is relevant. Jung's experience corresponds to Taylor's notion of Platonic eternity in which '[t]he really real, full being is outside time, unchanging' and where time is 'a moving image of eternity' (Taylor, cited in Main 2011: 152).
10 Shamdasani identifies this figure (see footnote 45; Jung 2009: 267).
11 The Jesuit came down from the woods and Jung, terrified, hastened to the highest point in the attic.
12 Mercurius as both spirit and matter is covered in chapter 9.
13 See footnote 96, in which Shamdasani identifies Izdubar as an early name for Gilgamesh (Jung 2009: 277).
14 See footnote 130 (Jung 2009: 284).
15 Shamdasani, citing a number of sources, summarises this Orphic figure in an extensive footnote. For example, he points out Jung's 1912 description of him as 'a god of love, androgynous'. In the *Black Books* he is described variously as 'the marvellous, shining one', as 'a golden bird' and as 'the messenger of Abraxas'. A more detailed description follows, replete with paradox, though with a clear bias toward positive spiritual qualities.
16 Note that Jung only officially introduced this metaphor in 1947, found in 'On the Nature of the Psyche'.
17 This is dated 2 August 1917 – the night of a full moon in Aquarius–Leo.
18 The lion–serpent could be considered a chthonic coniunctio, as was the subterranean phallus in the earth womb.
19 In *MDR* we read that another figure developed out of Elijah whom he called Philemon – a pagan with an 'Egypto-Hellenistic atmosphere' and with a 'Gnostic colouration' (Jung 1963/1995: 207).

20 In *MDR* Jung remarks about Philemon that 'at times he seemed to me quite real, as if he were a living personality. I went walking up and down the garden with him' (Jung 1963/1995: 208).

21 This painting has never come to light (see footnote 232; 2009: 306).

22 Jaffé included a footnote to this statement: 'as the spirit of quicksilver, the alchemical Mercurius was also an Anthroparion' (Jung 1963/1995: 210).

23 Consider, for example, the images of the *Rosarium Philosophorum* that appear in *Psychology of the Transference.*

24 For further context, see the chapter 'Bollingen' in *MDR*.

Chapter 6

A fish–snake synchronicity

In 'The Spirit Mercurius' (1943/1948), Jung establishes a Wotan–Mercurius identity. In the debate around Jung's alleged Nazi sympathies, there are often references to the figure of Wotan; only in a few instances, however, is a Wotan–Mercurius identity also mentioned (see Martin and Sherry, in Maidenbaum and Martin 1991: 9, 130). It would appear the deeper implications of this identity have not been explored. In light of this we should also remember that the picture Jung conjures of Wotan is sketchy and cursory compared to the subtle and sophisticated picture of Mercurius he creates.

In exploring this Wotan–Mercurius identity more deeply, including a consideration of Jung's alleged anti-Semitism,[1] I centre attention on a number of themes: Wotan and Germanic spiritual potential; the end of an Aeon; 1942 and 'The Spirit Mercurius'; and Jung's 1944 near-death experience.

Wotan and Germanic spiritual potential

At Eranos in 1942 Jung stated that the 'spirit in the bottle', Mercurius, in the German fairytale was identical to Wotan, a German national pagan god (Jung 1943/1948: 198). He had also already written of this god in 1936 in 'Wotan', wherein we read of the restless German spirit emerging as a released pagan god of war and finding expression in the Nazi party. Jung had an especial personal affinity for the god Wotan, even apparently into old age.[2] Such an affinity locates him spiritually in a male-pagan German tradition: the irrational frenzied warrior, but also the mantic diviner. In the words of Stein, 'His feeling for Wotan ... provides a metaphoric image of the psychic renewal Jung himself must have been feeling by way of identification with the upsurge of this youthful masculine energy in Germany' (Stein, in Maidenbaum and Martin 1991: 101).

Accordingly, it is generally accepted that Jung's position on National Socialism, at the beginning, was that it represented for him the emergence of a wild, pagan Wotan-like energy, bursting through the veneer of Christian Germany. In his view, the numinosity of this archetype entering collective consciousness had the ambiguous potential for either good or evil, depending on the engaging attitude of consciousness. In 'Wotan', we read:

> National Socialism was one of those psychological mass phenomena, one of those outbreaks of the collective unconscious, about which I had been speaking for nearly twenty years. The driving forces of a psychological mass movement are essentially archetypal. Every archetype contains the highest and lowest, evil and good, and is therefore capable of producing diametrically opposite results. Hence it is impossible to make out at the start whether it will prove to be positive or negative. ... The therapist's aim is to bring the positive, valuable, and living quality of the archetype – which will sooner or later be integrated into consciousness in any case – into reality, and at the same time to obstruct as far as possible its damaging and pernicious tendencies... If an archetype is not brought into reality consciously, there is no guarantee whatever that it will be realized in its favourable form; on the contrary, there is all the more danger of a destructive regression. It seems as if the psyche were endowed with consciousness for the very purpose of preventing such destructive possibilities from happening.
>
> (Jung 1936: 236–7)

In his view, it was especially the Germanic psyche that had great potentiality for transformation: 'The "Aryan" unconscious ... contains tensions and creative germs of an as yet unfulfilled future' (1934: 165). In contrast, he writes that the 'average Jew is already much too conscious and differentiated to be pregnant with the tensions of the unborn future' (ibid.: 166). In establishing the identity of Wotan in accordance with Mercurius, Jung also implies that the German psyche is capable of a profound alchemical transformation, perhaps to the level of the alchemist's *homo quadratus* or *homo altus*. Indeed, it has been suggested that Jung himself had undergone such an enigmatic transformation. For example, Erich Neumann (a Jewish Jungian) apparently believed that Jung, through his far-reaching integration of the collective unconscious, had become 'a new species of human being' (Neumann, cited by Kirsch, in Maidenbaum and Martin 1991: 70).

In light of the above, Jung may well have believed himself to have a Wotan-orientated destiny yoked to the German cause. Thus, with the rise of National Socialism and its Wotan-like swastika symbol in the early 1930s, it is more easy to understand how he may have been swept into an 'unconscious identification with events in Germany, and perhaps even with the power of Hitler' (Martin, in Maidenbaum and Martin 1991: 9).

In this context we can also recall his 1932 comment in the *Visions Seminars* about the square of Pegasus being 'the ruling principle of our times' and his assertion that 'people are now tremendously busy with squares as they were busy with the trinity before; all the old gods of India and Egypt and Greece were trinities' (Jung 1998: 731). For him, this 'most helpful symbol', which allows a spiritual transcendence by means of a libido principle (a coniunctio of spirit and instinct), represents a more complete personality, with the potential of healing the one-sidedness of a (trinitarian) neurosis (ibid.: 732).

He no doubt also recognised the alchemical black–white–red colour combination of the swastika.[3] However the anti-clockwise motion of this image, in his symbol-language, is problematic and prognostic of a regressive and 'sinister' activation of the archetype (Jung, in McGuire and Hull 1978/1990: 125).

In light of these remarks we can consider the opinion of Jung's Jewish secretary, Jaffé:

> Some of his observations from the years 1933–34 lead one to conclude that he set his hopes on a fruitful and peaceful development in Germany, and that he was willing to give National Socialism a chance in its early days . . . Only his deceptive hope that something positive, perhaps even a new culture, might emerge from the chaos can explain Jung's attitude.
>
> (Jaffé 1989: 91)

Building on such speculations, I also highlight Jung's friendship with the Indologist Professor Hauer, which apparently began in the late 1920s (Bair 2004: 434). More specifically, in 1932 at a seminar in Kusnacht, Hauer gave a presentation on Kundalini Yoga. Jung as respondent correlated his individuation process with Kundalini Yoga.[4] A few months later, in 1933, Hauer and Jung's professional paths apparently diverged, with Hauer forming the Nazi-orientated German Faith Movement and Jung taking up the position of president of the controversial German-controlled international journal *Zentralblatt* (ibid.: 434). Hauer's intentions were to modulate the 'eruption from the biological and spiritual depths' into a new religion for the Third Reich, ideologically rooted in pagan German romanticism (Samuels 1993: 463–70). Although Jung broke relations with Hauer due to such Nazi sympathies, it remains a curious anomaly that in 'The Spirit Mercurius' of 1942 he is still writing of the pagan, chthonic German spirit being alchemically transformed.

These circumstances suggest that Jung believed the Aryan Germanic psyche to have unique spiritual potential, and that his analytical psychology was a method to creatively transform this potential. More precisely, in 'Wotan', Jung emphasised that this pagan god also had a mantic side; he 'predicted that in time the divinatory side would also be revealed, and he seemed to be invoking this side by opening the article with a prophecy by Nostradamus and closing it with a cryptic reference to Wotan consulting the head of Mimir' (Sherry, in Maidenbaum and Martin 1991: 123). We should remember here that Jung was an avid user of the oracular I Ching and astrology, and apparently also even practiced phrenology (Bair 2004: 334). In light of these considerations it is possible he viewed his analytical psychology, with its use of oracles and divination, as the mantic side of this resurgent Wotan.

Concerning his 'prophecy' as Wotan consulting the head of Mimir in 1936, it would certainly appear so. In his 1945 essay 'After the Catastrophe' he referred back to this prophecy with the utterance 'the myth has been fulfilled' (Jung 1945: 194). By implication, he is here identifying himself with Wotan's mantic side.

The end of an aeon? A fish–snake synchronicity

In 1936, in the year of writing 'Wotan', whilst on a walk during his summer holiday in Bollingen, Jung stumbled upon a dead snake with a dead fish in its mouth. He was so amazed at this 'synchronistic event' that he made an image of it in stone (see Figure 6.1) at his Bollingen retreat (Hannah 1976: 236).[5]

We know Jung carved prophetic motifs on his Bollingen wall (ibid.: 341). I thus speculate that he considered this fish-snake event an augur of things to come; a prophecy. In his world-view at the time, the fish would signify Christianity (and possibly the Christian nations). The snake, simplistically, would represent paganism (the emerging Nazis?). In a letter in 1932 he wrote that animals in conflict, in terms of his dream interpretation method, represent a conflict still outside human consciousness, in the collective unconscious (Jung 1973–75: 96). In reading such an augur, in light of political tensions in Europe and in terms of his understanding of symbols, I suggest that he anticipated the pagan snake would be 'swallowing' the Christian fish: a victory of Nazi Germany over the Christian nations?[6] Or possibly mutual destruction, after an ambitious attempt by the snake to swallow the fish? Or perhaps 'a third thing' aligned to his concept of the transcendent function? Aziz elaborates:

> From Jung's point of view, the image was a depiction of how the new emerging pagan spirit, symbolized by the snake, was seeking to devour the Christian spirit, symbolized by the fish. The interplay of these two opposites, it should be pointed out, was full of import for Jung because he believed that through the clash of the pagan and Christian spirits a uniting symbol would arise that would be of particular healing significance to our present age.
>
> (Aziz 1990: 160)

Aziz, however, does not expand on this theme, and nowhere does he mention such figures as Mercurius or Merlin (symbols which represent such a unification of the pagan and Christian spirits). We can add to this Jung's idea of humanity being on the cusp of the Age of Aquarius, when the old symbols would die and new symbols would be born.[7] For example, in 1930, in the *Visions Seminars*, he states: 'Now if . . . about 2150 years after the end of Aries, a new symbol should be produced, it would be a sacrificed fish, because ours is the age, or the platonic month, of the Fishes' (Jung 1998: 110).

As mentioned in chapter 4, he initially believed the start of World War II to be the Christian 'End of Days'. In this view the rise of Germanic Wotan signified the beginnings of chaotic apocalyptic events: in Jung's view, an inevitable precondition for the birthing of the Age of Aquarius. Thus, with the eventual onset of World War II, he was witnessing the augury of the fish–snake synchronicity playing itself out on the European stage. In this schema of fatalistic unfolding, Jung also viewed Hitler in the role of an Antichrist and as 'an instrument of God' (Hannah 1976: 264). In the fracas of Europe through this period, it is also tempting to believe

Figure 6.1 Fish–snake engraving at Bollingen (personal photograph).

that in inflationary moments he perceived himself to be an 'instrument of God': as prophet and light-bringer for the imminent Age of Aquarius. In this schema his role resonated more with the mantic aspect of Wotan, and Hitler's with the fury aspect.

Such a perspective perhaps also affords insight into his alleged anti-semitism. It has been suggested that his acrimonious falling out with Freud and psychoanalysis fuelled what has been termed his 'Jewish complex' (Kirsch, in Maidenbaum and Martin 1991: 86). The turmoil in Europe in the 1930s was also a fertile environment for opportunism:

> In the face of the Nazi takeover, Jung, of course, had at least one ulterior motive, which is now well documented, of pursuing a vendetta against Freud and his close associates who had spent the twenty years since the break demonizing Jung as an unscientific woolly-headed mystic.
>
> (Naifeh and Smith 2003: 127)

As a movement, psychoanalysis competed with Jung's fledgling analytical psychology. In the years that followed, it could be argued that a 'magical contest' between these movements was brewing. Nazi Germany, with its anti-Semitism and imperialism, had the potential to vanquish psychoanalysis, with the possible outcome of instating Jung's analytical psychology as victor. This, at least, formed aspects of the cultural context from 1933 to 1939, when Jung controversially retained editorship of the Nazi-influenced *Zentralblatt*.[8] In light of these ideas, if we add a 'power complex' to his 'Jewish complex' and consider his views on the Aryan psyche, then we intuit an insidious aspect of his personality that may, at times, have opportunistically aligned with aspects of Nazi racialist ideology.[9]

1942 and 'The Spirit Mercurius'

> Mercurius, that two-faced god, comes as the *lumen naturae*, the Servator and Salvator, only to those whose reason strives toward the highest light ever received by man, and who do not trust exclusively to the *cognitio vespertina*. For those who are unmindful of this light, the *lumen naturae* turns into a diabolical seducer. Lucifer, who could have brought light, becomes the father of lies whose voice in our time, supported by press and radio, revels in orgies of propaganda and leads untold millions to ruin.
>
> (Jung: 1943/1948: 250)

By 1942 the balance of power between Nazi Germany and the Allies was precarious (Sherry 2001: 360): a time of deep uncertainty regarding the likely outcome. It was only in 1943 that the fortunes of war began to turn against Germany (ibid.: 363). In this context it is illuminating to consider Jung's Eranos lectures on 'The Spirit Mercurius' (delivered in the summer of 1942). A reading of this work, through the filter of a tension of Christian and pagan spirits, illustrates the extent of this struggle. A subtext can be discerned that suggests his position/s concerning pagan Nazi Germany and the Allies. To be sure, Jung admits to the value of such a reading of his works. For example, Hannah recounts that:

> When Jung's patients and pupils were having difficulty in facing the unconscious, he would often speak of the time he was writing Symbols of Transformation. He was haunted by bad dreams, and it still took him a few years to see that the book *Symbols of Transformation* could be taken as himself, as a picture of his own psychic condition, and that an analysis of the book, even at the time, would have led to an analysis of his own unconscious processes.
>
> (Hannah 1976: 100)

From this perspective, a reading of 'The Spirit Mercurius' captures the deep complexity and ambiguity of Jung's own psyche (conscious and unconscious); perhaps also a reflection of an internalised outer conflict between Nazi Germany and the Allies.

In light of this it is revealing to trace the protean shape-shifting of Mercurius in Jung's second lecture. This deity is described by him as corresponding 'not only to Christ, but to the triune divinity in general' (Jung 1943/1948: 222). A few pages on, Mercurius is described as an 'ambiguous, dark, paradoxical and thoroughly pagan god' (ibid.: 241). Could this be read in terms of his own affinity for the pagan German cause, yet also his firm stance in favour of the Christian Allies? Certainly, in the image of Mercurius, we get a 'united double nature' (ibid.: 218). Jung, with his deep Wotan–Mercurius affinity, is possibly also alluding to his own 'united double nature' on such crucial issues.

It is therefore interesting to discover that as late as 1942, he appeared to have access (directly or indirectly!) to the Nazi inner circle at the highest levels of authority. There is an intriguing story related by Hannah that would suggest he was involved in attempts to broker a truce with Nazi Germany in the year 1942. According to Hannah, the project involved a number of Swiss and German psychiatrists. One of the German doctors, because of his profession, apparently had access to Nazi headquarters. Jung also wanted Hannah to convey the message of the project to England (Hannah 1976: 273). However later, at Eranos in 1942, he recounted to Hannah that the plan had failed.

> At a concert one evening during the Eranos Tagung, he came to sit by me and murmured under cover of the music: 'Yours was an Abraham's sacrifice, we have had to give up the whole idea!' He added: 'The Nazis are too evil, no peace can be made with them, the whole thing will have to be completely destroyed, whatever it costs.' The next day, during the journey back to Kusnacht, he told me what had happened. When it was mentioned to Hitler, he had flown into one of his berserker rages, and the German psychiatrist had saved his life only by escaping to Switzerland, where he remained for the rest of the war.
>
> (Hannah 1976: 273–4)

Such an event, no doubt symptomatic of Jung's narcissistic personality, also brings to light his self-perceived role as 'secret agent'. Around this time he may also have reflected again on his fish–snake augury, this time reading it as meaning the brokering of a truce between Nazi Germany and the Allies.

Building on such themes, we note that in 'The Spirit Mercurius', he also writes that releasing Mercurius from the *vas* is alchemically incorrect (Jung 1943/1948: 202). In his view, this spirit needs to be transformed through alchemical procedures (ibid.: 203). It would appear that Jung intuited a greater potential of transformation of the German spirit. I aver that he believed history would have run a very different course if the engaging consciousness of the German people was such that it could have creatively modulated the wild, pagan spirit that had emerged in German cultural consciousness. Indeed, Mercurius is also described as a *process* that evolves from evil to good.

> If Mercurius is not exactly the evil one himself, he at least contains him – that is, he is morally neutral, good and evil, or as Khunrath says: 'good with the good, evil with the evil.' His nature is more exactly defined, however, if one conceives him as a *process* that begins with evil and ends with good.
>
> (Jung 1943/1948: 228)

In reading this excerpt as personal subtext, we can also detect a hope of redemption from his earlier 'flirtation with National Socialism'. He no doubt believed his analytical psychology, with its mantic leanings and emphasis on dealing with the shadow and individuation, were tools that could have effected a more benign and creative outcome for Germany – of a new beginning at the dawning of a new platonic month.

Jung's 1944 illness

Some Jungians have attributed his racial insensitivity to his 'inferior feeling function'. Sherry, for example, has interpreted Jung's 1944 heart event as a psychogenic consequence of his impoverished feminine and feeling side (Sherry 2001: 363–4). Like a snake shedding an old skin, Jung's personality and theoretical position repeatedly evolved. Kirsch relates that '[t]he outstanding fact about Jung is that he continually changed, that his unceasing confrontation with the collective unconscious produced a continuing transformation of his individuality' (Kirsch, in Maidenbaum and Martin 1991: 68). The year 1944, in particular, can be considered pivotal.

With the likely defeat of the Third Reich in 1944, a new era dawned. The Nazi dream of a 'thousand-year rule' was destroyed, along with a host of related esoteric beliefs. If Jung did harbour a 'united dual nature', with one side of his personality in Hermetic support of a German victory, then 1944 heralded a dramatic collapse of such an 'aspiration'.

In this context and in a confessional sense, Martin has identified the Jewish–Kabbalistic motifs in Jung's 1944 near-death visions (Martin, in Maidenbaum and

Martin 1991: 10). This theme is also more extensively developed by the Kabbalist and Jungian Sanford Drob (see Drob 2005: 33–54). In such accounts we see a Jung who has come to appreciate a depth of Jewish spirituality. We also witness here a deeper embedding of Kabbalistic imagery in terms of his individuation concept. This is certainly a radical departure from his earlier statement that '[t]he Jew, as relatively a nomad, never has produced and presumably never will produce a culture of his own' (Jung 1934: 165).

One also finds a de-coupling of Wotan–Mercurius identifications in his post-1944 writings. Mercurius has shape-shifted into a range of other figures. For example, a more notable shape-shift is into the figure of Merlin (Jung: 1963/1995: 255). In this context, it is interesting to discover that the word 'England' has been interpreted to mean 'Merlin's precinct'. This, no doubt, has something to do with the lack of popularity of Merlin in German literature. Indeed, he 'was never localized in the German-speaking countries' (Muller, in Goodrich 2005: 220). Here it is interesting to note that Jung had apparently often thought of himself as the reincarnation of the German Goethe. In light of this, it is notable that in later life he proclaimed: 'If I have lived before, I am sure I was at one time an Englishman' (Hannah 1976: 234).

A 'united double nature'

These ideas, often veering towards the speculative, contribute towards the general picture created by many Jungians, even those of the hagiographic ilk, that he 'slipped up'.

More specifically, my focus on the Mercurius side of the Wotan–Mercurius binary has allowed for an interpretation that, by including his concept of individuation, emphasised the transformative potential of the irrational and dangerous Wotanic spirit. This affords deeper insight into Jung's hope that National Socialism initially held potential for a positive outcome as a 'religious revitalization of the nation' (Sherry 2001: 363). I also speculated that Jung harboured 'prophetic inflations' and opportunistically viewed his analytical psychology as the mantic side of a new spiritual dispensation aligned to the dawning of a new astrological Age.

Furthermore, 1942 was highlighted as a crucial year, centred on his Eranos lectures 'The Spirit Mercurius' and his purported role as a 'secret agent'. Reading a subtext to 'The Spirit Mercurius' has also revealed a 'united double nature' that perhaps sheds further light concerning his ambiguous position on crucial issues. Consequently, the year 1942 in particular might be considered an addition to Adams and Sherry's chronological profile of Jung's *Significant Words and Events*, to be found in the appendix of *Lingering Shadows*.[10] Finally, I have noted a 'reinvented Jung' based on confessional interpretations of his 1944 illness, as well as a de-coupling of Mercurius–Wotan towards a Mercurius–Merlin identity, indicative of a shift of sentiment away from the politically sensitive Aryan–Germanic.

Not surprisingly, this analysis has drifted towards what could be considered a mantic perspective: Wotan consulting the head of Mimr, a fish–snake augury, the dawning of a new astrological Age. Hopefully, it has also shed some light on this most sensitive of issues. After all, in the words of Andrew Samuels, 'this, our drama' is of no small concern to followers of Jung (Samuels 1992: 3–5).

Notes

1 For a good overview of this issue see chapter 10 on 'Carl Jung, Anti-Semitism, and National Socialism' (Drob 2010: 161–207).

2 'Jung had several dreams with Wotan flowing, so to speak, beside him on the lake when he was at Bollingen' (Eugene Bohler, cited in Noll 1997: 146). Apparently Bohler was on intimate terms with Jung from 1955 onward (Noll 1997: 146).

3 See Hillman's 'The Yellowing of the Work' (2010: 204ff; also 229–30). In a footnote (page 205) he states: 'The omitted fourth (yellow) in the Nazi trinity of red, black, and white becomes the rejected Other (Jews)'.

4 A prominent image used in Kundalini is the double serpent coiled around the spinal column (a motif found on the god Mercury's caduceus).

5 An excerpt from Jung's letter to Pauli, in 1951, adds to the context of this event: 'Like the time I was working on the psychology of "Transformation Symbolism in the Mass," approaching it from the angle of alchemy, it happened that a serpent tried to swallow a fish that was too large for it and consequently choked. Fish is the other eucharistic food, and in this case it is seized not by a person but by the chthonic spirit, the mercurial serpent. (Fish = Christ. Serpent = Christ and the feminine darkness principle)' (Meier 2001: 68–9).

6 According to Jaffé, he had already coined the term *synchronicity* in 1930, during a memorial address to Wilhelm (Jaffé 1989: 25).

7 Jung had an especial affinity for the serpent, which appeared on his 'Gnostic ring'.

8 His acceptance of this position came a day before the summer solstice in 1933 (see Harms, in Maidenbaum and Martin 1991: 30). The astrological chart for this day indicates that the Sun and Moon were both in Gemini: sign of duplicity, and ruled by Mercury. The summer solstice, as St John's Day, adds further esoteric meaning.

9 Even his devoted Jewish secretary, Aniela Jaffé, has pointed a finger at him on the matter of wielding racial-oriented ideas at a historically sensitive time (Jaffé 1989: 86).

10 In their chronology, they include 1940 and 1944, but not 1942–43!

Chapter 7

An alchemical transformation mystery

Three days before St Valentine's Day, on 11 February 1944, Jung stumbled and broke his ankle. His condition worsened and resulted in a heart attack and subsequent hospitalisation. In such a condition he experienced being 'on the edge of death', complete with 'deliriums and visions' (Jung 1963/1995: 320).

As mentioned in the previous chapter, a number of interpretations for this have been put forward.[1] However, as far as I am aware, there is no literature that substantially locates them within his alchemical worldview and in the context of his preoccupation with the notion of the dawning of a new Platonic month.

Here, I shall take up this particular thread and interpret these visions from a Jungian-style alchemical perspective, in an effort to clarify how he might have understood this experience. My hypothesis is that he believed his ordeal to have been a profound alchemical transformation mystery that occurred at a most propitious historical moment. In this development I shall further argue that the figure of the alchemical Mercurius, in particular, features as a central concern. Astrologically I point out that the timing of this event, in the mid-1940s, coincided with Jung's observation that the precessed equinox would 'touch the first star of Aquarius' as the first waters from the jug/vessel of the Aquarian anthropos (see chapter 4).

An alchemical transformation mystery

Der Geiste Mercurius was published as a book a few months prior to this near-death experience. Had Jung died early in 1944, this creative labour on the quintessential psychopomp would have been one of his final published works. In his worldview it would perhaps have represented the concluding statement of his life, in the sense that he regarded his works as 'stations along my life's way' (Jung 1963/1995: 249).

The heart, for Jung, was also a most significant organ. In 1932, in the *Kundalini Seminars*, he identified the heart chakra *anahata* (the flighty 'white gazelle') with the unicorn and as the location of the *purusa*, the small 'inner man' or 'divine self' – an interface between the empirical and spiritual worlds and where the impetus towards individuation first begins (Jung 1996/1999: 39, 52).[2] Later, in *Psychology and Alchemy*, he associates the white unicorn with Mercurius (1944: 435ff). In light of this, it is probable that he understood his own seizure as a dramatic 'piercing of his heart chakra'; effectively a potent catalyst that furthered his own individuation. Indeed, in *MDR*, Jung claimed these visions were necessary as 'part of a completed individuation' (1963/1995: 328).

During this 'brush with death', he recounts some extraordinary events. At the beginning he described an out-of-body state, suspended in space and in view of the world. In this condition he beheld a part of the world as 'silvery' and tainted by rich and varied colours. After a while, he encountered a large, black, meteor-like floating rock. Upon entering a passageway into this rock, he was overcome by a range of powerful experiences: a stripping away of 'the phantasmagoria of earthly existence', a black Hindu who was 'expecting him', a sense of the meaning and purpose to his life and the perception that he would finally 'know what had been before me, why I had come into being, and where my life was flowing' (Jung 1963/1995: 322). In essence, it appeared he had been touched by the eternal: 'I can describe the experience only as the ecstasy of a non-temporal state in which present, past, and future are one' (ibid.: 327). Indeed, the specifics of his visionary descriptions are rich with alchemical allusions and imagery. I now touch on some of these.

In his first vision, we recognise the alchemist's paradoxical 'stone uplifted by the wind' (Jung 1943/1948: 212). This hard rock embodies 'darkness . . . and a strange cessation of human warmth' (Jung 1963/1995: 353). It evokes in him such ideas as 'a primordial defect in the ground of creation', but also has the benefit of engendering a powerful 'urge to create' (ibid.). These qualities are associated with the beginning stages of the alchemical opus, as the *prima materia* in its *nigredo* form.

Paradoxically, Jung's descriptions of being inside this space are also suffused with a sense of luminosity and heightened consciousness. For example, he writes that 'I had the certainty that I was about to enter an illuminated room and would meet there all those people to whom I belong in reality. There I would at last understand . . . what historical nexus my life fitted into' (Jung 1963/1995: 322). Here the cold and dark stone also has luminosity, warmth and meaning.

Outside this stone, he recounts viewing an image that is not unlike the alchemist's Hermetic *vas* as *unus mundus*: the world reflected in a retort. The iridescence of the experience gives it a sense of the 'first day of creation'. The colour textures he describes are also decidedly metallic: 'silver of the earth', 'bathed in a gloriously blue light', 'spotted dark green like oxidised silver', 'reddish-gold hue'. One is reminded of the bath of mercury into which the metals would be dissolved, often yielding a display of colours and metallic flowers.

It is also interesting to apply the concept of *time reversal* to his vision, as found in the alchemist's *contra natura* (contrary to nature). By doing this, we get the classic colour transformation sequence he identifies with medieval alchemy: *nigredo* (dark, floating stone); *albedo* (snow-covered Himalayas); *rubedo* (reddish-yellow desert of Arabia). More differentiated colours such as *verdigris* (blessed-green), *caelum* (deep blue light) and the *cauda pavonis* (all colours, as the 'peacock's tail') also feature in this vision. Each of these colours can be amplified with a range of meanings and associations that are derived from Jung's visions and memories and that correlate to alchemical notions. The particular example of the dark, floating stone as *nigredo* is illustrative.

Apart from the colours, Jung's visions as a whole also have affinities to the alchemical notions of the three coniunctios.[3] For example, upon entering the dark rock, 'I had the feeling that everything was being sloughed away; everything I aimed at or wished for or thought ... an extremely painful process' (Jung 1963/1995: 321). This correlates to the initial experience of the first alchemical coniunctio of the *unio mentalis*, whereby the soul leaves the recently 'deceased' body. In this coniunctio, the soul then unites with the spirit and achieves a heightened perspective and a lucid reality-sense, untainted by the illusory realm of projections (Jung 1955/1956: 465ff). Such states characterised many elements of Jung's visionary experience (see Jung 1963/1995: 321, 322, 326, 327, 328).

In the *second coniunctio*, the soul returns and incarnates back into the 'dead' body. It brings with it the objective insight achieved in the *unio mentalis*. This painful and limiting process requires the enticements of instinctual nature. Once achieved, the renewed adept, now in command of his/her instinctual nature, can then actualise insights gained from the *unio mentalis*. The experience is also said to revitalise the community at large.[4] In Jung's case, he 'grudgingly' returned from the grave to re-animate his body, eventually to regain his usual good appetite. Upon recovery, he entered upon 'a fruitful period of work' and went on to formulate his 'main business', as his *Mysterium Coniunctionis* (Hannah 1976: 288).

The *third coniunctio* apparently progresses from the previous two coniunctios to establish union with the more impersonal *unus mundus*. Jung describes this in terms of achieving identity between ego and the self, and admits it is a feat 'beyond individuation' (Jung 1955/1956: 535). According to Hannah, he also mentions that 'no alchemist ever laid claim to having gone beyond the second stage ... [though] Dorn was an exception in that he tried to reach a third stage' (Hannah 1976: 315). In this regard, he humbly admits: 'I cannot confess to have solved the mystery of the *coniunctio*. On the contrary, I am darkly aware of things lurking in the background of the problem – things too big for horizons' (cited in Hannah 1976: 294).

Despite this, Jung hints at what may be considered glimmerings of the third *coniunctio*, in his visionary experiences: 'One is interwoven into an indescribable whole and yet observes it with complete objectivity' (Jung 1963/1995: 327). In this paradoxical state we sense the ego–self identity to which he alludes. In essence, we can comfortably say that his visionary experiences had powerful resonance with all three alchemical *coniunctios*.

I now move to his final visions, of the Sacred Marriage or *hieros gamos*. In his understanding, this mysterious unification of opposites has an internal, personal aspect as well as an external, transpersonal aspect (Jung 1946: 291). As already mentioned, it also includes a quaternary structure of an above and a below, and a right and a left.

His vision as a whole reflects this quaternary structure. In his sojourn he traversed, in an intensely lucid and visceral sense, the spiritual (upper) realms when suspended in space, and also the chthonic (lower) realms when he emerged as a fish.[5] He also united the 'king' (right) and 'queen' (left) in the form of the *hieros gamos* visions. We might add that this Sacred Marriage was experienced internally and personally, through which he was 'The Marriage of the Lamb', yet also externally and trans-personally as a witnessing of the marriage of the gods Zeus and Hera (Jung 1963/1995: 325).

The alchemical Mercurius is also described by Jung as an essentially hidden deity, but capable of manifesting itself in empirical reality under extraordinary circumstances. In this form it is likened to the Holy Ghost, but differs as it includes not only the transcendent spiritual but also, and primarily, the chthonic and immanent as spirit of nature – the *lumen naturae* (see chapter 10).

Concerning this, Jung elaborates on his first *hieros gamos* vision, of the Cabbalistic marriage of Malchuth with Tifereth, by stating that they 'represent the male and female principles within the Godhead ... spheres of divine manifestation in which God emerges from his hidden state' (Jung 1963/1995: 325). Further, during this vision, he recounts sensing 'the "sweet smell" of the Holy Ghost . . . There was a pneuma of inexpressible sanctity in the room, whose manifestation was the *mysterium coniunctionis*' (ibid.: 326).

In the spirit of the Hermeticist project, we also witness in this *mysterium coniunctionis* a chimera of conflicting traditions (Christian, Cabalistic, pagan) representing, amongst other things, an essential spiritual–chthonic resolution that finds 'coherence' in the figure of the alchemical Mercurius – that paradox *par excellence*.

* * *

This visionary sojourn, in broad perspective, also has a likeness to the path of the alchemical Mercurius, as *filius macrocosmi* (son of the world). In 'The Spirit Mercurius', we read:

> The *filius macrocosmi* starts from below, ascends on high, and, with the powers of Above and Below united in himself, returns to earth again. He carries out the reverse movement and thereby manifests a nature contrary to Christ and the Gnostic redeemers.
>
> (Jung 1943/1948: 233)

Originating on earth, Jung *ascended on high* (with a sensation of flying and being suspended above the earth). In relapses of this condition, he witnessed the *uniting of the powers of Above and Below* (epiphany of the *hieros gamos*). Finally, he *returns to earth again* in his descent back into the three-dimensional reality of his physical body. Such experiences find further amplification in his later mentions of shamanism. Thus, no doubt inspired by Eliade's influential *Shamanism: Archaic Techniques of Ecstasy* (published in 1951), he wrote:

> The shaman's experience of sickness, torture, death, and regeneration implies, at a higher level, the idea of being made whole through sacrifice, or being changed by transubstantiation and exalted into a pneumatic man – in a word, of apotheosis.
>
> (Jung 1942/1954: 294–5)

Vas Hermeticum

Jung's idea that the alchemist projected a profound inner process onto an outer chemical transformation is especially relevant here. In particular, the most noticeable changes of the substance mercury and its derivatives, in the alchemical retort, would appear to have correlations to such phenomenological states. Here we should also remember the alchemical *correspondentia* in which metals have planetary correlates (see chapter 2). In the above description we also witnessed features of the Hermeticist notion of apotheosis as an ascent through the planetary spheres that results, ultimately, in the mystical goal of union with deity (see chapter 1).

Developing these ideas, we see the basic transmutations of the substance mercury: the initial stone is crushed (dismembered), heated (tortured) and emanates a display of colours (soul components). An 'indwelling being' is thus sublimated out as 'vaporous spirit' and re-formed as distillate as a mysterious, volatile, shining metallic-liquid (first coniunctio). Re-heating this quicksilver then produces a return to its original state, yet with an embodiment of luminosity as a pink earth-crystal (second coniunctio). In effect, there has been a journey of a 'chthonic spirit' being released from the earth, reconstituted in a purified form and then returned back to earth as luminous and living rock, as perhaps the alchemical *lumen novum*, all in a process that corresponds with a 'uniting of an above and a below'.

Furthermore, we might consider the differentiation out of a red and a white substance. As mentioned in chapter 2, this has been interpreted as a gendered differentiation from a 'hermaphroditic matter' to a 'brother–sister pair', followed by their subsequent synthesis by means of a *coniunctio* of, for example, the red king and the white queen (Jung: 1955/1956: 101, also 250, 462). In such images we get a further sense of the role of *artifex* and *soror mystica* in what Jung would have called a participation mystique of the opus (ibid.: 221). Inherent to such processes is also the alchemical belief in the intrinsic numinosity and animation of matter itself: as sacred and living substance.

Taken together, these processes afford an image of the coniunctio as an above (spiritual) and a below (chthonic), as well as a left (queen) and a right (king). Effectively, an alchemical process in the *vas* finds here a correlate in a supposedly profound ontological transformation of the alchemist. In effect, the practical side of the Hermetica (as alchemy) converges here with its theological goal as unity with the divine. This journey also captures the essentials of the alchemical opus as a torturous mystical rite which Jung likened to a mystery comparable, at least, to the passion of Christ (Jung: 1955/1956: 345). The substance suffers torments. The alchemist and *soror mystica*, aligned with the medieval conception of correspondentia, would typically identify themselves with this ordeal, which mirrors not only their own psycho-spiritual transformation but also a mysterious transpersonal process (ibid.: 221, 348, 505).

On the cusp of a new Platonic month

It is revealing to historically situate Jung's 1944 illness. At this time the world was beginning to emerge from what could be described as a crisis of apocalyptic proportions. As Hannah has pointed out his 'return from the grave' coincided with a major shift towards the restoration of peace in the world: "Synchronistically . . . D-Day, which was the beginning of the end of the Second World War, took place while Jung was still in Hirslanden hospital, but after he had overcome his illness and was well on the road to convalescence" (Hannah 1976: 284).

In a sense, the world was emerging from a conflict between the Christian and pagan spirits. At the approximate moment of victory of the Christian spirit, Jung was in recovery and emerging from the 'strange things that were happening to him'. His emergence as a fish hints at his identification (knowingly or unknowingly) with the victor spirit as the Christian Aeon of Pisces.[6] With this victory, the possibility of an alchemical transformation of the pagan Wotan–Mercurius Germanic spirit as cultural dominant now receded into the shadows of history.

Importantly, Jung's visions can be interpreted as being symbolic not only of his own 'completed individuation' but also as anticipatory of a new epoch of spiritual reality. In his worldview the first coniunctio, as 'separation of psychic opposites' as established in the Age of the Fishes, was to be followed by a 'synthesis of psychic opposites' in the second coniunctio in the Age of Aquarius. Applying such a framework, this visionary journey thus recapitulated the essential dynamic of the Pisces Aeon and also anticipated the imminent Aquarian Aeon.[7] Consequently, in light of the above argument, I postulate that Jung conceived his 1944 illness as an experience commensurate with a profound alchemical transformation mystery; as an apotheosis of mythic proportions that also finds a theological correlate in Hermeticism.

In summary: this visionary sojourn would seem to have stretched and extended Jung's known worldview – 'they were the most tremendous things that ever happened to me' (1963/1995: 326). He even mentioned to Hannah that 'his illness had been necessary, or he could never have known the full reality of the *mysterium coniunctionis*' (Hannah 1976: 279).

Thus, if Jung's pre-1944 analytical psychology was spawned as a result of his 'confrontation with the unconscious', then we can say that the more esoteric regions of his *magnum opus*, such as Dorn's coniunctios in the final part of *Mysterium Coniunctionis*, were the result of these visions.[8] Here we can also consider von Franz's *Aurora Consurgens* (von Franz 1996/2000) – effectively a commentary on the deathbed visions (of Thomas Aquinas!) of an individual whose life was immersed in the religious and spiritual problems of his day. I therefore posit that just as Jung's *Black Books* and *The Red Book* comprise the esoteric underpinnings to many of his writings (as creative articulation of his 'confrontation with the unconscious'), so his 1944 visions can be seen as key in moving towards a deeper understanding of his later works, such as *Aion* and *Mysterium Coniunctionis.* In addition, his earlier 'confrontation with the unconscious' is characteristic of depth and descent, whereas these visions are characterised by ascent and height. Eliade considers this descent–ascent and return journey in shamanistic terms as 'an almost complete schema of initiation: descent to the lower regions followed by ascent to the sky, where the Supreme Being grants shamanic power'; further, they 'repeat what the first (mythical) men once did in the dawn of time – go up to the sky and return to earth' (Eliade 1951/2004: 136–7). We witness here resonances with the legendary Hermes Trismegistus.

More critically, we should also remember that Jung had been researching alchemical literature since at least 1928. In light of this, there is the possibility his descriptions were constructed (wittingly or unwittingly) in an ambitious gesture towards self-mythification.

* * *

As a final consideration I remind the reader of the *Nag Hammadi Codices* discovered in 1945 in Egypt, a few months after Jung's near-death encounter (these were apparently only made accessible to a general readership in 1972; see chapter 1). Stephen Hoeller writes about this find:

> . . . when it seemed to many that the world would never recover from the greatest calamity of human history – at this very moment of deepest darkness and despair of the world soul, an Egyptian peasant, riding his camel while searching for fertilizer, came upon a number of ancient documents that possess the potential of aiding the West in the recovery of a substantial portion of its lost soul. At the very time when the sage C. G. Jung wrote and spoke about modern man in search of a soul, a long forgotten, or rather repressed, component of the soul of the Judeo-Christian religiosity and of Western culture in general emerged from the soil at the base of Jabal al-Tarif near the river Nile in Upper Egypt.
>
> (Hoeller 1989: 17)

One of these documents, the Hermetic Codex 'Discourse on the Eighth and Ninth', describes the final steps of the initiate's ascent beyond the seven planetary realms and thus of recognising his authentic being in relation to God, and of attaining godhood (Copenhaver 1992/2000: xxxix). In Hermeticism such a state of godhood, if achieved in life, is said to require the adept in a 'missionary call' to extol such a vision of God in an 'imperishable book' (Ebeling 2007: 17). We might think here of Jung's return to complete his magnum opus.

Notes

1 For a Hindu perspective of reincarnation on his visions see Tandan 2009: 402–8.
2 In alchemy the substance mercury's primary bodily association is to blood and the heart, and to white substances such as milk and semen (see Eliade 1978: 121, 124). Consider also the meaning of cinnabar, translated as *dragon's blood* (see chapter 2).
3 As he adapted them to his psychology from the alchemist Gerhard Dorn (see chapter 11 for a description of these coniunctios).
4 For example, see Jung's 'rain maker' story.
5 Hannah wrote that when Jung was recovering, he 'first re-experienced his body as that of a big fish' (Hannah 1976: 284).
6 The pagan spirit would more commonly be represented as a snake or dragon.
7 In astrology the foot is ruled by Pisces and the shin is ruled by Aquarius. The ankle, between these, might be considered a 'transition point' between Pisces and Aquarius.
8 In particular, his description of Dorn's coniunctios, as appearing in the final section of *Mysterium Coniunctionis*, was apparently the main part of this work that was formulated after his illness (see chapter 11).

Chapter 8

Merlin

In *MDR* we read that the engraved stone at Bollingen represented for Jung an 'explanation of the tower' and 'a manifestation of the occupant, but one which remains incomprehensible to others' and, further, that he was tempted to write the words 'Le Cri de Merlin' on the side of the stone facing the tower (Jung 1963/1995: 255).

Generally though, Jung wrote very little about Merlin and the grail legend, as this was his wife Emma's major project. However, although Emma was often asked to give lectures on the subject, she never managed to condense the enormous amount of material into book form (Hannah 1976: 259). Hannah writes that a reason for this is that she had not yet worked out 'the thorny problem of Merlin' (ibid.). After Emma's death, Jung asked Marie-Louise von Franz to finish the task. He was apparently 'exceedingly pleased with the result' (ibid.).

Apart from von Franz and Emma Jung, a strong Jung–Merlin conflation has been voiced in esoteric circles:

> [O]ver the past thirty years we have seen a striking development of depth psychology, particularly that of C.G. Jung, who had so much in common with Merlin that one esoteric group in the channel islands even sees him as his reincarnation and, like Merlin, a prophet of the Aquarian age (Begg and Rich 1991: 36).

However, more generally, in the post-Jungian literature, there would appear to be little official development of this theme.

Here I shall argue that Jung exhibited strong resonances with this figure. As preamble, I begin with a short commentary on Merlin (including a few words on Faust) and then clarify the relationship between this figure and Mercurius. I then formulate a number of symmetries between the historical Jung and mythical Merlin, and end with a brief contextualisation within the cultural milieu.

Commentary on Merlin

The figure of Merlin entered western imagination with the publication of Monmouth's twelfth-century bestseller *Historia Regum Britanniae* (The History of the

Kings of Britain). Apparently Monmouth derived the essentials of his narrative from a 'very ancient book' that has never been located (Thorpe, in Monmouth 1966: 15). A few years later Monmouth published his *Vitae Merlini* (Life of Merlin), written for a more exclusive readership. Other notable early works that contain poems on Merlin include *The Black Book of Carmarthen* (*c*. 1200) and the *Red Book of Hergest* (*c*. 1400).

Merlin's existence is generally accepted to have occurred in the fifth and first part of the sixth century CE. There have been attempts to concretise this figure as a historical personality. In general, however, this has been problematic – for example, see Goodrich (1988), Tolstoy (1985) and Phillips (2005), who identify three different personalities. To summarise: 'The evidence for an actual Merlin is limited to late written texts, circumstantial at best, and likely to remain so' (Goodrich 2005: 3). In the final analysis, many scholars would probably agree with Goodrich that 'Merlin is simply more interesting and complex as a textual tradition and a multifaceted literary character than as a single, hypothetical individual' (ibid.: 66). Apart from origins and historicity, it is also useful to briefly contrast the wizard Merlin with the Renaissance magus Faust.

> Faust's magic is wholly egocentric, for his worldly purposes alone. Therefore, the motif of magic links the archetypal figures of Merlin and Faust, yet the function of this magic is highly distinctive, the former's magic would shape a kingdom, a society, the latter's magic would shape an individual, in contrast to that society.
>
> (Singer, in Spivack (ed.) 1992: 96–7)

One might say the linear trajectory of the Faustian spirit has spawned the automated techno-world of industrial nations: the 'American Dream'. This is very different to the Merlinesque spirit whose 'cooperation with time (to say nothing of nature) may likewise bar him from a post-Enlightenment progressive world. Merlinic time is natural: circular, anagogic, relative' (Goode, in Spivack (ed.), 1992: 30).

The relevance of such a tension of spirits in our contemporary world is captured by the intuitive question posed by Spivack: 'Which of the two provocative mages seems to be winning out in our culture, the subtle medieval wizard or the striving Renaissance magician? The beguiling circle of wholeness or the beckoning straight line of aspiration?' (Spivack 1992: iii). Here one should be cautious of oversimplification. The 'Merlin of Mortlake', John Dee, for example, might be considered to be both magus and wizard – helping to inaugurate an era of technology, yet also championing a sacralised worldview. For now, however, I bracket off such wider concerns and progress by clarifying the relation between Merlin and Mercurius, as recounted in von Franz and Emma Jung's *The Grail Legend*.

Merlin and Mercurius

According to von Franz and Emma Jung, the 'efflorescence of the Merlin literature coincided in time with that of Occidental alchemy, and in the latter we find a personification of the arcane substance, which bears a striking resemblance to Merlin, namely the alchemical Mercurius' (Emma Jung and von Franz 1970/1998: 368). They further point out that the alchemists themselves compared Merlin with the alchemical Mercurius (ibid.: 371). In strengthening such an identity, we read further:

> It is remarkable how many features Merlin and the Mercurius of the alchemists have in common. Both are capable of infinite transformations. Both are compared, now with Christ, now with the Antichrist. Both serve as analogues for the inspiring breath of the Holy Spirit, or are derided as false prophets. Both have the nature of trickster, both are hidden away, both are the mysterious agent behind the transformation of the 'King' and are connected with the gods of love. Both are associated with Saturn, and both engender or themselves fall victim to insanity. Finally, both represent the mystery of a "divine vessel" which serves as the object of men's search. Both are connected with the experience of the divine in nature or in the unconscious.
>
> (Emma Jung and von Franz 1970/1998: 367–8)

In commenting on the historical background in which these two figures emerged, the authors further note:

> It is amazing how such a figure of the Self emerges almost simultaneously as Mercurius in Occidental alchemy and as Merlin in the grail legend. This indicates how profound the psychic need must already have been at that time for some such undivided personification of the incarnated Godhead that should heal the opposites of Christ-Antichrist.
>
> (Emma Jung and von Franz 1970/1998: 372)

They also speculate that the name *Merculinus*, which appears in the popular sixteenth-century *Rosarium Philosophorum*, is a hybridisation of Merlin and Mercurius (ibid.: 371).[1]

Apart from Mercurius, Merlin has also been associated with the Celtic deities Cernnunos and Lugh (Tolstoy 1985: 246; see also Emma Jung and von Franz 1970/1998: 375). According to Tolstoy, the 'antler headed master of the forest' is more descriptive of the wild forest-dwelling Merlin, and the many-skilled and magic-making hero Lugh is associated with the cultural Merlin as mage and advisor to the King (ibid.: 246).

With these preliminaries completed, I now progress to identify a number of biographical symmetries between Merlin and Jung. This also serves to clarify what might be considered relatively typical Merlinesque features.

Jung and Merlin

Van der Post attested especially to the knightly aspect of Jung's personality: 'the world of the knights of the Holy Grail, ever since the age of fifteen, had been his world in the deepest sense' (van der Post 1976/1985: 150–1). As a young man this was apparently an intense common interest between Jung and his future wife (Bair 2004: 78). His adulthood also had resonances with a Parsifal-like knightly quest.

However a shift from Parsifal to Merlin would appear to only have dawned in later life, no doubt influenced by his wife's research. Von Franz captures the intensity of such an identity: 'when ... Jung became acquainted with the details of the Merlin saga, he was shaken. Without in the least being aware of the fact, he had done and experienced so much which is reminiscent of Merlin' (von Franz 1998: 279). It is however unclear from von Franz's biography when exactly this 'revelation' dawned on him.[2] A clue might be evident in a statement in his *Answer to Job* (published in 1952):

> Myth is not fiction: it consists of facts that are continually repeated and can be observed over and over again. It is something that happens to man, and men have mythical fates just as much as the Greek heroes do ... It is perfectly possible, psychologically, for the unconscious or an archetype to take complete possession of a man and to determine his fate down to the smallest detail. At the same time objective, non-psychic parallel phenomena can occur which also represent the archetype. It not only seems so, it simply is so, that the archetype fulfils itself not only psychically in the individual, but objectively outside the individual.
>
> (Jung 1952a: 409)

If we read this as having personal relevance, then it may seem obvious that he identified himself here with the biblical Job in his No. 1 personality, reminiscent of his mid-life 'confrontation with the unconscious'. However, viewed from a broader perspective and in light of his having recently completed *Aion* and being immersed in *Mysterium Coniunctionis*,[3] it is more probable that he is reflecting on an uncanny symmetry between his life and that of Merlin.

Upon closer scrutiny, however, a literal comparison of Merlin and Jung is unconvincing. We need only consider the following: born of a virgin and a devil; capable of transformations, disguises, invisibility; magical feats of moving mountains, causing floods and thunder storms; a warrior in battles; prophesying, including the forthcoming kings of England; living in a forest with a wolf; talking with a piglet; triple death of being hung, impaled and drowned; entrapped in a glass castle; moving Stonehenge from Ireland, and so on.

Indeed, a study of Merlin alone is deeply complex. Spivack comments:

> To explore and define this archetypal figure, I begin with a composite biography of Merlin based on an amalgam of diverse medieval sources. As one examines this vast body of materials from the viewpoints of logic and continuity however, one is inevitably baffled by their glaring inconsistencies, their lack of progression, and their circularity. Nevertheless, to deeper inspection the central mythic event is clearly revealed.
>
> (Spivack 1992: 2)

It is this 'central mythic event' which I shall now try to illuminate by selecting a handful of more notable Merlinesque characteristics. In each case I view biographical Jung through such a lens and by utilising a predominantly symbolic thematic approach.

Unusual birth and child prodigy

Merlin was born of a virgin and a devil (incubus). 'The miraculous child therefore retains the uncanny powers inherited from his infernal father, but because of his mother's virtue and his own baptism, they will not be dedicated to the devil's purposes. Merlin will not be an antichrist' (Spivack 1992: 3).

Unusually, Jung's father and mother were both thirteenth children. So Carl Jung's birth, as the child of two thirteenth children, was considered 'highly auspicious (Bair 2004: 7).[4]

Carl's father and uncles were also all priests. He was therefore born into a deeply embedded Christian tradition. However, his mother made a far more 'pagan' impression on the young Carl. He describes her, during the night time hours, as being 'uncanny . . . she was like one of those seers who is at the same time a strange animal, like a priestess in a bear's cave' (Jung 1963/1995: 67). For young Carl, such a 'pagan' nature was a stark contrast to the veneer of her Christian persona (ibid.: 110).

Van der Post touched on this relationship: 'It was as if the "witch" in her (to pursue the word in the idiom of the pre-Arthurian world wherein it had its positive meaning) recognised that there was a "Merlin" in the son in need of protection of the magic she sensed to be in *Faust*' (van der Post 1976/1985: 88).

During childhood Jung's parents also slept in separate bedrooms (1963/1995: 33). He might well have wondered, at times, whether he was indeed the son of a virgin. More convincingly, we can say that his parental environment embodied a pagan–Christian ambiguity: a theme that permeates the legend of Merlin.

Merlin is also universally considered to have been a child prodigy, being simultaneously wise and knowledgeable as old man and youth. Jung was no doubt a child prodigy. At a young age he exhibited a voracious appetite for knowledge, including excursions into his father's library. The interplay between what he described as his No. 1 and No. 2 personalities during childhood also resonates with the idea of being simultaneously youth and wise old man. We might also reflect here on the nickname, 'Father Abraham', given to him by his classmates.

Two Merlins

The theme of duality permeates many aspects of Merlin's nature. Such duality has roots in Monmouth's writings.

> In order to be Ambrosius, serve Arthur, take part in Arfderydd and live in the Caledonian forest for fifty years, this Merlin would need three long

> lifetimes. . .The absurdity of this career was immediately apparent to Geoffrey's readers, who concluded there must have been two Merlins – a distinction that further established Merlin's dualistic nature and that prepared the way for future transformations.
>
> (Goodrich 2005: 5)

The two Merlins lived very different lives. The earlier Merlin, counsellor to kings, played critical roles in the establishment of the new kingdom of King Arthur and Camelot. He was also exceptionally learned in the magical and oracular arts. In this role he has been described as 'the perfect alchemist and astrologer' (Zumthor, in Goodrich and Thompson 2005: 146).

The critical juncture when he disappeared from the secular world is generally recounted as having been catalysed by the battle of Arfderryd in Scotland. Some scholars have regarded this encounter as a historical moment of advancing Christianity led by King Rhydderch and the departing paganism led by King Gwenddolau (see Jarman, in Goodrich and Thompson 2005: 112). This apart, the excessive slaughter and the heartbreak it caused during this battle sent Merlin mad, impelling him to forsake society and to lead a solitary and animal-like existence in the forest. It was only after many years in the forest that he eventually regained sanity and reintegrated back into the secular world, at least to an extent.

This, briefly, describes what has come to be known as the 'two Merlins'. Tolstoy traces historical antecedents, arguing for the two Merlins' mythic origins in the Celtic god of light, Lugh,[5] and the Celtic lord of the forest, Cernunnos. Von Franz and Emma Jung take a similar position, but use the mythical 'equivalent' of Wotan, instead of the Celtic Lugh:

> In Merlin the older image of God is probably resuscitated, an image in which aspects of Wotan are mingled with those of the archetypally related Kerunnus, an image of inner wholeness which presses its still unfulfilled claims on man.
>
> (Emma Jung and von Franz 1970/1998: 375)

The theme of cultural urban versus wild rural permeated Jung's life from childhood through to old age. *MDR* indicates that the first part of his life progressed toward an urban lifestyle. After his mother's death, however, there was a shift wherein he was opened more to the wild, rural side of his being, in the form of his Bollingen retreat. His excursions into Africa characterised a re-connection to so-called 'natural man'.

Such a primitive–civilised dichotomy characterises much of the Jungian worldview. Homans, for example, locates this feature as central to his project: 'I myself see Jung's psychology . . . as an attempt to integrate traditional and modern orientations to life. This is the sociological key to its formation' (Homans 1979/1995: 140). Van der Post captures a broader sense of this:

> Not the least of Africa's services to Jung, personally, was that it had confirmed and emphasised the reality of his own primitive nature which had

> already caused great conflict in him in his student days. He referred to the clash between his "country or natural mind" and the "town mind" in his encounters with professors and fellow students in the nineties at the university of Basle. This experience seemed to me to have blown into full flame the fire necessary for transcending two extremes that had long burned in him, not vicariously through Africa, but at home in his own context.
>
> (van der Post 1976/1985: 54)

Battle and madness

Prior to his madness, Merlin was involved in many military battles. The particular horror and devastation at the battle of Arfderydd, however, was the turning point that triggered his life change to an isolated forest existence.

A battle-aspect is also to be found in Jung's memories of himself. For example, Hannah recalls: 'He wrote that he often felt as if he were on a battlefield, saying: "Now you have fallen, my good comrade, but I must go on" ' (Hannah 1976: 91). Van der Post remarks on the title *Memories, Dreams, Reflections* as a 'session of a great old soldier remembering the battles he has fought' (van der Post 1976/1985: 172).

Van der Post also notes that Jung delivered a paper in Scotland in 1914 under great duress, as he thought he was going mad: 'I had to face seriously the chance of being called mad' (ibid.: 156). On the way back from Scotland, he heard the news that war had been declared. According to him, this event 'confirmed a feeling that nothing that had happened to me was not, in a sense, also happening to the life of my time" (ibid.). In effect, he is admitting to what he would call a *participation mystique* with his times. Perhaps it is a synchronicity that Jung's madness was brought more forcefully to his awareness in Scotland, where Merlin purportedly went mad.

Apart from World War I, this was also after the break with Freud and prior to his subsequent brush with madness, as his so-called 'creative illness' or 'confrontation with the unconscious'. At this time he also receded from active social life.

Forest existence, shaman, prophet

Von Franz and Emma Jung interpret the madness of Merlin and his forest existence in the following terms:

> His madness ... should be looked upon as an initiation by means of which he comes into closer contact with the otherworldly powers. As a result of his cure, he pledges himself, as many shamans do, to an isolated forest existence in the service of the divine.
>
> (Emma Jung and von Franz 1970/1998: 360)

No doubt they had Jung and his Bollingen retreat in mind. The legend also tells of a spring that emerged next to Merlin's abode, the waters of which were said to cure madness (Stewart 2009: 324). In her biography, von Franz elaborates:

> Jung's tower, like Merlin's, had at first no spring; Jung had to take his water from the lake. After a few years, however, a spring was discovered quite nearby; he had it captured and used it. It is true that it heals no form of madness, but the spring that Jung discovered in his psyche assuredly does.
>
> (von Franz 1998: 280)

We should add that Merlin also *engenders* madness. Accordingly, it is known that Jung's method, used without caution, can unleash a latent psychosis. Thus, to correct von Franz's more optimistic stance, we might say his method can both cure and engender madness.

Merlin's madness and his ability to talk with animals and to 'read the language of nature' are generally viewed as being related to prophecy. Indeed, in Jung's practice as analyst, we come across a similar 'reading of the language of nature', with a theoretical basis in his concept of synchronicity. The following account is illustrative:

> For example, when Jung analyzed in the ' "garden room", which was a small square room at the corner of his garden, directly on the lake,' he would take, Hannah relates, based on an account given by von Franz, 'every natural event, such as insects flying in, the lake lapping more audibly than usual, and so on, as belonging synchronistically to what was being said in the analysis'.
>
> (Hannah, cited in Aziz 1990: 85)

The idea of Merlin's prophetic ability in reading nature has, arguably, a correlate in Jung's *prospective function* as applied to the interpretation of not only dreams but also nature-related synchronicities.

Merlin's laughter

Merlin's laugh has traditionally been associated with prophecy and intuitive insight into human nature:

> This laughter is of a special kind, the irrepressible jubilation of a privileged being for whom the ignorance, candor, or shortsightedness of common humanity is visible ... his laughter is not the pure laughter of a fun-loving being. It has a darker origin and resonance.
>
> (Micha, in Goodrich and Thompson 2005: 301)

This 'darker origin and resonance' is further amplified by Lupack:

> Nowhere is Merlin closer to Satan, whose son of tradition claims him to be, than in his maniacal laughter ... The petrified laughter that lasts beyond death

> is so terrifying because it is laughter at all our human illusions that progress can improve the world, and laughter at the dream that we can change the human condition and so remake the world. It is a laugh that mocks and reminds us of our human failings that impede all our attempts at true progress.
>
> (Lupack, in Goodrich and Thompson 2005: 240)

Concerning Jung, it is no understatement to say his laughter was renowned: 'Even when he was well over eighty, when Jung was really amused he had a natural and infectious laugh, which seemed to come from his whole being and was hardly a whisper' (Hannah 1976: 41–2). Van der Post writes of his 'continuous love of laughter' and of how he laughed in 'such a wonderful way' (van der Post 1976/1985: 48). Bearing in mind the many people who attested to his uncanny intuition, it is possible that at times his laugh had something to do with prophecy.[6] His particular idea of the dream having a prospective function would support such a claim. As a critic of modern culture I also speculate that his laugh, at times, might have included a demonic element.

Lover

Apparently 'two feminine characters are more or less constantly associated with Merlin, although under various guises' (Berthelot, in Goodrich and Thompson 2005: 165). These two woman are his wife Morgue and the Lady of the Lake, known variously as Niviaene, Niniane, Viviane and Nimue. The personalities of these two women are very different: 'Morgue is a more stable character, especially in her relationship with Merlin, than is the Lady of the Lake' (ibid.: 167).

Niniane, his young 'fairy lover', enticed and bribed Merlin to teach her his magic (ibid.: 166). Upon agreeing to this request, she then used this against him by enchanting him into an eternal entrapment. According to different versions of the story this entrapment is in a hawthorn bush, a cave, a stone tomb or a magical glass castle.

Jungian scholars will easily recognise parallels here with his wife Emma and his younger lover, Toni Wolff. Arguably Jung 'enchanted Toni' and introduced her to the 'magical arts' of his analytical psychology. A dream Jung had around 1913, after terminating Toni's analysis, portrays her fairy-woman quality reminiscent of Merlin's Niniane:[7]

> . . . he dreamed that he and Wolff were hiking in the Alps together. They were in a rock-strewn valley. As they approached a mountain they heard the singing of elves. To his horror, she walked into this mountain and disappeared into it. He woke up in a state of panic.
>
> (Noll 1997: 94)

Back to Merlin, we discover versions of a more promiscuous wizard: 'every damsel who wishes to learn some magic has but to come and offer herself to Merlin.

Supposedly, in this narrative, the "wisest man in the world" has gathered around himself a kind of school in supernatural arts, mainly prophecy and (black) magic' (Goodrich 2005: 11–14).

Jung's womanising is notorious. According to Noll's (perhaps overstated) claim, 'from at least 1909 onward, he explicitly recommended the central tenet of Gross's philosophy – polygamy – to his male patients' (Noll 1997: 91). He also attracted a circle of women around him, known as the *Jungfrauen* (Anthony 1990: 72). Such popularity has also been associated to the establishment of a school or, more controversially and in the words of Noll, a 'cult'. Noll elaborates:

> I am convinced by the historical evidence that Jung believed himself to be a religious prophet with extraordinary powers. I further believe . . . he consciously devoted his life to a religious community centred on his personality and his teachings. This was his calling, and many in his earliest circle of disciples in Zurich during the first world war followed him because they believed he was "the new light", a charismatic prophet of a new age.
>
> (Noll 1997: xiv)

An interesting feature of Merlin's relationship with his female circle is that 'although [he] hands on his magic to the women, he withholds his prophetic and scriptural abilities' (Micha, in Goodrich and Thompson 2005: 71, 181). Jung certainly shared the 'magic' of his analytical psychology. However, he never openly taught 'prophetic ability' as part of his method. This is despite his own experiences of 'prophetic abilities' (for example his 'waves of blood' vision prior to World War I, Wotan and Nazi Germany prior to World War II, his Bollingen engravings).

Tower

Merlin eventually compromised his austere existence by accepting that a tower be built in the heart of the forest. In different versions, his tower is also referred to as an esplumoir (moulting cage), a castle and an observatory for astrological predictions. Emma and von Franz interpret his tower-observatory:

> Through this curious life in his forest observatory Merlin is, as it were, merged in the *unus mundus*, in union with the origins of all cosmic and psychic being, the unity of which is most clearly foreshadowed in the phenomenon of synchronicity, in which the astrological coincidences are indeed also a part.
>
> (Emma Jung and von Franz 1970/1998: 366)

Jung's Bollingen tower is clearly recognisable in this description. Much of his magnum opus (including *Aion* and *Mysterium Coniunctionis)* was written largely whilst at Bollingen. Furthermore, *Aion* is a historical description of the platonic month of Pisces synchronistic with the Christian Aeon, in the astrological worldview.

We should also remember that Jung engraved what he considered to be prophetic visions on the walls of his Bollingen retreat (Hannah 1976: 341).

King's advisor and 'secret transformation of the king'

Merlin was not only the guiding force behind Arthur's conception and destiny, but also his advisor and confidant once the new kingdom was established. He is also described as the 'secret transformation of the king' (Emma Jung and von Franz 1970/1998: 367–8). The motif of 'king's advisor' is mentioned in connection with Jung during both World Wars. Hannah recounts:

> He once told me of a very curious experience he had had in the middle of the First World War (it must have been about 1916). He had a whole series of dreams in which he tried to persuade the German Kaiser to make peace! But the Kaiser always refused, and at last – as Jung said – the unconscious gave up the attempt. He said the dreams felt strangely objective and he had sometimes wondered whether the unconscious had made any similar attempt with the Kaiser himself.
>
> (Hannah 1976: 132)

During World War II there were apparently similar dreams, but this time they involved Winston Churchill (ibid.: 293). More generally Jung's project, considered on a large scale, attests to the theme of 'transformation of the king'. It is helpful to remember that the word 'king', in analytical psychology, is often interpreted as the 'dominant value system of a culture or civilisation'. One only has to consider the title *Civilisation in Transition*[8] to appreciate the extent of this feature in Jung's thought.

Creation of a new world

Merlin also represents the creative dynamism and guiding force behind the establishment of a new world. He effectively leads humanity through the chaos and darkness of transition to a new order of civilisation. It would therefore appear that the theme of Merlin gains ascendancy in periods of dramatic cultural transition.

> The strongest literary and scholarly fascination with Merlin has coincided with the historical periods of Great Britain's greatest power and darkest moments – the Hundred Years War and War of the Roses, the Elizabethan and Victorian empire building, and the two World Wars – and in periods when our paradigms of science and reality itself are being redesigned.
>
> (Goodrich 2005: 68)

Gareth Knight amplifies this theme: '[Merlin] is the archetypal wizard or master of the wisdom whose function is to guide human evolution and establish patterns of civilization. He thus appears at various moments to guide, warn or advise or take action at critical points' (Knight, in Spivack 1992: 95). Dramatic cultural upheaval and renewal was a theme that preoccupied Jung, in accordance with his astrological worldview. According to Hannah:

> [He] had already spoken at some length in a seminar in 1929 of the great changes and upheavals that were to be expected as the age of the Fishes ended and as the Spring sign entered the sign of Aquarius, the water carrier. Since very few people heeded the warning in 'Wotan,' he had little or no hope that he would be heard again.
>
> (Hannah 1976: 337)

Pagan or Christian?

Merlin embodies 'a dynamic, dialectical interplay between paganism and Christianity' (Spivack 1992: v). This tension of religions places the figure of Merlin in a transitional historical and cultural context: 'Butler's understanding that magical contests present the "form of the conquest of a new kind of religion over an old" casts Merlin as a survivor of an old religion' (Spivack 1992: 30).

In light of this, Merlin would appear to be a shadowy presence from an older religion that 'looks back to a mysterious Golden Age relationship of man to nature' (Goode, in Spivack 1992: 32). In this view, the figure of Merlin emerges as a compensation and challenge to the prevailing orthodox Christian worldview and values of medieval Europe:

> Monmouth . . . represents the medieval Christian view that the ancient divinities of the Britons, by then already shrunk to demons, wanted to bring an Antichrist and son of a virgin into the world so that he might restore their waning power against the realm of the Savior.
>
> (Zimmer, in Goodrich and Thompson 2005: 266)

Here we need only consider Jung's championing of a *renovatio* of Christianity to include a pagan spirit. His description of Paracelsus, for instance, is reflective of his own personality: 'The Christian and the primitive pagan lived together in him in a strange and marvellous way to form a conflicting whole' (Jung 1942: 189). Like Merlin, Jung champions a 'third way' inclusive of both paganism and Christianity. Von Franz eloquently describes this:

> The harshness of [this] Christian moral dualism calls for a *tertium quod non datur*; for a symbolic solution through which life can continue to flow. One of the first such mysterious reconciling symbols is found in the emergence of the figure Merlin in medieval literature.
>
> (von Franz 1998: 25)

Merlin's death

There are a number of versions of Merlin's death: 'Two versions of [his] "death" recall Christ: in one he is bounded in a thornbush; in another he is imprisoned under a stone to return again' (Guerber, cited by Goode, in Spivack 1992: 27). Other versions include the so-called triple death and being buried alive in an underground tomb. I shall here consider the latter two accounts.

According to Tolstoy, Merlin's *triple death* has origins in an ancient Celtic ritual of being hanged upside down, drowned and impaled through the heart. In this version, at the moment of death, whilst hung upside down, impaled on a fishing stake and being drowned in the sea, Merlin has a vision of a renewed world at the bottom of the ocean. In this vision he also comprehends the relationship between our phenomenal world and the world of eternity (Blackburn, in Goodrich and Thompson 2005: 354). In some versions of the story he then transforms into a fish, as resurrected life.

These motifs can be linked to Jung's 1944 near-death experiences. The sequence of events included (a) a broken fibula (ankle), (b) a heart attack and (c) a lung infarct. These three injuries have the signature of the ritual triple death:[9] the broken fibula (being hung upside down), a heart attack (being impaled) and a lung infarct (drowning). Furthermore, in this 'death experience' Jung recounts extraordinary visions, reminiscent of Merlin's epiphany at the bottom of the ocean. We can also recount that this vision afforded him renewed creative vitality and inspiration. Furthermore, the motif of being *resurrected as a fish*, after this 'triple death', also occurs in his near-death experience, during the early stages of recovery. Hannah recounts:

> Jung must have still been in the depths of the unconscious, for he told Marie-Louise von Franz that he first re-experienced his body as that of a big fish. This was such a realistic experience that for some time, whenever he was fed with spoonfuls of soup, he felt anxious about whether it would not flow out again at his gills.
>
> (Hannah 1976: 284)

It can also be argued that this identification with a fish had a symbolic carryover into his creative life. His subsequent writing of *Aion* was a psycho-historical treatise on the Platonic Age of the Fishes (Pisces).

I now consider the account of Merlin being buried alive in an underground tomb. This motif has been interpreted animistically: 'to signify Merlin's totemic quality as a being immanent in nature, yet, at the same time, consubstantial with human life' (Watanabe, in Spivack 1992: 143). Some of Jung's Bollingen memories have this animistic quality, such as the sensation of being ubiquitous throughout nature (Jung 1963/1995: 252).

Although he wasn't 'buried alive in an underground tomb', we can say that his ideas and purported experiences of the third coniunctio (union with the *unus mundus*) correlate to this paradoxical idea of retaining individuality yet being immanent in nature and the world. We should remember that toward the end of his life he spoke of 'the other Bollingen', implying a preservation of personal identity, at least in the sense of an absorption into his No. 2 personality. An excerpt from his final recorded dream before death also portrays a Merlinesque absorption into the immanence of nature: '. . . a quadrangle of trees whose roots reached around the earth and enveloped [me] and among the roots golden threads were glittering' (von Franz 1998: 287).

* * *

By combining the context of this final recorded dream with an excerpt from *The Grail Legend*, it would seem clear that von Franz believed Jung to have become the *homo quadratus* or *homo altus* of alchemy: nothing less than an embodiment of the legend of Merlin responding to the time and culture in which he lived.

> The motifs of the Grail legend reach out beyond the Middle Ages into our time, and will perhaps reach even further. Merlin thus becomes the legend-entwined image of the whole man, the *homo quadratus* or *homo altus* of alchemy, in which the ordinary man has become one with the wholeness that transcends him.
>
> (Emma Jung and von Franz 1970/1998: 365)

In the language of analytical psychology, the statement 'has become one with the wholeness that transcends him' correlates to the idea of having achieved the third coniunctio as union with the *unus mundus*.

Jung, Merlin and a transition of the ages

One of Merlin's roles, as advisor to the King, was to prophesy the forthcoming kings of England (psychologically, these might be considered as 'collective dominants'). As astrologer, Merlin is also associated with the round zodiacal 'table'. He embodies the cycles and qualities of time. As also mentioned, he has been viewed as a figure that exists beyond the limited time constraints of the Arthurian age; a quintessential shaman and prophet who emerges during times of rupture and transition.

In Jung's worldview each astrological Age is a unique dominant expressing a quality of the transforming god-image. In particular, for him, the traumatic transitions between such Ages are moments when prophetic and spiritual guidance is most needed; when Merlin appears. In this context, Jung's life project could be viewed as an intense concentration and creative expression of the 'Merlin archetype', emerging at a moment, arguably, during the transitus from the Age of Pisces to the Age of Aquarius. The 'Merlin archetype', as immanence in the natural world and personification of it, also embodies a unique worldview that might be described as both holistic and Hermetic.

Notes

1 One might also ponder von Franz's pet name, *Marlus* (from Marie-Louise), used by her close circle of colleagues and friends.
2 She writes that this realisation occurred almost twenty years after his grail dream in India. This would place his realisation toward the end of his life (von Franz 1992/1998: 279).
3 Of all his works these are, arguably, the places where the theme of Merlin would be most fitting.
4 Merlin is associated with the number thirteen: he was entombed with thirteen magical treasures; the letter M is the thirteenth letter in the alphabet; he set up the twelve Knights of the Round Table with himself as the thirteenth, etc.
5 Lugh's festival (Lughnasa) is celebrated on 1 August, a few days after Jung's birthday on 26 July.
6 'Over and over again we have stories of Jung's ability to "read minds" ' (Anthony 1990: 100).
7 Consider also the following: 'Someone in the Inner Circle remarked that "Toni was all spirit. It was almost as if she had no body" ' (Down, cited in Anthony 1990: 31).
8 Volume 10 of the *CW*s.
9 Jung was aware of Merlin's triple death (see Jung 1955/1956: 81).

Part III

Magnum opus

> ... the milk [of Pegasus] takes the place of the water of Aquarius which is the alchemical virgin's milk – a synonym for the aqua doctrinae as one of the aspects of Mercurius ...
>
> (Jung 1973–75: 615)

Chapter 9

Synchronicity

Jung's magnum opus extends beyond his quintessential *Mysterium Coniunctionis*. At the beginning of this work he mentions a number of necessary preliminary works: *Psychology of the Transference*, *Aion*, 'The Philosophical Tree', *Synchronicity: An Acausal Connecting Principle* and *Answer to Job* (Jung 1955/1956: xv).

Arguably, *Mysterium Coniunctionis* is composed of three parts, the first two of which comprise Volume 14 of the *CW*s. The third part is *Aurora Consurgens*, authored by von Franz (von Franz 1955/1956: xv). Apparently Jung wanted all three volumes to be co-authored publications, following the alchemical tradition of adept and *soror mystica*. However due to a number of complications this did not occur, apparently to his great disappointment (Hannah 1976: 230).

Von Franz also collaborated on *Aion*, which resulted in her book *The Passion of Perpetua* – this work chronicled the psychological transition from antiquity to Christianity, whereas *Aion* dealt more specifically with the Christian era (ibid.: 300).

To summarise, Jung's magnum opus can be considered to be composed of the following works:

Synchronicity: An Acausal Connecting Principle
Answer to Job
'The Philosophical Tree'
Psychology of the Transference
Aion
The Passion of Perpetua (von Franz)
Mysterium Coniunctionis
Aurora Consurgens (von Franz)

I speculate that he also considered his wife's *The Grail Legend* (completed by von Franz) appropriate to be added to this list.

In a necessary scoping of this specific project, emphasis was placed on the following works: *Synchronicity*, *Aion*, *Mysterium Coniunctionis* and *The Grail Legend*. In particular, I endeavour to answer the following more focused questions aligned with chapters 9 to 12:

1 To what extent does a study of Mercurius add to an appreciation of Jung's synchronicity concept?
2 Does a dialogue between 'The Spirit Mercurius' and *Aion* result in a more differentiated understanding of Jung's concept of the self, as manifested through the so called Aeon of Pisces?
3 Can we consider Mercurius a 'key' that unlocks a valuable perspective on *Mysterium Coniunctionis*?
4 Does a study of Mercurius significantly add to an appreciation of a Jungian perspective on the grail legend?

I now proceed to address the first of these questions.

* * *

Mercurius does not feature in Jung's works on *Synchronicity* (1951b, 1952b). Likewise, major post-Jungians and physicists with specialist interest in synchronicity have not explicitly considered this figure to any great extent. The post-Jungian focus has been predominantly religious and psychological (Aziz 1990), cultural (Main 2004), spiritual (Main 2007; Sparks 2007), literary (Combs and Holland 1994; Rowland 2005), scientific as predominantly quantum physics (Peat 1988; Mansfield 2001) and scientific as chaos and complexity theory (Cambray 2009). A notable exception is von Franz, who has touched on Mercurius and synchronicity in various places scattered throughout her voluminous writings (for example: 1980, 1992, 1997). Nowhere in her works, however, do we find this specific theme as central concern.

More recently, perhaps due to English publication of the Pauli/Jung letters (2001), there has been some treatment of the Mercurius–Merlin theme (see Sparks 2007, and Miller 2009). This is understandable, considering that this figure appears fairly prominently and explicitly in Pauli's dreams, as revealed in the letters. Sparks and Arthur Miller, however, have also not dealt with this figure as a central interest. Others, writing with erudition on the Pauli/Jung letters, have not concerned themselves with Mercurius (Donati 2004; Zabriskie 2005. Lindorff 1995a and b, accessing the 1992 German language publication of the letters, touch very briefly on this figure).

Less directly, substituting the word Mercurius with the word trickster or Hermes[1] yields a fair amount of coverage. From a psychological and literary perspective, the general idea of synchronicity as trickster and as chance has been dealt with variously. For example, Murray Stein writes: 'with considerable justice, it can be said that the Greeks named the experience of synchronicity "Hermes"' (Stein 1983/2004: 19). Combs and Holland extend this to archetypal or universal tricksters and write of this figure as a 'divine jester' or 'juggler of reality', going so far as to state that 'synchronicity is . . . ultimately best comprehended in the language of myth' (Combs and Holland 1994: xxxi). Post-Jungians on Shamanism have also touched on synchronicity (for example Williams 1981; Ryan 2002). The figure of Mercurius, however, with its specifically western cultural colouration, loses much if interpreted predominantly in terms of narratives such as the Greek Hermes, shamanic trickster or 'trickster archetype'.

As pointed out in the introduction to this chapter, we should also remember that the figure of Mercurius takes us deeply into Jung's later and more esoteric works, such as *Aion* and *Mysterium Coniunctionis*. With the exception of von Franz (and Sparks, to a lesser extent), the above authors have not engaged, in any significant way, with these works in relation to the synchronicity concept.

In summary: the above authors, in my opinion, have not adequately dealt with Jung's synchronicity concept in relation to Mercurius. Here, I shall attempt to clarify this relation. The value of such a task, as I try to illustrate, is that it adds an especially *esoteric* perspective (emphasis on alchemy and astrology) to existing discourses on synchronicity, from angles such as the religious, spiritual, cultural, scientific, literary and psychological.

A study of the literature revealed a number of approaches one could pursue on this topic. For example, the correlation of medieval conceptions of the alchemical Mercurius in relation to the physics of Jung's day (emphasis on relativity theory and quantum theory) and in terms of more contemporary scientific trends (such as chaos, complexity and emergence theory), in the context of Jung's synchronicity concept, was particularly alluring and indeed occupied a fair amount of initial research.

However, in line with my emergent theme of a life-myth construction, I have chosen to rather more firmly situate Jung's synchronicity concept within his esoteric worldview, thereby arguing that his esoteric identity (hidden in earlier phases of thought) progressively came to the foreground in older age, with emphasis on his post-1944 writings. In particular, I shall develop the theme of the alchemical coniunctio in relation to Jung's formulation of the synchronicity concept. I begin with his astrological experiment regarding married couples and then progress to differentiating out his religious and physics quaternios as two 'big picture' elements of a *cultural* coniunctio. In expanding on the 'problematic fourth' in these quaternios, I look at Pauli's 'confrontation with the unconscious' and his relationship with von Franz. Finally, I locate these within Jung's (and von Franz's) belief in the transition from the Age of Pisces to the Age of Aquarius; as a *heiros gamos*.

Marriage coniunctio

In pioneering his concept of synchronicity, Jung could have chosen from a number of oracular-style techniques as experimental examples. His range of interests on such topics included the I Ching, ESP, astrology, mandalas, dreams and out-of-body experiences (see Bair 2004: 334). Of these, he chose astrology. Furthermore, instead of looking at common astrological concerns such as career, physical characteristics, children, personality traits, etc., he chose to look at sun and moon synastry

Figure 9.1 Mercurius engraving at Bollingen (personal photograph).

involving married couples (in alchemy, this relates to the coniunctio theme). Astrologically, such a choice of experiment could be considered fairly unusual.

For this trial he applied a statistical method in the hope of achieving empirical proof of an astrological 'truth'. Indeed, in the first round of experiments he did achieve an uncannily significant result. However, as von Franz has related, he was not altogether at ease with such a result:

> On obtaining this positive result Jung was, however, not quite comfortable. As he sat in front of his tower in Bollingen one afternoon, suddenly he saw, through the interplay of light and shadow, a mischievous face laughing out at him from the masonry of the wall (Later he brought this face out of the stone with chisel and hammer and perpetuated it as the trickster Mercurius). The thought struck him: Had Mercurius, the spirit of nature, played a trick on him? In a soberer and more sceptical frame of mind he repeated the experiment with a second batch of horoscopes and this time the result was substantially less

> improbable. In all probability, then, the first result had itself been a meaningful coincidence, in other words a synchronistic phenomenon!
>
> (von Franz 1998: 238)

This engraved trickster appears on his Bollingen wall (see Figure 9.1). Of significance here is that Jung chose what he would term *the archetype of the coniunctio* in this work. For him, this archetype was of critical relevance to his times. The splitting of matter and psyche in the Age of the Fishes, according to him, would reunite as a *heiros gamos* in the immanent Age of the Water-Bearer.[2]

As already mentioned in chapter 4, these coniunctio ideas are of particular relevance to Jung's portrayal of the alchemical Mercurius as marriage quaternion, as an above (spirit) and below (matter) and as bride (Queen Luna) and bridegroom (King Sol) – themes which are revisited again later, in chapters 10 and 11. In summary, the astrological experiment highlights the Queen Luna and King Sol coniunctio.

His synchronicity project, however, embodied greater ambitions. Specifically, with the help of the renowned physicist Pauli he struggled to pioneer a unified view of matter and spirit: effectively the other two components of this marriage quaternion.

Religious and physics quaternios

Towards the end of his work on synchronicity, Jung (with significant help from Pauli) constructed a quaternion hypothetical model that situated his concept of synchronicity in the contemporary scientific worldview. On the horizontal axis of this quaternion he placed 'Space–Time' on the left and 'Indestructible Energy' on the right. On the vertical axis he placed 'Causality' above and 'Synchronicity' below.

Here he also alluded to his already established ideas on the Christian *religious* quaternio as if hinting, in the spirit of a Renaissance 'grand auctour', at the possibility of equivalence between the religious and physics quaternios. He invokes here the three-four ambiguity as Christian Trinity in dynamic tension with 'the pagan quaternity which was ordinarily so beloved of the alchemists' (Jung 1952b: 513). In his religious quaternio, the problematic fourth takes on a plethora of forms, scattered throughout his writings. In the work on synchronicity, however, he chooses this fourth as the '*serpens quadricornutus*: the four-horned serpent who is the devil' (ibid.: 513), as shown in Figure 9.2.

This conception is heavily biased towards the masculine, suggesting that Jung was differentiating a masculine religious quaternion (spirit) and a feminine physics quaternion (matter) with a view towards a grand synthesis: his coniunctio idea.

The crucial factor for such a synthesis hinges on the 'problematic fourth' in both representations. It is here that the figure of Mercurius enters the picture, in that Jung has associated this figure with the fourth in both quaternios. For example, concerning the religious quaternion, we read in *Aion* of an 'anthropomorphised' fourth as Mercurius duplex, in the form of 'Mary or the Devil' (Jung 1951a: 252).

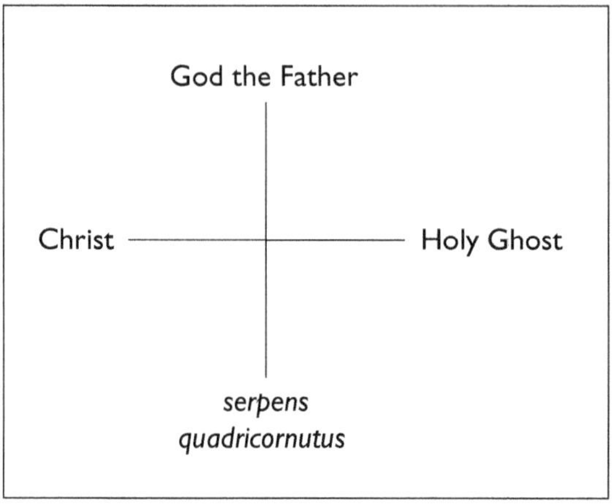

Figure 9.2 Religious Quaternio.

Then in *Mysterium Coniunctionis*, concerning physics and synchronicity, he identifies a more impersonal representation: 'It is apparent ... that the desperately evasive and universal Mercurius – that Proteus twinkling in a myriad shapes and colours – is none other than the "unus mundus," the original, non-differentiated unity of the world or of Being' (Jung 1955/1956: 462). Here he also considers synchronicity to be the 'para-psychological' equivalent to the concept of the *unus mundus* (see 463–4). These representations are depicted in Figure 9.3.

Here we see Mercurius as a common symbol of the problematic fourth, which traverses both the religious and physics conceptions, as 'third thing'.

It is noteworthy, however, that Jung does not attempt a grand synthesis of the religious and physics quaternios. His focus is on the fourth in the physics quaternio, as a principle of synchronicity. Yet it is through this concept that one can discern a motion towards such a synthesis. In the words of Main: 'because for Jung the psyche is partly spiritual, the connection of the psychic and physical in synchronicity may also provide for the basis for a partial integration of religion and science' (Main 2004: 177). Stein further elaborates:

> By including the principle of synchronicity as a fourth principle of science ... modern man, whose intellectual commitment is to scientific rationality and empirical method, would have a way of including transcendence and divine activity within a world-view that also paid full recognition to the space-time causality continuum.
>
> (Stein, cited in Main 2004: 127)

In effect, his synchronicity concept displays a 'united double nature', like Mercurius, in that it is associated with the 'recalcitrant fourth' in both representations: it

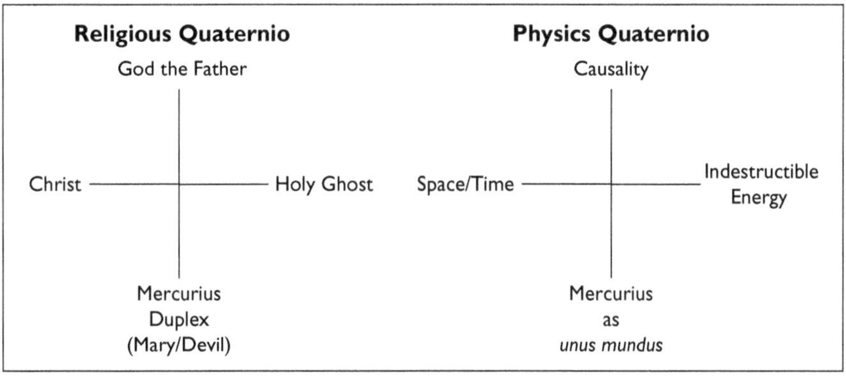

Figure 9.3 Religious and Physics Quaternios.

partakes of the nature of spirit (religious quaternio) and matter (physics quaternio). Of particular relevance here is that Mercurius functions as a more sophisticated symbol of problematic fourth in both systems, in that it draws us deeply into Jung's later writings, which he considered his most important (a claim I shall try to substantiate in chapters 10 and 11).

I now further expand on the problematic fourth by means of an exploration into Pauli's personal life, as portrayed in his letters to Jung. In doing this, I shall try to probe how Jung may have conceived of 'equivalence' (by means of the figure of Mercurius) between such seemingly disparate conceptions as 'Mary or the Devil' and 'unus mundus'.

Pauli and the problematic fourth

A reading of the Pauli/Jung letters reveals the extent of a shared interest centred on the 'problematic fourth'. In looking at this theme the relation between synchronicity and Mercurius, viewed through the eyes (so to speak) of Jung and Pauli, also becomes clearer.

Dealing with the 'problematic fourth' in the religious quaternion, Mercurius duplex in the form of 'Mary or the Devil' can be related, on a personal level, to the idea in analytical psychology of the anima and shadow as manifested via the inferior function, such as through dreams. This 'Jungian perspective' allows for a rapprochement between the microcosm of the personal and the macrocosm of the cultural. Thus, for example, Pauli's dreams and personal struggles with what can be termed shadow and anima-type figures can be related to larger cultural concerns; what Jungians might view as the shaping of a 'new myth' with the unique feature of bridging spirit and matter. I shall now elaborate on these ideas by looking at Pauli's dream figures, such as the Blond, the Persian, the Stranger, the Master and the Chinese woman.[3]

Pauli related persistent and enigmatic figures in his dreamscape. One of these he described as a tall, blond man, younger than himself (between 30 and 40 years old), with an uncanny and unconventional intelligence. He called this figure 'the Blond'. He also described another figure as dark and male, and termed him 'the Persian'.[4] In describing their relationship with each other, he wrote: ' "The Blond" and "The Persian" may be dual aspects of one and the same figure (they never appear together). The figure has an extremely "psychopompos" character and has a similar function as Mercury with the alchemists' (Pauli, in Meier [ed.] 2001: 30). Pauli expanded by noting that in 1948 these two figures merged and combined the two opposite poles as light and dark in a closer relationship, in a form he called 'the stranger'. He described this person as blond with a dark robe, or vice versa, and wrote to Jung that his work on 'The Spirit Mercurius' had greatly helped him in understanding this figure (ibid.: 43). Further, he stated this figure 'makes no distinction whatsoever between "physical" and "psychic," and he also applies mathematics to what we call "the hermetic world of the psyche" ' (ibid.: 44).

In a letter to Emma Jung, Pauli further characterised 'the stranger' by comparing him to, in particular, De Boron's version of Merlin, whereby his knowledge, rooted in chthonic origins, repeatedly takes him back to nature (Pauli, in Meier [ed.] 2001: 50). Expanding, he wrote: 'My dream figure is also "dual-layered"; on the one hand he is a spiritual light figure with superior knowledge, and on the other he is a chthonic natural spirit' (ibid.: 51). For Pauli, these characteristics contributed towards 'the stranger' being not so much an Antichrist, but a kind of 'Antiscientist', in the sense that he exhibits an aversion towards the one-sided approach taken towards science in universities of the day. Thus, in Pauli's dreams 'the stranger' occasionally sets fire to these 'symbols of his oppression' (ibid.: 51). Pauli further wrote concerning the stranger that 'If he feels he is being disregarded he does everything in his power to draw attention to himself, for example by means of synchronistic phenomena (which he calls "radioactivity")' and went on to explain that 'this "stranger" is something that did not accept the scientific world picture about 300 years ago and is now running around autonomously in the collective unconscious like a loose cannon' (Pauli, in Meier 2001 [ed.] 2001: 51).

Continuing, Pauli described the stranger as having not so much a destructive relationship with modern science, but rather an unconventional one akin to Merlin's ambiguous relationship with Christianity. For Pauli, 'the stranger,' like Merlin, wishes to be understood and acknowledged in contemporary culture and is therefore in need of redemption (Pauli, in Meier [ed.] 2001: 51). He wrote that 'what he is striving for is his own transformation, and in this ego-consciousness must cooperate in such a way that at the same time it broadens and grows' (ibid.: 79).

In these descriptions, 'the stranger' is cast as a human-like personality. However, Pauli also identified him more impersonally as 'the archetypal background constellated by the scientific concepts of our time' (ibid.: 40), with the aim of conveying a 'holistic concept of nature' (ibid.: 46).

A similar idea appears via another prominent figure in Pauli's dreams, which he related to the anima – described variously as 'The Dark One' and 'The Exotic One', but most often as 'the Chinese woman'. This anima figure, for Pauli, has 'knowledge' of a meaningful wholeness (Pauli, in Meier [ed.] 2001: 46) – a view he described as being problematic for the human mind (ibid.: 90), including his own. For him, 'she' was still insufficiently connected to his rational ego (ibid.: 88). Consequently, she 'first appeared as the bearer of "psychophysical secrets," ranging from sexuality to subtle ESP phenomena (and with the mantic of the *I Ching*)' (ibid.: 88). Thus, in learning from the Chinese woman, he began to experience resolution as a 'third thing' beyond such supposed dualities as science and mysticism (ibid.: 88, also Zabriskie 2005).

However, although this anima figure, for Pauli, can 'see' in a special way, she also has a limitation, being incapable of such rational processes as logical thinking, mathematics, physics, etc. Consequently, she requires the logos (Pauli) as a bridegroom, which results, in a later development, as the miraculous birth of the new light–dark 'stranger' – the son born from the river – for Jung, the 'age-old son of the mother' (Jung 1963/1995: 90, 117).

Together, the stranger and the Chinese woman are portrayed by Pauli as being deeply interrelated in a drama of not only personal but also cultural significance. For example, on a personal level he acknowledged having projected this twosome as an inner archetypal situation onto his difficult 'shadow-projection' relationship with his father, and a 'light anima projection' onto his stepmother (Pauli, in Meier[ed.] 2001: 151).[5] On a cultural level, he also commented on the dangerous and suspect constellation of the 'light anima' in a secret relationship with the shadow as Devil. Thus in 1956, no doubt influenced by Jung's later books, Pauli wrote:

> In my view, only a chthonic, instinctive wisdom can save mankind from the dangers of the atom bomb, which is precisely why the material-chthonic, ostracized by Christianity as unspiritual, requires a positive value sign. This manifests itself particularly in the fact that the dark-chthonic anima now seems to me superior, and its connection with the light (spiritual) side of the "Master" is a source of hope. So, for me, light and dark no longer coincide with good and evil. Down in the dark depths of the earth an assumption is required of the woman, not far from the person in heaven.
>
> (Pauli, in Meier [ed.] 2001: 140–1)

A further significant consequence of Pauli's creative encounter with these dream figures resulted in his pioneering idea (supported by Jung) of a *neutral language* that could apply equally to both psyche and matter. For Pauli, the language of the psychophysical background is a 'language of parables' that requires 'dedicated work' so that it can be translated into such a neutral language (ibid.: 40).

He also considered the language of analytical psychology to be insufficient for such a task and noted that concepts such as 'self,' 'archetype', etc. did not appear in his dreams. In contrast his own dream language, systematically created through '20 years of listening', was 'perfectly satisfactory' – a language composed of a lexicon of words such as 'spectral lines', 'isotope', 'radioactivity', 'nucleus', 'isomorphy' or 'automorphy' (Pauli, in Meier [ed.] 2001: 141–2). Indeed, in a letter to Jung he stated that 'I would have no need to translate it into the language of C. G. Jung's psychology, since I regard the latter as less differentiated than my own dream language' (ibid.: 141–2).

The relation between this dream language and creation of a *neutral language* would appear to have been a struggle in what might be described as Pauli's 'confrontation with the unconscious'. By way of example the following excerpt, in which Pauli reflects on a dream, affords a glimpse into such a process.

> My interpretation of the dream at the time (it was a proper examination, with the 'stranger' as examiner, in which the word 'automorphism' had the effect of a 'mantra') was that a generic term was being sought that was to cover both your concept of the archetypes as well as the physical laws of nature.
>
> (Pauli, in Meier [ed.] 2001: 79)

A key purpose of such an enterprise (of creating a neutral language) was, for Pauli, to assist in the quintessentially important 'creation of consciousness' (Jung's individuation). Thus, for example, the Blond's unconventional scientific contraptions and study of phenomena such as 'cosmic rays' would appear to have a scientific as well as a religious function of both personal and cultural significance. In this context Pauli notes that scientific observation by means of 'technical construction of apparatuses' and inner psychological observation by means of a 'methodically guided imagination' are, from the standpoint of the unconscious, 'one and the same' (Pauli, in Meier [ed.] 2001: 183).

Another relevant theme in Pauli's dreamscape concerned motifs around 'the new professorship'. This was not aligned to his day job, but is rather representative of a more complete and holistic conception reminiscent of the older seventeenth-century worldview but also inclusive of cultural developments such as modern science and analytical psychology. In this new position, he would be expected to articulate not only such ideas as his neutral language and cultural problematics, but also ethical and personal matters.

Thus in a dream he recounted in 1952, the Chinese woman communicates with him by means of a mime-like ballet and leads him through a trapdoor, down steps and to an underground auditorium where he is expected to deliver a lecture to strangers. Whilst waiting, the Chinese woman dances rhythmically up the stairs into the open air and then back down again, in a continual motion which reminds Pauli of 'the circulation of light'. During this dance, whilst her arms are outstretched, the index finger of her right hand is pointing downward and the index finger of her left hand is pointing upwards. The effect of this dance is that the upper and lower worlds 'magically' diminish. As Pauli then begins to mount the rostrum of the auditorium, he wakes up (Pauli, in Meier [ed.] 2001: 89–90).

This dream illustrates the psychopomp-like role of the Chinese woman. In Jung's psychology, she functions to 'stitch together' consciousness (upper world) and the unconscious (subterranean) in an intriguing and sensual dance, as *eros* in the individuation process. In further applying Jung's concepts, the 'new professorship' could signify his potential new persona as learned and esteemed in not only the scientific values of the upper world (intuition and thinking as his dominant functions), but also the lower and chthonic (feeling and sensation as his inferior functions). In this view, the dynamics of his individuation (circulation of the light) impel him towards not only greater personal wholeness but also a new persona role. In all, situated in the bigger picture of his worldview, he perceives himself as facilitating a process of redemption of the Merlin figure. Indeed, in a letter to Jaffé, he wrote: 'I want to recognize [Merlin], talk to him again, bring his redemption a little nearer. That, I believe, is the myth of my life' (Pauli, cited in Miller 2009: 196).

In summary, we see how Pauli viewed the dynamics of an 'inner archetypal drama' as manifesting in his personal life (shadow-anima) as well as through compelling cultural problems. This afforded an expansion of Jung's characterisation of problematic fourth as Mercurius duplex, in the form of 'Mary or the Devil' and also in terms of the 'impersonal world' (such as the psychophysical background, etc.). Thus, through these figures, we have been drawn closer to concerns related to the problematic fourth pertinent not only to the religious quaternion but also to the physics quaternion, thereby adding depth to how both Jung and Pauli understood the symbol of Mercurius. In the journey towards unravelling all of this, the central 'life-myth' of Pauli has also been identified as 'the redemption of Merlin'.

Pauli and von Franz

Apart from Jung, Pauli also had an 'intense' and 'tumultuous' friendship with von Franz. Indeed, rumour has it there was a romance between them (see Miller 2009: 213–14). Scholars of Jung would also probably agree that von Franz was the most influential first-generation follower to further the concept of synchronicity. For her, the individual experience of a synchronicity wherein matter and psyche mirror each other and are meaningfully related can be understood in terms of an *alchemical coniunctio*:

> ... there is a sort of *coniunctio* of matter and psyche and at the same time an exchange of attributes which always takes place in the *heiros gamos*. So it is really true that a synchronistic event is an act of creation and a union of two principles normally not connected.
>
> (von Franz 1980: 116)

In considering cultural perspective, she further wrote that 'the rationalism of the seventeenth century ... had one advantage after all: it drove father-spirit and mother-matter so far apart that now we can reunite them in a cleaner way' (von Franz 1992: 157). No doubt, in her view, the 'marriage' of physics and psychology (especially analytical psychology) was the context for such a cleaner unification. Perhaps she also viewed the intense intellectual affinity (and romance) between Pauli and herself in a mystical way, commensurate with such a *coniunctio* theme.

For example, von Franz gave partial articulation to the 'psychophysical secrets' as characterised by Pauli's Chinese woman in her writings on the *I Ching*. In this context, building on Jung's assertion that 'synchronism is the prejudice of the East, causality is the modern prejudice of the West' (cited in Peat 1988: 22), she has done fairly extensive work relating the concepts of *unus mundus* and synchronicity to the Chinese holistic worldview. She states this succinctly: 'Chinese thought presumes that the whole of nature is a psycho-physical unity or has a unitary wholeness, which, however, escapes observation that concentrates on details' (von Franz 1992: 26).

Adding to this perspective von Franz, in sympathy with Jung, also championed such astrological conceptions as the imminent arrival of the Age of Aquarius, when opposites such as psyche and matter would reunite. Considering such an astrological worldview, her rendezvous with Pauli could well have taken on esoteric connotations (in their roles as helping to catalyse this New Age) – at least in her opinion.

The alchemical coniunctio

In overview: the concept of a partial synthesis of the religious and physics quaternios, through problematic fourth, coalesced around the coniunctio theme and played out in the minds of Jung, Pauli and von Franz as an internal drama anticipatory, in a prospective and visionary sense, of a coming *heiros gamos* of psyche and matter on a grand cultural scale (Pauli, in Meier [ed.] 2001: 87).

Pauli was optimistic about this new possibility, though uncertain about its timing: 'whether and when this *coniunctio* will be realized I do not know, but I am in no doubt at all that this would be the finest fate that could happen to both physics and psychology' (ibid.: 122). He was of the opinion that this was the 'intention' of the unconscious which, he averred, was forcing itself 'vaguely and sketchily' into the consciousness of individuals. For Pauli, this would all 'require just as great an effort on the part of many people in what may be a distant future as has the development of science and technology in the last 300 years' (ibid.: 142).

Thus we see convergence of opinion by both Pauli and Jung on the essential idea of a *coniunctio* between psyche and matter as future possibility. Pauli though, sceptical of Jung's astrological beliefs, would appear to have had no interest in locating this in terms of Platonic months. For Jung, in contrast, this was central. For him this *coniunctio* would coincide, synchronistically, with the esoteric idea of the dawning of the Age of Aquarius (after the separation of psyche and matter during the Age of the Fishes). In such a worldview the images of vertical fish (spirit), horizontal fish (matter) and container of the water-bearer capture, to an extent, key elements of the transition between these Platonic Aeons.

In alchemy, these elements find amplification in such images as the alchemical retort and the two mercurial substances. For example, medieval alchemy had, for Jung, already anticipated resolution by means of a 'marriage' in such images as the union, in the alchemical retort, of two beings of contrary natures such as the winged and wingless dragons (as representative of the spiritual and chthonic) into a 'third thing' which conflates with the Mercurius–Merlin phenomenon. It would appear that Jung further believed, optimistically, that such a historical split and subsequent union had creative potential; that a quantum leap of consciousness (a 'creation in time') would become a more commonplace potentiality for individuals synchronistic with this New Age, just as his idea of the god-image incarnating (and being contained) and undergoing an alchemical transformation through the process of individuation.

In summary: from the above, we see a persistent theme emerging around the idea of the alchemical coniunctio. The astrological experiment involved Sun and Moon signs of married couples (bride and bridegroom). The problematic fourth in the religious and physics quaternios highlighted the essential idea of 'father spirit' and 'mother matter' as coniunctio of the above (spirit) and below (matter). Descriptions of Pauli's confrontation with the unconscious and his relationship with von Franz have offered further expansion on such themes, as inclusion of the personal. In effect, we have witnessed dynamics of the quaternion structure of the coniunctio as Queen Luna (right), King Sol (left), a spiritual father (above) and a chthonic mother (below) in the microcosm of a personal drama (as Pauli's confrontation with the unconscious and relationships with Jung and von Franz) and in the macrocosm of cultural worldview in transition (as psychophysical *heiros gamos*, and as emerging New Age).

Notes

1 Here I re-emphasise the differences between the figures of Hermes and the alchemical Mercurius (see chapter 1).
2 These themes are developed further in chapters 10 and 11.
3 See also Sparks 2007, especially chapter 3, 'The Stranger Knows', for further commentary on Pauli's dream-figures.
4 See Sparks 2007: 103–7, in which 'the Persian' is related to Zarathustra in relation to the Christian Platonic month.
5 Pauli's father's wife was much younger than his father (of interest in light of Jung's archetypal motif of Eros-Logos as old man and young woman).

Chapter 10

Aion[1]

In a letter to Victor White, Jung wrote that *Aion* 'came to me as a shock' and said that he felt 'utterly unequal to such a task' (2007: 103). *Aion*, with its astrological basis and use of the synchronicity concept, can be considered a radical departure from his more 'conservative' earlier thought. In a private conversation with Margaret Ostrowski-Sachs, Jung explained:

> Before my illness I had often asked myself if I were permitted to publish or even speak of my secret knowledge. I later set it all down in *Aion*. I realized it was my duty to communicate these thoughts, yet I doubted whether I was allowed to give expression to them. During my illness I received confirmation and I now knew that everything had meaning and that everything was perfect.
>
> (cited in Edinger 1996: 13)

Concerning 'secret knowledge', one is also reminded of the alchemical belief that the doctrine can manifest as a 'gift of the Holy Ghost' and as a revelation of nature, as opposed to book or taught knowledge (Jung 1951a: 162). We also read that it is the 'wonder-working "divine" water of alchemy, whose double aspect is represented by Mercurius' (ibid.: 180), and further that 'sometimes Mercurius is a substance like quicksilver, sometimes it is a philosophy' (ibid.: 155).

The purpose of this ambiguous substance–philosophy would also appear to be nothing less than to achieve spiritual transfiguration. Jung wrote that '[i]n the Indian "quicksilver system" the arcane substance is called *para-da*, "leading to the other shore"; in the West it is Mercurius' (Jung 1951a: 152). Therefore, just as mercury is transformed into such products as gold and the philosopher's stone as lapis, so the alchemist first needs to become 'fixed in the mercury'. Jung further explains: 'Fixation in the Mercurius of the wise would then correspond to the traditional Hermetic knowledge, since Mercurius symbolizes the Nous; through this knowledge the self, as a content of the unconscious, is made conscious and "fixed" in the mind' (ibid.: 168–9). Framed in the terminology of analytical psychology, this would surely read as 'achieving realisation of the self, through an individuation process'.

The central theme of *Aion*, however, constellates around the concept of the self as manifested through the history of Christianity. Edinger has described this endeavour as 'the cultural history of the human race as though it were the case history of a single patient' (Edinger 1996: 12). More subtly, Rowland, by utilising Bakhtin's concept of the chronotope (briefly, a space–time unity), considers *Aion* to be a historical map of the psyche in the four dimensions of space-time: 'it is an attempt to offer history as a form of psychic energy' (Rowland 2005: 155).[2]

Perhaps the most significant theme of *Aion*, subtitled *Researches into the Phenomenology of the Self*, concerns 'the relations between the traditional Christ-figure and the natural symbols of wholeness, or the self' (Jung 1951a: x) within the context of the 'Christian Aeon' of Pisces. Here, Jung claims the cultural and religious history of Christianity unfolded in space and time according to the astrological narrative of the precession of the equinoxes. According to him, this coincidence between religious and cultural history and the star narrative is a case of synchronicity. *Aion*, amongst other things, is therefore his attempt to substantiate this claim by invoking major spiritual trends (Gnosticism, Hermeticism, Christianity, alchemy, etc.) and cultural moments (Reformation, Renaissance, etc.) contained within this time span. Importantly, for Jung, *Aion* also traces a *cultural individuation* whereby the polytheistic pagan *anima/animus* stage has progressed to a monotheistic Christian *self* stage (Jung 1951a: 268). Effectively, *Aion* chronicles an operatic drama (cultural individuation) of religious, spiritual and cultural forms as reflecting a dynamic expression and regeneration of the self: the idea of a transforming god-image (ibid.: 192–4).

* * *

In what follows, I shall look specifically at Jung's conception of Mercurius in the context of *Aion*. My rationale for doing this is that first, Jung's treatment of this theme is tacit and obscure; second, this has not been done in the post-Jungian literature (of which I am aware). In addition, as I shall illustrate, such an enterprise clarifies both the figure of Mercurius and important themes of *Aion*.

My method is to establish a dialogue between 'The Spirit Mercurius' and *Aion* by means of a study on the themes of (a) Christ and Mercurius as symbols of the self, and (b) the idea of astrological Aeons in relation to the idea of a transforming god-image. Throughout, a fidelity to original texts is ensured by restricting references almost entirely to Jung's writings, with emphasis on 'The Spirit Mercurius' and *Aion*. The rationale for this method is to reveal 'what Jung really said' in the context of these less studied works. I then conclude with a broader discussion.

Christ and Mercurius: symbols of the self?

> Hesitantly, as in a dream, the introspective brooding of the centuries gradually put together the figure of Mercurius and created a symbol which, according to all the psychological rules, stands in a compensatory relation to Christ. It is not

> meant to take his place, nor is it identical with him, for then indeed it could replace him. It owes its existence to the law of compensation, and its object is to throw a bridge across the abyss separating the two psychological worlds by presenting a subtle compensatory counterpoint to the Christ image.
>
> (Jung: 1943/1948: 245)

In *Psychological Types*, Jung gives a 'working hypothesis' definition of his concept of the self. Here we read of it variously as expressing the 'unity of the personality as a whole' and as a '*transcendental* concept' describing 'psychic totality, consisting of both conscious and unconscious contents'. He further cites empirical manifestations of this phenomenon as found in dreams, myths and fairytales, such as 'king, hero, prophet, saviour, etc., or in the form of a totality symbol, such as the circle, square, *quadratura circuli*, cross etc.', and also as a '*complexio oppositorum*, a union of opposites' (Jung 1921: 460–1). For Jung the self is an enigma, an idea 'so difficult to visualize in itself that a great many different expressions are required in order to bring out its various aspects' (Jung 1951a: 196).

For western Christian culture he considers the particular figure of Christ, our culture hero, as embodying 'the myth of the divine Primordial Man, the mystic Adam' (Jung 1951a: 36). He continues by identifying the psychological position of the Christ symbol with the archetype of the self (ibid.: 37). Further, he cites various qualities of the Christ figure to illustrate aspects of a *complexio oppositorum*. For example, as deity he is eternal, yet as the historical man Jesus he is unique and historical.

Jung also identifies Christ with the *principium individuationis* that leads towards a '*mysterium coniunctionis*, the self being experienced as a nuptial union of opposite halves' (Jung 1951a: 64). In this context his cross as bride, tree, church, etc. represents mystical union with the feminine. The cross as passion, as division into four and as representing upper (spiritual) and lower (chthonic), as good (redeemed thief) and evil (unredeemed thief), are all used by Jung to corroborate the identity of Christ as a symbol of the self and the dynamism of his life as individuation process (ibid.: 64–5).

However, in Jung's view, there are two particularly glaring problems with the idea of iconic Christ as archetype of the self. First, he does not possess a shadow; second, the feminine is missing. The first of these concerns the missing evil, chthonic, instinctual polarity of the archetype (ibid.: 43–4).

In this schema the Christ symbol lacks wholeness due to a missing evil and material–chthonic. Jung further elaborates such a 'deficiency' by comparing the Christ image to his concept of the archetype: 'The Christ-image is as good as perfect (at least it is meant to be so), while the archetype (so far as known) denotes completeness but is far from being perfect' (Jung 1951a: 69). For him, the one-sided archetypal manifestation of Christ was deeply unsettling.[3]

Apart from a missing shadow, Christ also lacks the feminine. Although the feminine has, to an extent, been appropriated as the 'death marriage' to the cross-tree as bride and as the Church (ibid.: 39), there is no overtly feminine aspect such as wife, sister or lover in the life of the historical Jesus as represented in traditional Christianity.

In Jung's view these missing components have given rise to psychological compensations in the form of the Antichrist as shadow and the idea of Christ having had variously a sister or a bride and/or exhibited androgyny, as found, for example, in gnosticism and alchemy. In summary, the idea of Christ as a symbol of the self is compelling yet deficient. It lacks many glaring aspects of a *complexio oppositorum*. Indeed, it invites the question of whether there is a more satisfactory symbol that complements such 'deficiencies'.

The missing shadow and missing feminine

Jung considers the Antichrist to be 'the shadow of the self' (Jung 1951a: 42). For him the Christ–Antichrist dyad thus forms complementary aspects of an original unitary archetype.

In further developing the idea of an initial unitary archetype that has divided, Jung relates the mythic motif of two brothers harbouring enmity towards each other, one dark, the other light, such as the Egyptian Set and Horus; yet in a situation wherein both are united in the greater figure of Osiris (ibid.: 123). He identifies the same motif associated with Christianity, from various non-traditional sources. In one example he cites, God is said to have had two sons: Christ and his elder brother Satan (ibid.: 57, also 81). Here we get the same idea of a common root whereby Christ and Antichrist are linked as brothers to a greater or ultimate deity. Jung also highlights primitive Christian views that Christ shared many 'symbols or "allegories" in common with the devil ... the lion, snake, bird, raven, eagle and fish' (ibid.: 72). For him, this all points towards an initial unitary archetype that combines the spiritual and chthonic, and thereby has potential for healing the dangerous split archetype.

Apart from a missing shadow, Jung also pointed out the missing feminine in Christ as god-image. Here, once again, he took recourse to non-traditional sources to indicate a tendency towards resolution. For example, he noted that in some medieval depictions, Christ is shown to have breasts. He also noted from various sources the idea that Christ differentiated out a woman from himself, thereby implying an initial androgyny. Citing an important version of such a motif, he also noted that after splitting himself into man and woman on a mountain-top, Christ and his feminine part then performed the *heiros gamos* by copulating (ibid.: 205–6). Once again, such images indicate an original unitary archetype (Christ–female consort) that splits and then reunites in the idea of the *heiros gamos*.

For Jung, such compensatory elements to the missing shadow and feminine in the Christ-image can be found in undercurrent Christian culture (such as Christian mysticism, Hermeticism, Gnosticism and alchemy). However, he points out that mainstream Christianity does not entertain such ideas as integrating evil and the feminine or of a paradoxical god-image (ibid.: 42). For him such deficiencies underpin an epic spiritual struggle that stretches across the roughly 2,000 years of the Aeon of Pisces.

Christ's older brother?

In the concluding pages of *Aion*, we read: 'The Other, the fourth, corresponds in ... the "Christian Quaternity" – if such an expression be permitted – to Mary or the devil. These two incompatible figures are united in the Mercurius duplex of alchemy' (ibid.: 253).

This is perhaps the most explicit statement Jung makes in *Aion*, in the sense of Mercurius as 'resolution' of the missing shadow and feminine in the iconography of the Christian deity. Further, his words 'if such an expression be permitted' suggests that *Other* as *missing fourth* finds only partial expression in Christian imagery. Here he hints at deeper subtleties, as captured in the figure of Mercurius, that attract a plethora of symbolic and mythic notions beyond the ethnocentricity of a strictly Christian worldview (as we have amply seen). Indeed, he here hints that 'The Spirit Mercurius' is key in moving towards a fuller understanding of this conceptual difficulty.

* * *

In 'The Spirit Mercurius', he more clearly locates the figure of Mercurius relative to the Christian deity. Here, this figure is described variously as 'a chthonic trinity' (1943/1948: 221), as 'God's reflection in physical nature' (ibid.: 237) and as the alchemist's analogue of the Holy Ghost (ibid.: 229). In these aspects, Mercurius is described as a compensatory image of the Christian deity. More particularly, Jung briefly develops (in this text) the relationship between Mercurius and Christ.

Historically, Mercurius can be linked to the supposed founder of alchemy: Hermes Trismegistus. Christ's historicity, on the other hand, is based on the life of Jesus of Nazareth. In this context, Jung uses alchemical references to construct the view of Mercurius as first-born son of God, and therefore as Christ's 'older brother' (1943/1948: 222–3). Building on this view, he points out a 'compensatory symmetry' in which Mercurius arises from below, ascends to heaven and then returns to earth in a motion which unites the above and the below, in contrast to Christ and the Gnostic redeemer's journey from heaven to earth and back to heaven (ibid.: 233).

These 'two brothers', Christ and Mercurius, are both described by Jung as symbols of the self. In an attempt to resolve this conceptual difficulty, he wrote that 'we are actually confronted with two different images of the self, which in all likelihood presented a duality even in their original form. This duality was not invented, but is an autonomous phenomenon' (ibid.: 246). Expanding on this, he writes that 'Christ appears as the archetype of consciousness and Mercurius as the archetype of the unconscious' (ibid.: 247). He further writes that 'in the beginning there were two figures, one bright and one shadowy, and only afterwards did the light of consciousness detach itself from the night and the uncertain shimmer of its stars' (ibid.). Here we find resonance with the already mentioned ideas of the light and dark brothers, such as Horus and Set.

Here I recall Jung's V6 definition of the self, as essentially unitary and inclusive of both consciousness and the unconscious. This contrasts with his idea of an intrinsically *dualistic* self as 'autonomous phenomenon', as portrayed in 'The Spirit Mercurius' and reminiscent of ideas already discussed as the split archetype: light–spiritual fractured from the chthonic–instinctual. In 1951 Jung associated polytheistic–pagan deities with the anima–animus stages, and monotheistic deity to the self stage of cultural individuation (1951a: 268). In this sense, he is being conceptually inconsistent by positing two co-dependent archetypes of the self in 1943/1948.

A further difficulty is the idea of the 'two brothers' as Christ and Antichrist. This leads to the logical conclusion that Antichrist = Mercurius; a conclusion Jung cautioned against.

> To the Christian mentality, the dark antagonist is always the devil. As I have shown, Mercurius escapes this prejudice by only a hair's breadth. But he escapes it, thanks to the fact that he scorns to carry on opposition at all costs. The magic of his name enables him, in spite of his ambiguity and duplicity, to keep outside the split, for as an ancient pagan god he possesses a natural undividedness which is impervious to logical and moral contradictions. This gives him invulnerability and incorruptibility, the very qualities we so urgently need to heal the split in ourselves.
>
> (1943/1948: 245–6)

I also reiterate that intrinsic to the idea of Mercurius is a progressive transformation, from arcane substance through to completed lapis, aligned to his concept of individuation as a process which begins with an activation of the shadow and 'ends' with the self. Depictions which emphasise his darker, pagan, and ambiguous aspects thus correlate to his alchemically 'untransformed' state (ibid.: 228). Therefore, in the beginning stages, we can say that Mercurius is contaminated with the repressed shadow of Christianity as devil.

Christ, Mercurius and the 'missing feminine'

In contrast with the Christ image, the alchemical Mercurius has numerous associations and even identifications with the feminine. We can recall an earlier quote from *Aion* where Jung related the feminine aspect of Mercurius to Mary. In 'The Spirit Mercurius', however, the feminine images invoked are decidedly pagan: 'Lilith or Melusina' (Jung 1943/1948: 199), '*foemina* or *virgo*' (ibid.: 212), 'Aphrodite' (ibid.: 216). Especially in the cases of Lilith or Melusina, we see the chthonic polarity of the archetype that is missing in the image of Mary.

Sexual and romantic imagery are also integral to the image of Mercurius at various stages of alchemical transformation. Expanding on this, we note that initially Mercurius as arcane substance displays a unitary and undifferentiated hermaphroditism. Jung, quoting Khunrath, describes this as 'begotten of the hermaphroditic seed of the Macrocosm' (1943/1948: 219). Such an initial unitary state is also described as being capable of differentiating into a male with a female soul, or the reverse. In all this the themes of love, passion and libidinous lust are central. Thus 'as his own divine consort he easily turns into the goddess of love, just as in his role of Hermes he is ithyphallic. But he is also called the "most chaste virgin" ' (ibid.: 226). Indeed, 'Mercurius represents the "continuous cohabitation" which is found in unalloyed form in the Tantric Shiva-Shakti concept' (ibid.: 231).[4]

Symbols of the self: snake and stone

In *Aion*, apart from the more obvious complementary features of Christ and Mercurius as self symbols as indicated above, are a range of other symbols. Prominent amongst these are serpent and lapis (stone). A Christ–serpent identity is mentioned (1951a: 186, see also 247). However, he highlights that the serpent is more usually associated with Mercurius. For example, the serpent of Eden is represented as more knowledgeable, wise and 'trickier' than Adam: 'she is older than he' (1943/1948: 245). Expressed variously as *anima mundi*, *deus terrestris*, *serpens mercurialis*, etc., it is also none other than the alchemical Mercurius. As such it is described variously as a 'vegetation numen', a 'blessed greenness', a serpent dwelling in the interior of the earth and 'the pneuma that lies hidden in the *stone*' (ibid.: 245).

This 'tricky spirit' is said to eventually become transformed into the *lapis*, considered one of the main alchemical accomplishments. In alchemy the redemption of the 'spirit slumbering in matter' consists of not only its extraction, but also a transformation that ultimately reconciles this spirit back with matter. This partially explains the alchemical terminology of Mercurius as 'son of the world' or *filius macrocosmi* (1951a: 66), compared to Christ as 'son of man' or *filius microcosmi*. Here, Jung's bias is predominantly towards a *Mercurius–lapis* identity, though he also makes strong associations to a *Christ–lapis* identity (ibid.: 67).

Commentary

Finally, of related concern is Jung's later (post-1944) understanding of the archetype. In *Aion* the notion of archetype as solely intra-psychic is modified to include the extra-psychic or world which, according to him, imbues them with numinosity and a 'cosmic' character (1951a: 196). Building on this view, it is interesting that he also considers the lapis not only a symbol of achieving psychic unity through individuation, but also in terms of a supraordinate or *transcendent* unity (ibid.: 170–1). In such depictions he alludes to an enigmatic ontological dimension to individuation that includes world and nature, beyond the intra-psychic and personal. Ultimately, it was perhaps such intimations that contributed humility to his understanding of alchemy: 'Unfortunately, we today are not so far removed from the Middle Ages: we still have to overcome considerable difficulties before we can begin to understand the real purpose of alchemy' (ibid.: 157).

In summary, I highlight that looking more closely at 'The Spirit Mercurius' in relation to *Aion* results in an expansion of Jung's conception of the self beyond his 'official' 1921 definition from *CWs* V6 to include at least the following features:

1 the self, and archetype in general, as extension beyond the personal intra-psychic to include the world/cosmos as extra-psychic;
2 a regenerative self, manifesting as transformation of the god-image through space and time and as cultural individuation;
3 a co-existing 'dual self-image' in the form of Christ–Mercurius manifested historically in the Judaeo-Christian tradition.

I now consider the second theme, as the idea of a transforming god-image synchronistic with the astrological Age of Pisces.

Astrological aeons: a transforming god-image?

An astrological and synchronistic worldview underpins the theme of *Aion*. For example, Jung makes the rather grandiose claim that '[t]he course of our religious history as well as an essential part of our psychic development could have been predicted more or less accurately, both as regards time and content, from the precession of the equinoxes through the constellation of Pisces' (1951a: 95).

The subject matter of *Aion* is largely focused on the roughly 2,000 years of the Age of Pisces 'synchronistic' with the Christian story. Thus, the symbol of the fish is of particular interest. For Jung the fact that Pisces is a double sign (two fishes) has great explanatory value: it portrays a 'splitting of the archetype' into opposites. The most notable of these is perhaps the 'doctrine of the two sons of God' as the Christ–Antichrist schism, as touched on earlier. *Aion* chronicles the historical unfolding of this 'splitting process'. Thus, he associates the first fish of Pisces with the 'sublime and spotless' Christ, and the second fish with the 'reign of the Antichrist'. There is 'a reign of a "thousand years" and of a "coming of the Antichrist," just as if a partition of worlds and epochs had taken place between two royal brothers' (ibid.: 44).

In Jung's interpretation the qualitative nature of the Christian religion at the beginning of the Pisces Aeon was psychologically one-sided, and therefore doomed to a dramatic swing from 'good' (Christ) to 'evil' (Antichrist). Accordingly, 'the coming of the Antichrist is not just a prophetic prediction – it is an inexorable psychological law whose existence . . . brought [a] sure knowledge of the impending enantiodromia' (1951a: 43). He further believed the transition periods (after the first thousand years, and then again at the end of the Age of Pisces as the 'end of days') to be turbulent and apocalyptic. For him, biblical insight such as the Book of Revelations implies that the 'anima Christiana' possessed prophetic knowledge (ibid.: 36). In *Aion*, Jung as 'prophet of the past' attempts an empirical study to prove this.

Within such a context, he championed the idea of the god-image or *Imago Dei* as evolutionary, regenerative and dynamic; effectively as a transformation that runs 'parallel with changes in human consciousness' (ibid.: 194, see also 260). Here, he aligns himself with the Gnostic and alchemical idea that the 'world-creating Deity is not conscious, but may be dreaming' (ibid.: 192).

I now progress chronologically, starting with the beginning of the Age of Pisces and moving through the roughly 2,000 years of this Aeon up to the beginning of the Age of Aquarius.

The First Fish: Christ and a new astrological Age

In 7 BCE, sky augurs suggested a momentous event in the story of humanity. Specifically, there were three Saturn–Jupiter conjunctions in Pisces. One of these occurred on 29 May with the Sun in Gemini. The conjunction itself occurred at the equinoctial point at the cusp between Aries and Pisces (1951a: 77). Such a conjunction of two large and bright planets in the night sky would have created a spectacle: the star of Bethlehem.[5]

Jung remarks on the birth and death of Christ in the context of this changing Age: 'to the extent that Christ was regarded as the new aeon, it would be clear to anyone acquainted with astrology that he was born as the first fish of the Pisces era, and was doomed to die as the last ram of the declining era' (ibid.: 90).[6]

Jung's identification of Christ's birth with the Sun in Gemini (29 May) also feeds into his general argument of the Christ image's essential duality which differentiates out into the Christ–Antichrist myth, reminiscent of the Egyptian brothers Horus and Set, 'who in a sense prefigure the drama of the Christian myth' (1951a: 78). He further highlights the idea of Jesus as double personality, 'part of which rises up from the chaos or *hyle*, while the other part descends as pneuma from heaven' (ibid.: 79). Here I add that the duality of Gemini traditionally has the planet Mercury as its ruler. This image of Christ exhibiting a 'united double nature' is reminiscent of Mercurius.

However, in secular Christianity, the Christ image has no shadow or feminine. This image that upholds values of perfection, purity and spiritual aspiration is essentially represented for Jung by the first fish of Pisces. This initial fish appears head upward and vertical relative to the ecliptic, and thereby signifies for him the lofty spiritual aspirations that characterised the first millennium of the Aeon of Pisces. In his interpretation this created a dangerous splitting of the unitary archetype into spiritual–chthonic and male–female oppositions and repression of the chthonic and the feminine (a wound of the Christian religion).

The first-millennium vertical fish then gives way to the second-millennium horizontal fish in a movement whereby spiritual values swing into the opposite as materialism: the reign of Christ gives way to the reign of the Antichrist.

Transition point: the middle of an Aeon

Returning to the mid-point of the Aeon, Jung writes that this augured a contrariness of spirit: 'heresies sprang up everywhere like mushrooms, and at the same time Christ's adversary, the second fish, alias the devil, appears as the demiurge' (1951a: 150). During this transitional period, he described seismic shifts in the prevailing religious spirit characterised by the emergence of a variety of new religious movements, such as the influential Joachim de Flora's Holy Ghost Movement, yet also the start of 'devilish developments' and the 'evaporation of Christianity' due to the emergence of a new spirit of rationalism and materialism (ibid.: 150).

In particular, he emphasised the influence of Joachim de Flora and his condemned teachings about the dualistic, ambiguous and ambivalent 'archetype of the spirit' that allowed for symbolic, as opposed to literal, interpretation of Christian doctrine (1951a.: 86). He writes that Joachim de Flora unknowingly motioned towards a resolution of the Christ–Antichrist split (ibid.: 86, also 82). Further on, he elaborates, 'the numinosity of this feeling was heightened by the temporal coincidence – 'synchronicity' – of the epoch he lived in with the beginning of the sphere of the 'antichristian' fish in Pisces' (ibid.: 85).

Jung identifies the rise of Latin alchemy in the forthcoming twelfth and thirteenth centuries as a continuation of this spirit (ibid.: 87). Thus, in the Middle Ages, we get such ideas as the 'chymical wedding', the *lapis philosophorum* and, of course, a prominence of the figure of Mercurius (ibid.: 39, 254). Such uniting symbols have been interpreted by Jung as psychic compensations for the Christian 'split archetype'. In particular, he highlights the development of the concept of Mercurius as 'the partly material, partly immaterial spirit that penetrates and sustains all things ... In the form of a snake he dwells inside the earth ... [and was also] believed to have a human shape as the homunculus or *homo altus*, and was regarded as the chthonic God' (ibid.: 232).

In alchemy we also see the motif of the fighting winged and wingless serpents (sometimes dragons) as representative of the two substances of Mercurius. In this image we get a serpent–dragon correlate to the two fishes of Pisces.

The second fish: the Antichrist

To summarise the above: the enantiodromian spirit that began in the middle of the Aeon gathered momentum through such notables as Joachim de Flora and continued with the Latin alchemists originating in the twelfth and thirteenth centuries.

Jung then shifts to the sixteenth century and the time of the Reformation, where the precession of the equinox coincides more definitely with the beginning of the tail of the second fish (1951a: 94).[7] Here he invokes a prophecy of Nostradamus about a 'usurper from the North' that he believes corroborates his views on the unfolding drama.

In affirming such a prediction he refers to the Catholic–Protestant schism in the sixteenth century as stirrings of an enantiodromian shift in which the preceding Gothic spiritual strivings of the first vertical fish were replaced with the horizontal 'antichrist' fish of Pisces in a new zeitgeist characterised by colonial expansionism and the rampant exploitation of nature, 'so that today we are confronted with a crisis of Western civilization whose outcome appears to be exceedingly dubious' (ibid.: 95).

Jung thus also associates the second fish with the Renaissance and a time during which the spirit of Christianity 'underwent strange pagan transformations, exchanging the heavenly goal for an earthly one' (1951a: 43). Continuing, he understands the Enlightenment and French Revolution as further progressions of such a spirit. Ultimately, he believed this would all culminate in the 'end of time', as anticipated by early Christianity, and as manifested in the times in which he was living (ibid.: 43). In particular he reflects on the identification of Martin Luther, catalyst of the Reformation, as the 'second Antichrist' predicted by Nostradamus to appear after 1792.[8] He makes the further comment that the Nazis considered Hitler a continuation of Luther's uncompleted work (ibid.: 102).

The Age of Aquarius

Jung thus considered Nazism an embodiment of the Antichrist that appears at the Christian 'end of days'. It is also evident that he considered a dualistic, ambiguous and ambivalent 'archetype of the spirit' to have entered cultural consciousness during the build-up to World War II as well as during the war and in the following decades, not unlike what occurred at the mid-point of the Aeon. For example, we can reflect on his 1943 analysis of 'The Spirit in the Bottle' wherein he writes of a 'storm bird' being loosed upon the world (1943/1948: 203). The inevitable apocalyptic scenarios such as World War II, for him, were thus the Christian myth approaching its 'end-game' (1951a: 62).

For Jung, the transition of the current astrological Age (from Pisces to Aquarius) was particularly dangerous due to the extreme splitting of the archetype and due to a progressive erosion of the god-image (in the second millennium) that characterised the Pisces Aeon. He warned of such a 'sinister reality . . . demonstrated before our eyes by the splitting of our world: *the destruction of the God-image is followed by the annulment of the human personality*' (ibid.: 109, also 70–1). Here, he is no longer referring to World War II (now over) but to events contemporaneous with the 1950s; that is, to the prospect of nuclear holocaust. Indeed, for him, the Christian 'end of days' (after all) had not reached fruition during World War II.

However, he is not entirely pessimistic. He views the forthcoming Age of Aquarius as having profound capacity for resolution. Here we need only dwell upon the major images of Aquarius: human, angel, container, 'sweet' water. In such images, one can discern such quintessential symbols as anthropos, grail cup, *aqua vitae*.

Indeed, a major theme for Jung in terms of this New Age concerns the problem of the opposites. For example, he writes: 'If, as seems probable, the aeon of the fishes is ruled by the archetypal motif of the hostile brothers, then the approach of the next Platonic month, namely Aquarius, will constellate the problem of the union of the opposites' (1951a: 87). On this theme he considers alchemy, in particular, as embodying the potential to heal such a split: 'we need to find our way back to the original, living spirit which, because of its ambivalence, is also a mediator and uniter of opposites, an idea that preoccupied the alchemists for many centuries' (ibid.: 86).

In a footnote to this excerpt, he refers specifically to 'The Spirit Mercurius'. It is also notable that he chose the symbol of the serpent to represent cultural transformation or 'the turning-point of the great drama' (1951a: 256) and wrote that 'like a snake changing its skin, the old myth needs to be clothed anew in every renewed age if it is not to lose its therapeutic effect' (ibid.: 181). Such ideas are particularly interesting in light of his Hermetically inspired belief that the Aeon of Pisces was giving way to the Age of Aquarius. For him what was previously shadowy and subterranean was being brought to the 'light of day' through his life project in the *kairos* of a new dawn.

To summarise: a dialogue between 'The Spirit Mercurius' and *Aion* revealed an interpretation of Mercurius as a 'living myth' projected as divine numinosum onto the astrological constellations. In the Age of Pisces we saw Mercurius duplex incorporating both Christ as the first 'spiritual' fish and the Antichrist as the second 'matter' fish, yet taking on the role of 'uniting third' as a coniunctio to be transformed into a unitary spirit–matter amalgam in the *vas* of the water bearer in the Age of Aquarius. In this conception the 'turning of the Great Wheel' as the precession of the equinoxes synchronises with the alchemical transformation of the god-image. In this grand narrative the Age of Pisces and Christianity was considered a mere chapter in the epic struggle of human consciousness in relation to the divine numinosum.

Notes

1 For a discussion on the word *Aion*, see Jung 1984: 430; also Edinger 1999: 35 and Rowland 2005: 153–4.
2 For a more elaborate description of the chronotope, see Rowland 2005: 142–55.
3 For example, in a conversation with Miguel Serrano in 1959, Jung muses: 'do you know what the Self is for Western man? It is Christ, for Christ is the archetype of the hero, representing man's highest aspiration. All this is very mysterious and at times frightening' (Serrano 1977: 56).
4 It is perhaps worth mentioning that the adept's commitment to the *Opus* in the first place can come about through a love-wound, as the 'dart of passion' of Mercurius (Jung 1943/1948: 231).
5 Although Jung does not state this, the fact that it occurred on the cusp of Aries and Pisces might be construed as a synchronicity in that a microcosmic event (the birth of a special child) and the macrocosmic event (bright star on the cusp) coincided at a point of great cosmological and cultural significance as the dawning of a New Age. The benefic Jupiter and malefic Saturn conjoin at that particular astrological spot: the very cusp of the New Age that signals a shift from the Aeon of Aries to the Aeon of Pisces.
6 That is, the Age of Aries, the ram.
7 See chapter 3 on John Dee, for a glimpse into this historical period.
8 Jung considered possible candidates for the first to include Luther, Nero and Mohammed (1951a: 102).

Chapter 11

Mysterium Coniunctionis

Mysterium Coniunctionis, which took Jung roughly twelve years to write, is generally considered to be the most significant part of his magnum opus – his 'last great work' (Jung 1955/1956: v). The theme was initially inspired by Kerenyi's essay on the Aegean Festival scene from Goethe's Faust and by such works as Rosencreutz's *Chymical Wedding* (ibid.: xvi). According to von Franz, the first draft of this work was completed in 1944. She adds that when she saw Jung after his illness, he said: 'What I wrote in the *Mysterium* is true, I don't need to alter the text. But I only know now how real these things are' (von Franz 1966/2000: xiii).

The initial draft of this work was apparently a rather slim volume consisting of 'a nucleus of basic concepts tied together logically, in the form of a hypothetical construct' (Heisig 1979: 108). According to James Heisig, Jung's copious alchemical insertions bloated this original theme beyond recognition: 'the original cluster of ideas had all but perished under the weight of its embellishments' (ibid.: 108). Heisig further writes that 'strands of guesses, facts, suspicions, and hypotheses are all woven together in a torrent of seemingly endless allusions, which only the most encyclopaedic of minds could ever hope to sort out' (ibid.). Indeed, he notes that no significant development on the psychology of religion (beyond what can be found in *Aion* and *Answer to Job*) can be found here (ibid.: 89). Consequently, his treatment of *Mysterium Coniunctionis* is practically non-existent.

In contrast, Edward Edinger's hagiographic opinion is that this work is likely to be 'a major object of study for centuries' (Edinger 1995: 17). According to him, Jung is here functioning as a mediator of contents from the collective unconscious: 'he is transmitting them through what I can only call a magisterial consciousness' (ibid.: 18). He considers this work as being of quintessential significance: '. . . if you take it as a whole, the net result is an exceedingly rich picture of the anatomy of individuation, with all its interconnecting images dissected out for us' (ibid.: 20).

In his *Mysterium Lectures*, Edinger considers 'The Spirit Mercurius' to be an appendage to *Mysterium Coniunctionis* (Edinger 1995: 32). Toward the end of his commentary he states: 'The symbolism of the spirit Mercurius is so important to all our accounts with the autonomous psyche, both in ourselves and in our patients, that it should be uppermost in our consciousness' (ibid.: 296). However, despite such importance, he does not deal exclusively with this figure (to any great length) at any point in his commentary. His work is also strongly biased toward clinical rather than cultural concerns.

Overall, I am of the opinion that Heisig exemplifies a general post-Jungian tendency to mostly detour around this work. Indeed, the relative scarcity of scholarship on *Mysterium Coniunctionis* can be flagged as a curious omission.[1] In addition, it is of interest to point out that Mercurius features as *the* most prominent character in this work, as borne out by a perusal of its index:

Christ:	1/2 page
Anthropos:	1/2 page
Self:	1/2 page
Mercurius:	2 pages

As a development on *Aion* which explicitly deals with the Age of Pisces, it is tempting to surmise that this climactic work coincided (in Jung's mind) with the approach of the Aquarian Age. To corroborate this idea I point out that in 1929 (and again in 1932), he 'prophesied' the dawning of the New Age in the decade of the 1940s – the decade in which he worked on *Mysterium Coniunctionis*. During this decade, with the precession of the equinoxes touching 'the first star of Aquarius', he was embroiled in the 'uniting of opposites' that were supposedly sundered in the Age of Pisces. For Jung, quoting Taoist philosophy, heaven and earth had been sundered for 'unfathomable reasons' and could 'come together again only if the wise man re-establishes Tao in himself by ritual meditation' (1955/1956: 419). He equates such a Taoistic 'marriage of heaven and earth' to the alchemical *mysterium coniunctionis* (ibid.: 463–4).

* * *

My method here is to develop a fair amount of exposition focussed on identifying the role of Mercurius as featuring in *Mysterium Coniunctionis*. A rationale, once again, is to ensure a fidelity to 'original texts' in light of scarcity of scholarship in this particular area.

My chosen themes allow for a degree of narrative coherence coalesced around the theme of Mercurius. I begin by establishing a broad mythic framework, after which the major components of the coniunctio as Sol and Luna are identified. This is followed by their marriage and the subsequent birth of the *filius philosophorum*. The idea of Sol (transformation of the god-image) and Luna (return of the feminine) are then expanded upon and the idea of the coniunctio is extended to include Dorn's three coniunctios. I then finish with a brief look at von Franz's *Aurora Consurgens* and a final discussion.

Throughout, one should bear in mind the historical circumstances of this decade, as well as Jung's personal situation. Most notably, World War II erupted in 1939 and continued up to 1945. Furthermore, on a personal level, Jung was intensely engaged intellectually with such notables as Pauli (physics) and Victor White (Catholicism). This was also a decade during which his health suffered, not only during his 1944 near-death experiences but also through recurrent bouts of ill health and depressive malaise, as evident in the various letters during this period.

An alchemical myth

In chapter 10 I focused predominantly on the figure of Mercurius in relation to Christ. In *Mysterium Coniunctionis*, however, Jung substantially broadens the range of meanings of Mercurius in relation to Christianity.

In this work, we come across two quaternio representations; one alchemical and the other Christian. Concerning the Christian quaternio, the vertical axis is composed of *Pater Auctor* (top) and *Spiritus Sanctus* (bottom) and the horizontal axis has *Filius Salvator* (left), *Diabolus Antichristus* (right). Concerning the Alchemical quaternio, the vertical axis is composed of *Principium Mercurius* (top) and *Filius Mercurius* (bottom) and the horizontal axis has *Filius, Frater, Pater, Sol* (left), *Filia, Soror, Mater, Luna* (right) (1955/1956: 101–2).

These are further developed by identifying a *three-part process* in the form of an origin, a drama and then resolution in what would appear, superficially, to be two mutually exclusive 'myths'. For the alchemical myth, the beginning is an origin as *Mercurius*. In the development we get *Sol* and *Luna*, which then leads to the final goal as the *Filius Mercurius*. For the Christian myth, the beginning is the *Auctor Pater*. This develops into a conflict of *Salvator* and *Diabolus* and the final goal of *Paraclete* or *Holy Ghost* associated with the Church or Kingdom of God (ibid.: 103).

In the Christian model, the *Auctor Pater* is an all-knowing deity, as God, who creates the world and universe according to a preconceived design. Once created, he (mostly) disappears from the world, but then reappears in the form of a God-man as Jesus Christ: son of God, son of Man. In this schema Christ's adversary, the devil, tempts humanity into a sinful life which is instinctually fulfilling but leads to damnation in the hereafter. Individual humans find themselves in a conflict between Christ and the Devil. Redemption is possible through the *imitatio Christi*, leading to everlasting life in a transcendent Kingdom of Heaven after death. Although humanity is essentially alienated from deity, there are times when direct experience and guidance from God can occur, under extraordinary circumstances such as through God's presence as the Holy Ghost.

In the alchemical model, the principal deity is one of immanence that exists in the very fabric of matter and materiality, as a *Deus Terrenus* dispersed (ubiquitous) throughout nature. In its natural form this hermaphroditic slumbering deity is largely unconscious of itself and is also hidden to secular consciousness. It is, like the Christian God, a hidden deity or *deus absconditus*. However, unlike the Christian deity, it requires redemption through the labours of the alchemist. By means of the opus the alchemist effectively engages with this being and struggles to redeem it through a torturous ordeal of transformations and successive alchemical operations. Paradoxically, this being also guides the process. All being well, the alchemist is also transformed and redeemed, though this is apparently only a secondary concern (1955/1956: 349).

Within the opus, the original hermaphroditic matter as the *Principium Mercurius* gets differentiated out into gendered opposites, as Sol and Luna (Rex and Regina, etc.), as the active and passive aspects of Mercurius duplex respectively (ibid.: 101). Through an alchemical mystery wedding, as the *coniunctio*, Sol and Luna then unite and give birth to the *Filius Mercurius* as lapis, which combines Sol and Luna into an enigmatic unity.[2] This many-named lapis – as *filius macrocosmi*, *filius regius*, *filius Mercurius*, etc. – is considered the saviour of the natural world who thereby completes the work of the Christian redeemer, who was the saviour of humanity only (ibid.: 34, 216).

These descriptions, admittedly simplistic, afford insight into how the Christian and alchemical conceptions are both similar and different. Of note is the extent to which the figure of Mercurius features in the alchemical myth. Indeed, Jung emphasises that 'The opus is a … transformation whose subject and object is the elusive Mercurius' (ibid.: 218).

A further important difference in the alchemical and Christian 'myths' concerns the idea of the opus as a passion. Thus, according to Jung, the transformations and operations on the various substances in the retort signified for the alchemist not only a transformation of the deity slumbering in matter, but also corresponded to a profound psychological and spiritual transformation of the adept, which he likened to a passion. However, this passion is described as different to the 'imitation of Christ'. Rather, it is described as 'the exact opposite', as a 'spontaneous' and 'involuntary experience of the sacred [alchemical] legend' whereby the 'true man' as a Christ image is assimilated to his self. He emphasises that such a torturous passion 'happens not to the alchemist himself but to the "true man," who [he] feels is near him and in him and at the same time in the retort' (1955/1956: 349).

Such ideas, to an extent, correlate to the Christian mystics' personal experience of divinity through the grace of the 'blessed greenness' of the 'spermatic and procreative' Holy Ghost (ibid.: 113, 375). However, for the alchemist, such grace had a subtle difference, as it was thought of as emanating from nature through Mercurius in his form as a *spiritus vegetativus* or as the *lumen naturae* – a figure with origins from an immanent alchemical deity as opposed to a transcendent Christian deity (ibid.: 127). Another crucial difference is the deeply feminine connotations of alchemy. The royal art is thus described as 'queen of the alchemist's heart, she is at once his mother, his daughter, and his beloved, and in his art and its allegories the drama of his own soul, his individuation process, is played out' (ibid.: 381).

* * *

I now expand on the alchemical quaternio and three-stage process by looking at the main protagonists of this drama as Sol, Luna and Mercurius, and their 'magical correspondences'.

Sol, Luna and magical correspondences

In medieval alchemy, 'magical correspondences' refer to the idea of sympathies between levels of the natural and supernatural world. Most notably these are the inorganic, the human, the heavenly and the divine (1955/1956: 184). In such a worldview the element gold, for example, corresponds to the sun, to the king, to aspects of the human psyche and to God.[3] In *Mysterium Coniunctionis* two sets of magical correspondences that feature prominently include:

Sulphur – Sol – King (masculine)
Sal – Luna – Queen (feminine)

In each case an alchemical substance (Sulphur, Sal) corresponds to a celestial body (Sun, Moon) and to a royal figurehead (King, Queen). These are also represented as opposites, with the inclusion of Mercurius, in the following way:

Sulphur – Mercurius – Salt
Sol – Mercurius – Luna
King – Mercurius – Queen

In these schemas the figure of Mercurius plays a central and mediating role. As already discussed, this figure appears as the original alchemical 'substance', as a mysterious hermaphroditic *Principium Mercurius* who then differentiates out into an active part as red–sulphur–Sol–King and a passive part as white–Sal–Luna–Queen.

Jung amplifies each of these with a plethora of alchemical material. He reveals that each substance, though exhibiting unique properties, also shares many characteristics. The tendency to consider sulphur and salt as mutually exclusive opposites, for example, is shown as deficient. Each displays a subtle complexity and has intrinsic similarities to its so-called opposite, reminiscent of the Chinese yin–yang symbol. For Jung, this is of vital significance in that alchemy is an unconscious compensation of an overly rationalistic worldview: 'the eternal images are far from consistent in meaning' (1955/1956: 333).

Despite the rich ambiguity of such conceptions as Sal, Mercurius and Sulphur, there is nevertheless a clear bias toward relatively specific meanings.

The marriage of Sol and Luna

Sol and Luna, as the active and passive aspects of Mercurius, differentiate out of an original 'hermaphroditic matter' – the *Principium Mercurius*. The marriage of masculine–spirit as Sol and feminine–matter as Luna, as the coniunctio, was considered by Jung to be the 'central idea' of alchemy (1955/1956: 89, 457). This marriage is also said to take place in a 'third thing' which has commonality with both luminaries: '*Mercurius masculinus* and *Mercurius foemineus* are united in and through *Mercurialis menstrualis*, which is the "aqua"' (ibid.: 462).

Jung expresses the same idea in the alchemical myth, wherein the original one world (*unus mundus*) gets divided into two as heaven (spirit) and earth (instinct) – such a division apparently being necessary to bring the potential *unus mundus* into reality as the 'ten thousand things' of the empirical world (ibid.). Within this spirit–instinct binary lies a ubiquitous and hidden 'third thing' that partakes of both natures, and which is capable of re-uniting the split by means of a 'holy matrimony'. Alchemically, this 'third thing' as Mercurius is the mysterious and paradoxical 'fluid' that catalyses a love relationship as the 'sweet smell of the Holy Ghost', a spiritual water, *aqua permanens, aqua aeris* (aerial water), etc. As the medium in which the coniunctio of Sol and Luna takes place, it is the marvellous sea that 'mitigates and unites the opposites' (1955/1956: 461–2).

By magical correspondences, the coniunctio combines on different orders of existence. These include: substances in the retort; Sol and Luna; heaven and earth; king and queen; the psyches of the alchemist and his *soror mystica*. The coniunctio itself also requires a range of imagery to capture its multifarious facets as a process in which 'extreme opposites unite' (ibid.: 166). The 'spagyric marriage' is thus portrayed as not only erotic but also a tension of oppositions. For example, in one version we read of the woman being pursued by a 'grey haired, winged, ithyphallic old man. He is named . . . Flowing Light . . . and she is Dark Water' (ibid.: 149). In another, we hear of it as a struggling of the winged and wingless birds or dragons (ibid.: 117, 151). Elsewhere it is the mating or fighting of 'dog and bitch' or 'cock and hen' (ibid.: 29, 147). More profoundly, it is also the 'marriage of heaven and earth' (ibid.: 419). Less mysteriously, Jung describes it as an 'archetypal drama' wherein 'immemorial human emotions clash together' and as 'the moral task . . . to bring the feminine, maternal background of the masculine psyche, seething with passions, into harmony with the principle of the spirit – truly a labour of Hercules!' (ibid.: 41). In effect, he notes that the alchemists drew upon a wide range of variants on the *heiros gamos* theme in their attempts to 'express the all but incomprehensible nature of the mystery' (ibid.: 470). Despite these multifarious coniunctio motifs, the one Jung most often cites is Sol and Luna, inclusive of their magical correspondences, uniting within a dissolving bath, in a condition not unlike a chemical 'dynamic equilibrium' (ibid.: 24).

This motif is amplified with the mythic image of Gabricus dissolved into atoms in the embrace of his sister–wife Beya. Jung further describes such a death experience in terms of a 'histolysis in the chrysalis state', thereby identifying the coniunctio with the quintessential image of a transformation mystery as caterpillar–chrysalis–butterfly (1955/1956: 272, 283). Elsewhere he amplifies using Christian iconography, whereby Luna (as Virgin and/or the Church as Mother-beloved) carries the disintegrated King Sol (as Christian dominant) in her body, where they together form a 'single homogenous solution' (ibid.: 315).

Jung continues by noting that in the histolysis state, the '*scintillulae* are put together to form the gold' or 'the fishes eyes are tiny soul-sparks from which the shining figure of the filius is put together' (1955/1956: 53). In effect, a 'transconscious process' as the union of consciousness and the unconscious produces an embryo as homunculus or lapis (ibid.: 272, 381). He adds that such a phenomenon cannot be grasped rationally as, by definition, 'the unconscious is unconscious and therefore can neither be grasped nor conceived' (ibid.: 381). Consequently, he is of the opinion that such things must remain the 'mystery of the queen' or 'the secret of the art' (ibid.: 381).

* * *

We should remember that the coniunctio of Sol and Luna includes all the magical correspondences identified in the previous topic. For Jung this union certainly has an intra-psychic factor, though he also entertains the possibility of it having an external reality (1955/1956: 300). If we include the idea of synchronicity as a coincidence of psyche with the world or of ego with the unconscious, then the idea of the coniunctio and birth of the lapis as a 'being' created through a wearisome opus takes us into some interesting speculative territory!

Birth of the 'filius philosophorum'

Jung writes that 'usually' the lapis is the child from the coniunctio of Sol and Luna and therefore 'the lapis exactly corresponds to the psychological idea of the self, the product of conscious and unconscious' (1955/1956: 371). Alchemically, the duplicity of Mercurius (ego-consciousness as Sol and unconscious as Luna) is thus cancelled out in the unity of the stone (ibid.: 79). The lapis could be said to have integrated its Sol and Luna parents into its own being, and thus to have given birth to its own parents as regenerated unity.

The birth of the lapis, synchronous with such natural events as an earthquake or an eclipse, also vivifies the idea of it as a *filius macrocosmi* (son of the world). As a *mysterium coniunctionis* this entity combines not only the inorganic (stone) but also a human-like form as youth or hermaphrodite (1955/1956: 227–8). Its magical properties include incorruptibility, food of immortality (*cibus immortalis*), ability to multiply itself indefinitely, and so on (ibid.: 372–3). Indeed, it is also described as 'an Anthroparion, a kind of goblin, a familiar who stands by the adept in his work and helps the physician to heal. This being ascends and descends and unites Below with Above, gaining a new power which carries its effect over into everyday life' (ibid.: 227–8). In effect, this was the alchemist's birth of the whole man: 'this "Man," being indescribable, is an intuitive or 'mystical' experience' (ibid.: 171). The numinosity of such experiences, according to Jung, also compelled the alchemists to describe the lapis in superlative terms – most notably by establishing a lapis–Christ parallel and, more specifically, by identifying it with the Messiah as second coming (ibid.: footnote 158, 318). More mysteriously, he describes the lapis as 'a fabulous entity of cosmic dimensions which surpasses human understanding' (ibid.: 63).

Importantly, the lapis here does not replace the Christ image, but rather completes and renews it (1955/1956: 361). Put slightly differently: 'the symbol of the stone, despite the analogy with Christ, contains an element that cannot be reconciled with the purely spiritual assumptions of Christianity' (ibid.: 450).

The lapis is thus aligned to his conception of the self as realised through the individuation process and as the unification of consciousness with the unconscious through the transcendent function. In effect, 'it is a half physical, half metaphysical product, a psychological symbol expressing something created by man and yet supra-ordinate to him' (ibid.: 454).

* * *

The above descriptions are a development on Jung's 'alchemical myth' (compared to chapter 4). An original 'hermaphroditic substance' differentiates out into Sol and Luna (with their magical correspondences) and re-unites in the coniunctio to give birth to the *filius philosophorum*.

I now expand on such themes by identifying cultural problematics appearing in *Mysterium Coniunctionis*. These include transformation of the western god-image, the missing feminine and the idea of Dorn's three coniunctios. After this I consider, briefly, *Aurora Consurgens*.

Transformation of the god-image

The idea of an ageing and ailing deity in need of transformation and renewal is a prominent theme in *Mysterium Coniunctionis*. For Jung, this is a perennial phenomenon in human culture since prehistory, in that 'Man's ideas and definitions of God have followed one another kaleidoscopically in the course of the millennia' (1955/1956: 367).

Here, the terms 'God' and 'king' get contaminated in meaning. King refers more to an earthly incarnation of 'God' as the mythic God-man. More precisely, for Jung, the image of the king is 'the carrier of a myth ... the statements of the collective unconscious' (ibid.: 258) with the power, characteristic of a symbol, to vitalise the psyche by means of a life-giving 'pneuma' (ibid.: 264). Such an archetypal image, for him, is not static but rather 'signifies a dynamic process whereby the human carrier of the mystery is included in the mysterious drama of God's incarnation' (ibid.: 265). Such a 'dynamic process' would typically include renewal of the ailing king by means of an alchemical transformation mystery (inclusive of features such as a death, a *heiros gamos* and rebirth) into a reborn form of incorruptibility and wholeness (ibid.: 266).

Alchemically, in relation to Christianity, this corresponds to the idea of the 'corrupt arcane substance', the drowning king and the redeemer son as *filius* who represents his renewal. In the grail legends, it is the motif of the ailing king and his redeemer as Parsifal (ibid.: 280–1). For Jung it is also a motif implicit in Christianity itself – in the form of the 'figurative language of the Church', whereby the Christian deity as 'bearded old man' was worshipped in Christ as rejuvenated

Son (ibid.: 281). He also adds that the idea of Yahweh as wrathful *senex* being transformed into a God of Love as *puer* in the New Testament was not only championed by the alchemists, but was also believed in ecclesiastical circles (ibid.: 361).

In Jung's view deity personified as king represented, in alchemy and the grail legend, a symbol of the religious collective dominant – Christianity (in the Middle Ages and onwards) – as ailing, in crisis and in need of transformation and renewal (ibid.: 280–2, 360). For him the medieval man, 'not remotely conscious of this problem', struggled to resolve it through unconscious projections such as in alchemy (ibid.: 360). In this view, the alchemist's 'king' was therefore God himself, who had grown old and was being renewed as their sacred and enigmatic *filius philosophorum* through the art (ibid.: 367). Indeed the magnitude of the problem for Jung, some centuries later, was such that it 'can hardly be grasped even today – which is why the psychological interpretation of the One, the *filius regius*, meets with the greatest difficulties' (ibid.: 360).

Furthermore, for him, the urge for renewal of an ageing god is all the stronger and more traumatic the more it is consciously denied, as is the case with a Christianity that stubbornly adheres to a dogma (ibid.: 282, 325). For others, disillusioned with Christian dominants, such renewal is welcomed as liberating and revitalising (ibid.: 325). Alchemically both positions are represented in such imagery as the drowning, dismembered or devoured king and, positively, as an ecstasy in consummation of the chymical wedding. Thus the melting of metals, or dissolution of metals through acids, and a recasting into a new amalgam provides a metaphor for the relativisation and renewal of such dominants (ibid.: 325, 347). Renewal of the king by means of 'a bath into which all the planets pour their "influences" ... expresses the idea that the dominant, grown feeble with age, needs the support and influence of those subsidiary lights to fortify and renew it' (ibid.: 358–9). Thus the king is reborn and experiences an apotheosis described variously as 'wonder of the world', and further as 'the most elect, subtile, pure, noblest', and so on (ibid.: 328). Psychologically, Jung interprets this as the production of a new dominant of consciousness (ibid.: 355). In such imagery we get the idea of the Christian 'king' being melted and dissolved, and also renewed by means of a 'regression' into a pagan-like polytheism.

Thus for Jung, although such stirrings of renewal may find creative expression in visionary individuals sensitive to archetypal dynamisms, such as the medieval alchemist, their transformative impact on society can only take effect 'when the time is fulfilled' (ibid.: 308).

Applied to analytical psychology and the microcosm of the psyche, the 'ailing king' would typically represent a mid-life crisis whereby the dominants of consciousness were beginning to falter, early hints of which may be mirrored and anticipated in dreams (ibid.: 358, 359, 368). Renewal of the king thus corresponds to a descent of ego-consciousness into the unconscious.[4] In particular, Jung stresses the 'archetype of the nuptial union' as the means by which the unconscious resolves its contradictoriness (ibid.: 81). Thus the ailing king, after an ordeal, eventually achieves rebirth as a new totality that joins consciousness and the unconscious, symbolised by the son as *filius* (ibid.: 369).

In such a portrayal of the renewed dominant there is a paradoxical unity of opposites that includes king and queen in an amalgam of light with dark, the muddy with the clear, and so on, in a life-affirming wholeness wherein 'wisdom herself [can] ... celebrate her carnival' (ibid.: 334).

Return of the feminine

In chapter 9 I mentioned how Jung completed the Christian Trinitarian formulation by including a fourth as Mercurius, in the form of 'Mary or the Devil'. Here, I highlighted his idea of a transforming god-image whereby the Christian worldview is portrayed as being under tectonic stresses – a situation supposedly prefigured by the alchemical 'king in crisis'. In this context the Catholic Assumption of Mary in 1950 was, for him, a momentous event that finally institutionalised an archetypal truth; that is, the god-image as a quaternity that finally included the 'numen of feminine deity' (1955/1956: 186, 469). For him this event also signalled a sacred or archetypal marriage as a *heiros gamos* of the masculine spirit with feminine matter (ibid.: 244). Within the bigger picture of his thinking, this was an important movement toward renewal of the Christian God image synchronistic with the beginning of a new Platonic Aeon. He also located the assumption of Mary within an earlier alchemical frame of ideas as found, for example, in such images as Reusner's Pandora (Figure 11.1). Mary's coronation is paralleled here by the releasing of a 'monster' from matter, described also as the *anima mundi* and the *filius macrocosmi* (ibid.: 188). He also refers to this being in Reusner's *Pandora* as 'the re-arisen Primordial Man, who is the cosmos' (ibid.: 317).

Jung continues by stating that this image also contains in it 'the great secret', in that the assumption, by including matter, brings with it the 'prince of this world' as the devil. The assumption of Mary thus includes, according to him, a sophisticated nuance as a drama of redemption wherein the Christ–Devil split seeks resolution. The devil here is represented as the darker side of Mercurius duplex (1955/1956: 188).[5]

Furthermore, Mary's association with the Church and its congregation (on earth) means that the Assumption, viewed as a sacred marriage, unites the congregation with Christian heavenly deity and therefore represents, for Jung, the return of the kingdom of heaven on earth (ibid.: 317). If we extend the meanings of Mary here to include the main alchemical associations as *Luna – Sophia – Sapientia Dei – anima mundi*, effectively the feminine half of Mercurius (ibid.: 322), then we get a better idea of what he was trying to convey. The Assumption as a divine *heiros gamos* thus unites king Sol with queen Luna – the 'unlocking of paradise' or the 'advent of God's Kingdom on earth' (ibid.: 317). This brings with it the plethora of meanings he associates with these images: psyche and matter, transcendent and immanent, heaven and earth, masculine and feminine, Christian and pagan, consciousness and

Die Gab Gottes. 253

Non

Figure 11.1 'The extraction of Mercurius'; Reusner's *Pandora*, 1582; p. 253.

the unconscious, etc. This is a marriage that is followed by the birth of the *spiritus mercurialis* as sun–moon child, homunculus, etc.

In the same place Jung further writes that 'in a psychological sense Mercurius represents the unconscious, for this is to all appearances that "spirit" which comes closest to organic matter and has all the paradoxical qualities attributed to Mercurius' (1955/1956: 491). Psychologically the 'extraction of Mercurius' as redemption of the feminine numen (as Mary and her alchemical connotations) is therefore interpreted as being achieved 'through the pains of the opus' (ibid.: 322). His equivalent for the opus, of course, would be the concept of individuation with emphasis on the role of the anima, at least in this context. The assumption of Mary as coronation, apotheosis and marriage is thus interpreted psychologically by him as a *coincidentia oppositorum* whereby the conscious and unconscious unite in a mystical marriage (ibid.: 380).

Jung saw in this the possibility of a *renovatio* as a dogmatic Christianity having integrated its mystical other. In this context he writes that 'the regenerated dominant also brings the corpus *mysticum* of mankind (Ecclesia as Luna) into glorious reality' (1955/1956: 372). Following the alchemical drama, the *heiros gamos* of Christian dogma as Sol and its corpus mysticum as Luna gives birth to a 'third thing' as sun and moon child in the form of the *filius philosophorum* or *Mercurius-lapis*. For the alchemists, in Jung's view, this also entailed either the knowledge of 'God in nature' being integrated into the Church as a rebirth of dogma or, more heretically, as the investment of nature with 'a mystical significance, whose mysterious light outshone the splendid incomprehensibilities of Church ceremonial' (ibid.: 326).

Dorn's three coniunctios[6]

The coniunctio, represented previously as a marriage of Sol and Luna or King and Queen, finds further elucidation in the final part of *Mysterium Coniunctionis*. Here we read of *three* coniunctios as various stages of a mystical journey. In this form Mercurius, by means of a celestial journey and return to earth, is said to unite the powers of Above and Below, and thereby effects a mystical marriage of Heaven and Earth (1955/1956: 16). In this action deity, previously split into opposites, is restored to its original unity (ibid.: 23). Mercurius, in particular, features centrally in this 'mystical journey'.

The first coniunctio

Prior to the first coniunctio is an original half-animal condition of unconsciousness as 'an inextricable interweaving of the soul with the body' in a *unio naturalis* (1955/1956: 488–9). Separation of this 'enchained soul' from the body concerns the first coniunctio.

In this coniunctio, the *unio mentalis*, the soul leaves the body to unite with the spirit. Effectively, the departed soul leaves the body behind as a dead corpse to unite with the spirit, where it experiences a 'divine influx' (ibid.: 473). Here, quoting Dorn and Leibniz respectively, the spirit is described as 'a "spiracle [spiraculum] of eternal life," a sort of "window into eternity" ' (ibid.: 470–1). This is the goal of spiritual discipline as mind overcoming one's instinctual animal nature, with the further purpose of visualising the self 'as a "window" into eternity' (ibid.: 535, 542).

According to Jung, the *unio mentalis* corresponds to the goal of Christianity in its seeking after a spiritual position and a conquering of bodily desire. The centuries-old Christian aspiration is thus, for him, a 'separation of psychic opposites' as spirit and instinct in the *unio mentalis* (ibid.: 475, 524–5).

The second coniunctio

The second coniunctio entails the return of the soul-spirit to re-animate the 'dead body', and thus the incarnation of pristine consciousness achieved from the first coniunctio back into the phenomenal world – a process represented as a 'chymical marriage'. Such an experience requires a re-engagement with the instinctual nature and with the passions as the soul returning to its 'natural inclinations', but now with spiritual control derived from consciousness attained in the *unio mentalis* (1955/1956: 475).

More subtly, the second coniunctio for Dorn is the spirit-soul uniting with a cosmic *imago Dei* as a 'secret truth' hidden in the materiality or physiology of the body. By means of various sensual magical procedures that invoke the spirit-soul of the *unio mentalis* into this bodily *imago Dei*, a manifestation of the soul-spirit becomes incarnated as a subtle, celestial, 'sky-coloured' fluid, the *caelum*. Such a magical procedure, for the adept, would appear to be the manifestation of the 'potential world' as 'nothing less than the kingdom of heaven on earth' (ibid.: 487, 478–9, 531–2, 542–3). The *caelum* is thus also described as 'the very essence of the body, an incorruptible and therefore pure and eternal substance, a *corpus glorificatum*, capable and worthy of being united with the *unio mentalis*' (ibid.: 542–3).

In terms of analytical psychology, all of this entails the difficult task of actually applying insights and numinous experience of the self as paradoxical wholeness, derived from the first coniunctio through analysis (inclusive of mandala work), into the context of lived experience (1955/1956: 476, 528, 531–2). Indeed, the 'elusive Mercurius' here would appear to have become truly transformed, such that 'the centre experienced proves to be a *spiritus rector* of daily life' (ibid.: 544).

The second coniunctio as re-animation of the body, according to him, also echoes a larger cultural movement reminiscent of the medieval correspondentia. The meaning of body here extends beyond the human form (and the retort), to include the natural world. Transcendent deity returns to animate a dead (disenchanted) natural world which finds expression in the alchemical fascination with the *numinosum* of matter. In this schema, Christ (representative of the *unio mentalis*) is 'wedded' to the *Imago Dei* in matter which produces the *lapis*, in the second coniunctio. Here, it is important to remember the alchemist's lapis idea incorporated the Christ image.

Effectively, spirit and matter are re-united as a 'synthesis of psychic opposites' in a *chymical wedding* (to use a specific symbolic image). Put differently: the immanent spirit of matter (Below) sublimates into an ascent to wed the descending and concretising transcendent spirit of heaven (Above) in a process of mutual transformation (1955/1956: 451, 536). From this synthesis comes resolution in a 'third thing', such as in the image of the liquid *caelum* or stony *lapis* as a 'transcendental entity that could be described only in paradoxes' (ibid.: 536). An analogy is the *filius philosophorum* as that reborn and transformed Mercurius – that 'paradox par excellence' (ibid.: 43–4). For the alchemists, it represented the goal, as successful production of the lapis (ibid.: 533). For Jung, the second coniunctio was thus the goal of medieval alchemy, perceived as a developmental progression and as a healing of an ailing Christianity.

The third coniunctio

Jung, following the alchemist Dorn, also speculated on a third and final coniunctio: conjunction with the *unus mundus*. In this conjunction the combined spirit–soul–body now merges with the universal ground of being.

He invokes a range of descriptions in an attempt to articulate the concept of the *unus mundus*. As 'one world' it is described variously as the potential world of the first day of creation; eternal Ground of all empirical being; the suprapersonal atman; matter as intrinsically deified; a transcendental psychophysical background; an underlying unity of the empirical world; and the underlying unitary nature of body and psyche (1955/1956: 534, 535, 537, 538).

In these descriptions we get a bridging of what we generally think of as the opposites of psyche and matter. The emphasis though is not on the empirical world of multiplicity or the ego world of perceptions, but rather on an underlying (hidden) unitary psychophysical background. Jung uses Plato's cave parable to amplify: the shadows we see on the cave wall are likened to our empirical reality (ibid.: 538). In this sense the *unus mundus* is viewed as 'hidden' or as the unconscious but, in another sense, as a modality we could describe as 'more real than real', or perhaps as the mystic's spiritual reality. Union with the *unus mundus* in the third coniunctio is therefore described by Jung as the *mysterium coniunctionis* and as a new synthesis characterised by 'many far-reaching changes of consciousness' (ibid.: 539).

Aurora Consurgens

Both Jung and von Franz cautiously championed the view that the original *Aurora Consurgens* was the transcription of the visionary experiences of Thomas of Aquinas during a near-death experience, and possibly on his deathbed (von Franz 1966/2000: 428–30). Von Franz, in reflecting on Jung's 1944 near-death visions, further comments: 'Might it not be that St. Thomas Aquinas too, only experienced on his deathbed, when the Song of Songs flooded back into his memory, how real Wisdom and a union with her can be?' (ibid.: xiii).

For Jung, the original text of *Aurora Consurgens* represented an example of how the medieval Christian worldview came to terms with alchemy in the thirteenth century (1955/1956: xvi). In this context von Franz notes that Aquinas, after a lifetime of immersion in the Christian worldview, experienced a flood of compensatory symbolic material from the unconscious (von Franz 1966/2000: 322). For her this eruption can be understood, using the key of alchemical symbolism, as a 'treasure of the doctrine' which is 'concealed in the darkness of matter' and which appears as a 'gift of the Holy Ghost', in which the wisdom of Sophia (as anima) functions as a psychopomp to God (ibid.: 186–7, 194). Importantly, von Franz notes that the author, entering the post-mortal land, beholds in the Holy of Holies 'not the Godhead, but the mysterium coniunctionis of sun and moon' (ibid.: 320).

Von Franz further remarks that Aquinas apparently died having contemplated God in an ecstatic vision, whilst dawn was breaking (von Franz 1966/2000: 428–9). Indeed, *Aurora Consurgens* means 'rising dawn'. She associates this phrase with 'the moment of mystical union with God' (ibid.: 205) and, psychologically, as 'the luminosity of the unconscious' (ibid.: 204). This theme, resurrected as part of *Mysterium Coniunctionis*, thus also carries with it nuances of the birth of a new Platonic month.

A particularly prominent figure in the visions is the Shulamite as the dark, feminine side of God. Von Franz links this figure to Wisdom, as the *anima mundi* immanent in matter who enters the author's consciousness as anima to consummate a coniunctio, resulting in the birth of a Sun–Moon child in the future as the *lapis philosophorum* (ibid.: 212). This feminine deity is thus described as being 'friendly to man', with the intention that the 'ordinary man' be the place chosen for God's birth, in which both his dark and light sides find expression (ibid.: 233–4). Thus the author is exalted, for a time, into Wisdom's male partner as the 'King of Glory' in the *mysterium coniunctionis* (ibid.: 359). Similarly, the author is also described as having experienced inflationary identifications with the child of this union as the *filius philosophorum* (ibid.: 356). Later, however, his role shifts more humbly to that of a mere 'guest at the banquet' (ibid.: 359).

Von Franz notes the calming effect of such visions in their capacity to convey a feeling of immortality (ibid.: 338). She further compares these experiences to Dorn's third coniunctio: 'after the self has been experienced as a divine centre within the psyche, this experience expands into a feeling of oneness with the whole cosmos' (ibid.: 340). We further get the idea of an apotheosis into a 'God-man' in the idea of the lapis as a divine–human figure (ibid.: 354).

In summary: the author's visions are viewed by von Franz as a condensed opus in which the hidden, material, feminine aspect of God 'imprisoned in matter' is redeemed and wedded to the manifest, masculine deity by means of the alchemical labour (ibid.: 242). From this union the enigmatic *lapis philosophorum* as a transformed Mercurius is born. In essence, she considers the author (versed in alchemical lore) to have undergone a completed individuation process by means of these climactic visions (ibid.: 403–4). Accordingly, for von Franz, the visions are of relevance not only for their age, but prospectively as the resolution of a problematic Christianity.

Commentary

In summarising Jung's position, we could say he believed the Christian worldview had lost its interdependent relation to instinct in what amounted to a dangerous split between spirit and the chthonic. Spirit had concretised into a belief system overburdened with dogmatism and at odds with instinct. Optimistically, however, he considered this 'separation of psychic opposites' as intrinsic to the evolutionary process itself – whereby the separation creates an energic tension that facilitates a differentiation of consciousness. However, he sees a problem when such a separation results in an extreme and dangerous polarisation, inaugurating an enantiodromian correction toward an opposite movement as a 'synthesis of psychic opposites'. For him such a movement was already anticipated in the medieval alchemical worldview as a preoccupation centred on a union of opposites, as embodied in their coniunctio symbolism. He was of the opinion that Christianity had to more openly integrate such a worldview in order to renew and heal itself. In effect it had to reunite spirit and instinct in a relatively harmonious and interdependent regulatory system, in a new ritual that also reconnected one, through an anamnesis, to an original wholeness of a cosmic and divine identity – the *anthropos* as archetype of man (1955/1956: 418–20). In this sense, we could say that he believed alchemy contained a key that could unlock a renewal and rebirth of the Christian worldview.

In this view the religious dominant of the western nations, in the form of the patriarchal Christian deity, was in need of renewal. In alchemistic allegory, the ailing king was to be 'dissolved', 'mutilated', 'devoured', etc. before undergoing a transformation and rebirth as the *filius philosophorum* (son of the philosophers); effectively an image that incorporates a 'mysterious conjunction of opposites'. The neglected feminine, chthonic aspects of deity, and a holistic worldview that included the natural world, would find redemption in this new amalgam of greater wholeness. Importantly, it would also involve a reintegration of all that was dangerously repressed in the Christian Aeon of Fishes, such as the pagan-oriented worldview.

In this context Dorn's first coniunctio could be viewed as a recapitulation of the 'split opposites' (psyche–instinct) in the first fish of the Age of Pisces. His second coniunctio would then be the union of the second (matter) fish with the first (spiritual fish) begun mid-Aeon and to be fulfilled in the grail-like vessel of the coming Age of Aquarius – a theme corroborated by precession through the astrological Pegasus, as a further symbol of the *coniunctio* of instinct and spirit. The third coniunctio might then be considered a visionary experience, as 'holistic grail' of an even more complete spirit–matter unity, intimated by the symbols of the Aquarian Age.

The theme of a 'synthesis of psychic opposites' also translates into a cultural zeitgeist of peacemaking. Here I recall that Mercury causes the two entwined 'fierce' serpents of the caduceus to agree (ibid.: 229). Thus, in identifying the one 'golden serpent' with the Christian spirit, the other 'silver serpent' would represent the pagan spirit and mystical feminine. In this schema, renewal of Christianity is envisioned as an engagement with its Other, inclusive of the pagan 'adversary'.

By means of an alchemical mystical marriage these spirits combine and give birth to a renewed form as one with a 'united double nature'. Similarly, the caduceus could also be cast as an image that unites a Sun religion (Christian worldview) with a Moon religion (Muslim worldview) – see the Dream Analysis Seminars (Jung 1984: 321–435).

In this view, a new cultural dominant was thus beginning to emerge from the collective unconscious: a dominant that found early articulation in certain visionary individuals of medieval alchemy and that was now hatching, through mediums such as Jung's magnum opus, into the cultural landscape of a new Platonic Aeon. In this context I aver that one of Jung's intentions with *Mysterium Coniunctionis* was to effect in the reader, through an invocation of symbols, an alchemical-like process of transformation – as an 'immersion in the mercury' as the 'highest mystery of the Whole work' (Figulus, cited in Giegerich 1999: 137) – in which the figure of Mercurius functions as an agency that stitches together a plethora of oppositions and confounds one's rationalism, thereby opening one toward a revelatory gnosis.

Overall, it would appear that in *Mysterium Coniunctionis* Jung was seeking to articulate a *renovatio* of the Christian god-image not only as a fringe psychological theory (embedded in his analytical psychology) but, more ambitiously, within the very fabric of the mainstream Christian 'myth'. For him, the separation of psychic opposites in the Aeon of Pisces as a dualistic sign (two fishes) would now experience a healing in a synthesis of opposites in the unitary and grail-like image of the Aquarian water-bearer.

Within this operatic drama, the figure of the alchemical Mercurius takes centre stage variously as *metaphor of transformation*, as *image of wholeness* and as new cultural dominant as the *filius philosophorum*, emerging from the chaos of cultural rupture and renewal – effectively as a quintessential *transcendent function* capable of healing and renewing an ailing Christianity.[7]

Notes

1 This said, most Jungian works on alchemy quote from and often discuss aspects of *Mysterium Coniunctionis* (for example, Hillman 2010, Grinnell 1973/1989).

2 This basic transformation forms the subtitle of *Mysterium Coniunctionis* – the separation and synthesis of psychic opposites.

3 An event involving the sun, such as an eclipse, would therefore be considered an auspicious time for the 'king' and would also have a bearing on the substance gold in the alchemical retort and to the divine as Deity.

4 Here we should remember that the unconscious, for Jung, is not only a chaotic contradictoriness but, due to its 'hermaphroditism', also contains revitalising qualities with the capacity for 'spontaneous and autochthonous reproduction' (1955/1956: 177).

5 If we consider the Pandora image as prefiguring the dogmatic inclusion of the mother of God as Christian dogma in the Catholic Church, then the forthcoming event would appear to be the emergence of the *spiritus mercurialis* in collective consciousness – at least in the alchemical worldview as portrayed in this image.

6 See Hillman, who links colour symbolism to the coniunctios (Hillman 2010: 154ff). See also Edinger for further reflections (1995: 275ff).

7 Consider von Franz: 'Mercurius is the transcendent function, who in alchemy is the bridge ... He is the spirit of the unconscious ... He brings the opposites together' (von Franz 1997: 184).

Chapter 12

The grail legend

I now venture a synthesis that combines Jung's alchemical and astrological myths within the frame of the grail legend. My rationale is that this serves to further clarify and contextualise Jung's multifarious representations of the alchemical Mercurius and thus also allows for a life-myth construction centred on this figure. My approach is to first consider Emma Jung and Marie-Louise von Franz's *The Grail Legend* and discern specific narrative elements of interest. After this, I make a few critical observations and then identify a 'loose end' in their (and Jung's) treatment. This is then addressed under the title of *Jung and the Holy Grail.*

Emma Jung and von Franz: the grail legend

For Emma Jung and Marie-Louise von Franz the grail legend, viewed psychologically, captures the symbolic essence of an unresolved Christianity and of its struggle for resolution in a prospective sense. For them, the unresolved aspects of Christianity have resulted in psychological problems especially related to 'loss of soul,' sexuality, the feminine, the problem of the opposites and of the unconscious – all of which, they believe, have contributed significantly to the dire situation of the world (Emma Jung and von Franz 1970/1998: 17–19).

For them the grail legends, like alchemy, are compensatory to a one-sided Christianity in crisis (the ailing king), and therefore represent a struggle for the psychological and spiritual redemption of 'Christian man' in the form of an ongoing creative engagement with powerful and numinous archetypal dynamics. Thus, in a way, they cast grail-legend authors (especially Chretien and Wolfram) as alchemists in the grip of 'the spirit of the unconscious' undergoing a passion as alchemical opus in a venture to revivify the 'Christian myth'.

Of especial relevance here is the esoteric aspect of these so-called archetypal dynamics, such as the astrological worldview of Platonic months, whereby major growth moments of consciousness are identified as being synchronistic with important astrological events. An example would be the coincidence of Christ with the beginning of the Age of the Fishes (Pisces). In essence a prophetic *esoteric* interpretation can be discerned amidst the literary, psychological and religious interpretations. More specifically, differentiating out how Emma Jung and von Franz have portrayed the shape-shifting forms of the alchemical Mercurius, in particular, tends to reveal this perspective.

I now discern, briefly, how this figure appears in key images and motifs in Jung and von Franz's rendition as, variously, the grail itself, the ailing grail king's heathen adversary, Perceval as *natural man*, Merlin, epochal ages and 'an unresolved problem'. This is followed by the second theme of this section, *Jung and the Grail Legend*.

Symbols of the grail

Emma Jung and von Franz associate von Eschenbach's four grail objects (lance, sword, vessel and stone) with the four functions, as lance – intuition, sword – thinking, vessel – feeling and stone – sensation (Emma Jung and von Franz 1970/1998: 154), and thus to Jung's quaternary structure of the self.

Alchemically, they tie each of these symbols to Mercurius: the vessel to the enigmatic *hermetic vas* (ibid.: 142), the sword to Mercurius' permeating spirit and life urge (ibid.: 89), the lance to Mercurius' arrow of passion as *telum passionis* (ibid.: 90) and the stone to Mercurius–lapis (ibid.: 151). Together these are reminiscent of his *quadratus* nature. The authors also further develop each of these four images.

For example, the grail vessel is described as 'a font or piscine [in which] transformation into a spiritual being is effected', as a 'wondrous vessel ... goal of the quest ... in which life giving powers inhere', as 'the individual psyche as vessel for the influx of unconscious contents' and where 'the archetype of the Self is transformed' and thereby as a container wherein the god-image and the Christian contents are continually reshaped, developed and matured (ibid.: 137, 141, 145, 156–7). Furthermore, as a uterus, it is where the birth of the *filius philosophorum* as Mercurius–lapis takes place (ibid.: 142). They also point out that the grail, like the alchemical *vas*, can be poisonous, fiery and dangerous (ibid.: 145).

Continuing, they identify the *content* of the grail with the 'blood of Christ', interpreted as 'the mystical continuation of Christ's being ... through the ages' (ibid.: 124) and as the feminine element – as feeling, pressing toward consciousness (ibid.: 100). The blood is also not only the blood of Christ but also refers to the alchemical 'stone that drips blood' (ibid.: 96–7). Once again, a paradoxical notion is presented – in this case, of grail contents being associated with Christ's blood and, alchemically, to 'blood of the stone'.

Such images combine Christian spiritual transcendence (heaven) with pagan chthonic immanence (earth) into a 'third position', in a conceptual entanglement that finds expression in the figure of Mercurius.

The Fisher King

The grail king is depicted as wounded Christian dominant split off from instinct: chthonic, ecstasy, intoxication, etc. (ibid.: 106). Thus, his wounding in the genital area by a pagan opponent's lance is interpreted psychologically as an impulse (lance) from the unconscious (heathen layer) that brings the problem of the instinctive/chthonic/erotic painfully to consciousness (ibid.: 91, 155).

The pagan opponent is interpreted as the grail king's shadow. Grail king as personified Christian god-image is thus contrasted with a pagan opponent, as the 'shadow of God' personified as Wotan and, by association, Mercurius (ibid.: 196–7). This opposition is cast as being highly polarised: as Jung's 'warring brothers'.

They associate the grail king's redemption not only with symbols of his wounding (sword, lance), but also compensatory feminine images (vessel, stone). The pagan opponent as shadow, according to them, can also be viewed as 'father of the anima', as a dark spirit of nature seeking fulfilment in instincts. Thus, apart from the masculine pagan shadow, they also associate the grail king's redemption as having something to do with the feminine, moon, soul of nature; effectively, as a struggle to resolve an anima problem (ibid.: 205, 211).

Perceval

Perceval, as successor to the grail king, is portrayed as an embodiment of 'Christian man' destined to achieve salvation for an unresolved Christianity (ibid.: 77, 243). His task is recognised as the restitution and completion of the Christ image, in accordance with the Jungian concept of the self. Perceval is thus cast as questing modern man faced with the 'colossal task' of dealing with the problem of evil and of the feminine; the legacy of a problematic Christianity (ibid.: 159). As a simpleton living with his mother in the forest, he is interpreted as *natural man*, embodying a naive and unconscious completeness (ibid.: 111).

At the beginning of his adventures Perceval enters the forest, symbolically entering the unconscious. Psychologically, the authors interpret this as questing Christian man embarking on a 'confrontation with the unconscious'. In this forest, for example, Perceval meets and overcomes the feared red knight, an alchemical parallel being the red *prima materia* that requires transformation. Here we also see the transformation of Perceval, who has killed and, to an extent, integrated the red knight, symbolised in the wearing of his clothes (ibid.: 5–7). The red knight, interpreted in the Christian myth as devil/antichrist, is thus defeated and partially integrated.

Later, in the grail castle, Perceval witnesses the enigmatic grail procession but fails to ask the grail king about the meaning of his suffering. Consequently, the grail king is not healed, Perceval is disgraced and the kingdom remains in desolation. Emma Jung and von Franz interpret his failure as related to the initial fall of Adam and Eve in the Garden of Paradise, when they ate from the Tree of Knowledge despite it being taboo. However, according to Emma Jung and von Franz, the myth of redemption now requires a questioning attitude in acknowledgement of 'Christian man' as possessor of consciousness (ibid.: 335).

Merlin

For Emma Jung and von Franz, the mysterious figure of Merlin represents a 'personification of wholeness' connected with both the wounding and the healing of the grail king (ibid.: 279). He is therefore coupled not only with the grail king's heathen, Wotan-like adversary, but also with an invisible 'guardian spirit' standing behind Perceval: 'He [Merlin] seems to know all about the grail' (ibid.: 361); further, he is not only the 'mysterious instigator of the quest', but he '*is* the mystery of the grail' (ibid.: 373).

They thus proclaim that underneath the Christian Trinity as collective dominant (ailing grail king) lies a 'Holy Grave' in which a dead anthropos (Merlin–Mercurius) awaits redemption (ibid.: 328–9). Further, they interpret 'the sword that shatters on the grave of the anthropos' as the ineffectiveness of traditional Christian thinking in solving the grail problem (ibid.: 247). For them, Jung's later thought (as historical continuation of the alchemical worldview that values holism) holds more promise. Thus, in sketching out the detail of this 'dead anthropos' they struggle with Jung's three–four problem by proposing 'Mary or the grail vessel' as the fourth, which thus completes the Father–Son–Holy Ghost Trinity (ibid.: 342).

In this schema the grail is associated with the Christian problematic of matter, the feminine and evil. The grail here is also described as sharing characteristics with the Holy Spirit, especially in its capacity to resolve and unite the opposites, wherein 'God's love and terribleness come together in wordless union' (ibid.: 341). Thus Perceval, as carrier of the Holy Spirit, is revealed as the 'chosen one' destined to unite widely sundered opposites.

Here Emma Jung and von Franz are of the opinion that the medieval mind was premature for such an enigma, resulting in a bursting forth of the archetypal symbol of Merlin. Their further elucidation of Merlin thus depicts resolution of this three-four problem in the form of grail as fourth (ibid.: 346). For them, this fourth brings with it completeness as a totality symbol: '. . . in the final analysis, Merlin is not simply the Antichrist which is joined to the Trinity as the Fourth but is also an incarnation of the primal Father God in whom the Father, Son and Holy Spirit are embodied' (ibid.: 355–6). Here we can recall the four objects of the grail, *Mercurius quadratus*, and so forth.

The authors highlight that, according to St John, the slain man as anthropos will return 'at the end of time' (ibid.: 249). For them, this augurs the return of a complete symbol of the self as new Messiah; effectively as 'the return of Merlin', who embodies 'the mystery of individuation'. Here they point to further powerful images in selected versions of the grail legends, to corroborate such prophetic utterances. For example, they interpret the image of 'babe in the tree' as the 'birth of a new redeemer' and link this to Jung's individuation concept (ibid.: 248).

For Emma Jung and von Franz this all augurs profound healing for 'modern man', having lost his soul and in problematic relation to matter, evil and the feminine. Indeed, in their opinion, the 'bewitched land' would be lifted in a new world characterised by an 'age of connection between God and man . . . an age of continuing realization of God's challenge to man' (ibid.: 324).

Three ages

In this context Emma Jung and von Franz, reflecting Jung, highlight the idea of three ages in the evolution of the god-image, as championed by the thirteenth-century Joachim of Floris. These correspond to Old Testament (Yahweh), New Testament (Christ–Antichrist) and third age as the age of the Holy Ghost (ibid.: 318).

Here the Old Testament god-image is portrayed as a predominantly undifferentiated unity, with original Adam as microcosmic reflection. Christ is viewed as a *transitus* out in the second age, as a New Testament worldview and with the Antichrist as his 'warring brother'. The third age, as age of the Holy Spirit, is characterised as a more symbolic approach toward experience and understanding of Christianity (ibid.: 298, 322). Perceval is here portrayed as redeeming *tierz hom* or 'third man', who resolves the split Christ–Antichrist dichotomy and also restores fertility in a spiritual wasteland (ibid.: 77, 298).

Summarising their view: in each Age, the god-image moves closer toward human-level integration. The Old Testament Father-God is wholly other to human experiences (Yahweh–Job). The New Testament Christ is God become man in a single incidence. The third age is the possibility of God being born in the psyche of the human individual.

By inference, these epochs correspond to Platonic months: the first Age to Aries, the second to Pisces and the third to the Age of Aquarius.[1] Such a demarcation is not explicit in Emma Jung and von Franz's account.[2]

An unresolved problem

In von Eschenbach the grail legend finds resolution through Perceval who, on his second witnessing of the procession in the grail castle, asks the grail king what ails him. By this action the king is restored to health and the bewitched land is redeemed.

Perceval marries his beloved and ends his days in hermit-like service of the grail. He grows old with the grail, suggesting that his identity progressively blurs into the figure of Merlin (identified with the grail). Accordingly, Emma Jung and von Franz state that 'Perceval and Merlin are in the final analysis one; Perceval as questing Christian man, Merlin as pagan wholeness' (ibid.: 392). Concisely, their view is that Perceval personifies Christian man who, through a laborious individuation, eventually achieves wholeness in the self as Merlin.

In summary, it would appear that completion is achieved: 'Wolfram was able to bring the symbol of wholeness – as represented by the grail stone and the marriage quaternion – closer to the consciousness of his age' (ibid.: 399). The choice to emphasise a German version of the Legends (von Eschenbach 1980) is also not incidental:

> In Wolfram, the German spirit has been united with the cultural values of the Orient in an uncommonly fruitful manner, and it would seem as if it were possible to humanize, i.e. to integrate, a more considerable part of the figure of Merlin through this detour connected with the assimilation of the East.
> (Emma Jung and von Franz 1970/1998: 398)

This said, they also diverge from such a 'happy ending'. According to them, Perceval failed in that he chose holiness instead of humanity; he should have brought the grail to King Arthur's round table, as symbolic of incarnating experience of the divine into everyday communal existence. Likewise Merlin, for them, does not find a satisfying conclusion. As allegorised in the *Vita Merlini*, by choice, he rejects the daemon of scientific spirit and power politics, preferring his forest existence (ibid.: 392).

Merlin's final end is also described as problematic. Bewitched by his fairy-woman Ninianne, he remains apart from the world in a glass castle. Emma Jung and von Franz interpret this as the archetype of wholeness (anthropos–Merlin–Mercurius) being, once again, neglected and relegated to the unconscious by the collective Christian dominant, still suffering an anima problem. Here they contrast Merlin's 'anima bewitchment' with Lao Tse's more wholesome end, in a voluntary retreat from the world, accompanied by his dancing girl (ibid.: 396–7).

Ultimately, for Emma Jung and von Franz, the hidden man as anthropos is only partially redeemed in this legend. Merlin 'lives', and indeed his voice can be heard in the forest ('Le Cri de Merlin') and emanates from the stone (ibid.: 392). For von Franz individuation, as heeding Merlin's cry, allows for the fuller integration of this living symbol for the benefit of both individual and culture. Throughout she effectively reveals early Jung as a questing Perceval and mature Jung as a Merlin.

Commentary

In overview of Emma Jung and Marie-Louise von Franz's analysis, I highlight the usefulness of the grail legend and especially the alchemically influenced Chretien/Wolfram versions, as they are more accessible than the obscure alchemical texts. The grail legend also offers a framework that can be used to view Jung's more challenging writings, such as *Aion*, *Mysterium Coniunctionis* and his alchemical works. In particular, they are an attempt to capture the story of Christianity from an esoteric perspective. In the Jungian worldview, this is invaluable, as the esoteric conflates with the archetypal undercurrents that compensate and renew the Christian dominant.

However, viewed more critically their analysis suffers limitations, being so embedded within the Jungian paradigm. A problem emerges if one attempts to discern a crisp conceptual picture from the richly associative webs, such as the Wotan–Mercurius–Merlin–Anthropos–Heathen contaminations. These figures are not adequately contextualised, in my opinion. Consequently, the task of discerning a coherent narrative around the figure of Merlin–Mercurius, in particular, proved to be challenging.

A further difficulty arose in the authors' use of Platonic ages. There are a number of references to the previous epoch as the Age of Pisces, and also to Jung's *Aion*. We get prophetic allusions such as 'the return of Merlin' and 'the coming of the anthropos at the end of time'. We are also reminded that 'the end of time' refers to the end of a Platonic age, such as at the end of the first millennium or the end of the Age of the Fishes. However, there is no explicit mention of the idea of the dawning of the Age of Aquarius. Indeed, the word *Aquarius* does not feature in this text.

Of the above concerns I now choose to focus on the latter in terms of the Age of Aquarius in relation to the grail legend. In particular, I shall construct the idea that Jung's 'life-myth' can be better understood when viewed from such a perspective. As we shall also see, the images and symbols that emerge correlate strongly with central characters and motifs in the grail legend, and thus also with my research theme.

Jung and the grail legend

I now formulate a grail-legend perspective on Jung, underpinned by a few key excerpts from his life and works. The excerpts I shall look at include: a shattered knife and split table during his student years; two images from *Liber Novus*; the Dream Analysis Seminars (1928–30); the first star of Aquarius (1940–50); and the Bollingen tower stone engraving of a woman milking Pegasus (1958). These are used, together with developments from preceding chapters, to hypothesise how Jung may have constructed his 'life-myth' from an esoteric perspective.

Shattered knife and split table (student days)

Perhaps the two most prominent symbols of the grail are 'vessel' and 'sword', as quintessential images of feminine (womb) and masculine (phallus). Conceptually, these can be abstracted to 'circle' and 'line'.

In this context, it is of interest to recall a couple of Jung's student memories at age 23. Specifically, he recalls one summer afternoon studying in the room adjoining their dining room, where his mother was knitting. Suddenly and unexpectedly, a loud 'pistol shot' rang out in the dining room. Upon rushing in, he noted that their seventy-year-old walnut dining room table had split from its rim to beyond the centre, about three-quarters of the way through.[3] Jung remarks here on his flabbergasted mother responding darkly, in her No. 2 voice: 'Yes, yes . . . that means something' (Jung 1963/1995: 126; also 1973–75: 180).

The next curious incident occurred some two weeks later when he arrived home in the evening to find his mother, the maid and his 14-year-old sister in a 'great state of agitation', as about an hour earlier there had been another 'deafening report'.

Jung eventually discovered the most likely source of this event. In the breadbasket, beside a loaf of bread, was the breadknife, snapped into four pieces: the handle and the three other pieces were each in a corner of the breadbasket. Flabbergasted at this further inexplicable event, Jung questioned 'why and how had the table split and the knife shattered?' (1963/1995: 127). These events left him 'completely at a loss', with the implication that perhaps they embodied an enigmatic riddle.

Concerning the knife, we can recall Emma Jung and von Franz's interpretation of the *broken sword* as a failure in the thinking of the age, incapable of grasping the paradoxical nature of the opposites; effectively, as a split-off shadow. A bread knife, in particular, attaches religious symbolism in the phrase 'our daily bread'. The pieces of the knife in each corner of the basket could be interpreted as mirroring a 3 + 1 problem (the riddle of Merlin), characteristic of one of Jung's conceptual fixations, as we have amply seen.[4]

If we now look at the circular table as a symbol of the self, then the sudden split three-quarters of the way through can be interpreted as an intense awareness of a split god-image (the table 'hosted' the Christian family together in daily prayer, possibly over two or three generations) that also constellated a three–four theme. This event occurred with only his mother in the room, as if to emphasise a problem connected to the feminine. Here we should remember that for Jung, the split god-image is also what characterised the Age of the Fishes, with its exclusion of the feminine in divinity.

These two inexplicable events could thus be interpreted as the young Carl, in the throes of his studies, being made aware of an explosive problem posed by the 'mysterious other', as unconscious psyche exteriorised. In this regard, I emphasise Jung's conceptualisation of the alchemical Mercurius as a 'spirit of the unconscious' extended to include world and physical matter.

It is possible to interpret a wider range of Jung's 'anomalous experiences' within the context of the grail legend and in terms of the theory of synchronicity. In this context, Main writes: 'It is as though a mythic motif and archetypal theme of great importance within Jung's work were shaping his anomalous experiences or being expressed through them' (Main 2012: 23). In further locating the possible significance of such phenomena, Main continues: 'Jung's attention to anomalous experiences and his theorisation of them in terms of synchronicity can therefore be seen as part of his strategy for rediscovering a deeper source of spirituality in order to re-sacralise the modern world and thereby address the crisis of modernity' (ibid.: 27).

I now move on to highlight a couple of images from *The Red Book*, with a view to corroborating the idea that Jung was deeply (yet Hermetically) concerned with the idea of the dawning of a New Age.

Liber Novus: The Red Book (1914–28)

The very first image to appear in *Liber Novus* portrays a ship reminiscent of medieval Europe, as if hinting at a voyage or 'mystical peregrination'. It also illustrates domains of the natural world in cross-section, extending from subterranean through to the celestial, as if to amplify the idea of great depths and great heights. Of particular interest, though, is the undulating zodiacal band at the top of this image, where we see a bright star located on the glyph of Aquarius.

Here we should remember Jung's view that the first dream or image brought to an analysis often contains remarkable insight into the client's life. This same insight, applied to our image, reveals the idea of a sea voyage, as well as super-sensory perception of natures' depths and heights;[5] all under the 'guiding star' positioned in Aquarius. This suggests that Jung's intent with *Liber Novus* was to pioneer new psycho-spiritual territory associated with the dawning of a New Age.

The second image I select appears on page 121 of *Liber Secundus*, from November 1919.[6] The inscription for this image features the only explicit reference to the word 'Aquarius' in *The Red Book*, and also the only place where we find an alchemical word (*lapis philosophorum*). As part of the inscription, we read: 'it expands into *space* through ... breadth, height, depth, *and time* [italics mine]' (2009: 305, footnote 229). This is reminiscent of Einstein's conception of a unitary space–time continuity, and thereby hints at a possible 'intuitive resolution' of the 'three–four' problem. It might also be compared to Jung's Bollingen stone, where we see a similar four (or $3 + 1$) 'streams of Aquarius'.

Speculation aside, it is especially interesting to locate this image. In the year of its making Jung professes to having discovered the 'goal of psychic development' in the form of 'the mandala as an expression of the self' and states that 'I had attained what was for me the ultimate. Perhaps someone else knows more, but not I' (1963/1995: 222).

His 'confrontation with the unconscious', as recorded in *The Red Book*, thus includes a grail-like discovery of 'the ultimate'. Indeed, much of *The Red Book* can be framed as a Perceval-like grail quest. For example, in this work we witness a battle with a red knight, the overcoming of a dragon, a supernatural castle, Philemon as Merlinesque character, etc.

Dream Analysis Seminars (1928–30)

It would thus appear that by 1920 Jung had discovered the mandala as grail-like 'goal of psychic development'. From approximately this time onwards I speculate that he considered his life as being 'in service of the self' and therefore, by association, to the grail.

The Dream Seminars of 1928–30 make clear that he considered his analytical psychology in terms of a grail-like vessel of rebirth, likened to the idea of a mystical sect of the magical vessel (krater), where one is reborn.[7] For example, during one of the seminars he remarks: 'It was just as if a modern man wrote to a friend: "I strongly advise you to go to the krater at Zurich for analysis – to the *Jungbrunnen*"' (Jung 1984: 429, see also 328).[8]

In these seminars he chronicles a case study of a successful businessman suffering, during a mid-life crisis, from a spiritual malaise and also a 'sexual problem' (his wife having lost interest in him). In a sense, he is suffering from the grail king's 'wound in the genital area' (psychologically speaking) and an ailing faith. Wounded and retreating from the world, he embarks on a process of introversion. Like the Fisher King, he ponders the 'waters' of the unconscious, where he catches 'fish' in the form of his dreams.

In another sense Jung, in Merlinesque fashion, invokes in him his heroic and adventurous side and thereby functions as his guide in a mysterious venture with the unconscious. Indeed, one could frame this 'ordinary businessman's' experiences in terms of Perceval – in a quest to redeem his soul and to discover the secret of healing, renewal and his relation to the divine.

Thus, in analysing dream [23] of this man, for example, Jung elaborates on a dream-figure of a Jewish hermaphroditic personage singing loudly and in a different key in the church hymn. After a lengthy discussion of this dream he arrives at 'the interesting conclusion . . . that this figure is God' (Jung 1984: 504; also 506 – dream [23] is on page 479).

The motif of a 'divine presence' emerges again in dream [25], in which a man falls from a strange, gas-filled, yellow, triangular-shaped vehicle described as something between an airship and an aeroplane, from a distance higher than a house and in the dreamer's neighbourhood (ibid.: 574). In the next dream [26] the man's wife gives birth to triplets, but only the third survives (ibid.: 557).[9]

In analysing these dreams, Jung expands on the idea of three ages as 'successive revelations' or 'periodical manifestations' of divinity (ibid.: 606). The yellow air vehicle is interpreted as transcendent Trinity above and the three children as successive manifestations of the divine, recapitulated historically (culturally and personally) up to the present:

> His three stages are representations, so to speak, of his three successive conditions – spiritualism, the Father; theosophy, the Son; and psychology, the Holy Ghost. Now, the fact that the two are dead would refer to the first ones. The Father is dead, the Son is dead, and the Holy Ghost is alive.
>
> (ibid.: 605)

He goes on to state that 'the third would be the Empire or Kingdom of the Holy Ghost, that is the thing to come' (ibid.: 606). Elaborating, he says: 'And now, people think that the coming of the New Age – Aquarius – will be the third condition, the new revelation of the Trinity' (ibid.: 607).

In dream [28], the patient is called to a swimming pool by a child. However, instead of a swimming pool he is led to a large bed. He lifts the bed cover and finds a giant tortoise. He takes a chisel-like implement that appears in his hand and taps the tortoise's head with the wooden handle. At this, the tortoise opens its mouth and spits out a living child (ibid.: 642).

In analysing this dream, the tortoise is identified with the primitive yet living quality of the unconscious and its chthonic nature. The slaying of this 'monster' of the unconscious then yields up its 'treasure' as the divine child. This child is averred to be the same 'third child' from dream [26], and thus corroborates for Jung his notion of the birth of divinity within the psyche at the dawning of a New Age (ibid.: 650).

These statements affirm the idea that Jung considered his psychology a means by which the incarnation of divine presence (Holy Ghost) in the psyche of the individual can be catalysed, and that this represented a momentous new spiritual development synchronous with the dawning of a New Age. Based on this premise, and in the context of my general construction, I claim he believed his message as captured in *The Red Book* to be of vital significance.

Specifically, I propose the following resonances: Old Testament (first Age – Age of Aries), New Testament (second Age – Age of Pisces) and *Liber Novus* (third Age – Age of Aquarius). As an important qualification, the 'third Age' as the divine numinosum potentially experienced by many individuals (and integrated by means of an individuation) implies *The Red Book* is merely *one* example of such an expression (Christiana Morgana's Visions, from the *Visions Seminars*, were also transcribed and illustrated in her own 'precious book'). This said, Jung's specific circumstances lend themselves to 'esteemed status'. Indeed, at the end of his 1929 seminar, he stated that Leo personalities (he was a Leo) would be deified in the coming Age of Aquarius:

> When the sun came into Pisces, Virgo became the autumnal sign, and astrology has connected that fact with the worship of the Virgin Mary. When we get into Aquarius, we shall have Leo opposite, so we would have a deification of lion attributes – the worship of the sun or sun-like personalities.
>
> (ibid.: 423)

I now continue to expand on such ideas in an effort to further clarify the relationship between the grail legend, alchemy and the dawning of a New Age. My focus shifts to the decade of the 1940s.

The first star of Aquarius (1940–50)

For Jung the Age of Pisces sundered the opposites (sword), whereas the Age of Aquarius would re-unite them by means of a renewing and transformative *vas* (vessel). Dominant symbols of the constellation Aquarius include the anthropos and vessel filled with life-giving fluid, as we see in Figure 12.1.

In looking at this sky narrative in terms of the Great Year flowing 'backwards in time', as Jung does (1998: 733), we see how the two fishes flow into and become contained in the *vas* of the water-bearer. Amplifying this image using alchemical ideas, it symbolises the two mercurial substances being alchemically transformed into a 'third thing'. Thus the first, vertical 'spiritual' fish (Christ) gets combined with the second, horizontal 'matter' fish (Antichrist) to become a third thing, as a spirit–matter coniunctio.

Figure 12.1 Constellations of Pisces, Pegasus and Aquarius.

These ideas link astrological ages to the grail legend. In this view, the onset of the Age of Aquarius starts as the precession of the equinox begins to 'touch' the stars associated with the 'water' from the vessel. This can be interpreted, esoterically, as humanity beginning to experience the first waters of the healing and fructifying grail.

* * *

As already mentioned, Jung believed the dawning of the New Age would begin in the 1940s with the precession of the equinoxes approaching 'the first star of Aquarius'. This was also the decade during which he worked on part of his magnum opus, *Mysterium Coniunctionis*: a work I would characterise as a creative struggle with divine shadow in an effort to contain and unite the opposites sundered in the Aeon of Pisces. In addition, world events that transpired around this fateful decade included:

1939 World War II beginning
1945 Nuclear bombs destroy Hiroshima and Nagasaki, ending World War II
1945 UFO sightings
1950 Assumption of Mary

Close to the middle of this decade, in 1944, Jung suffered near-death visions which culminated in a number of lucid experiences of the Sacred Marriage. In chapter 7, I argued that he could well have believed this experience to have been an apotheosis. Its timing in the midst of the precessed equinox, arriving at the first star of Aquarius, is further suggestive that the 'myth of his life' coalesced around this esoteric theme.

Some months later, in 1945, World War II came to an end with the bombing of Hiroshima and Nagasaki. For Jung, the harnessing of star energy for human purposes was one of the terrifying 'promethean' consequences of the incarnation of divinity in the human psyche (Jung 2007: 237; see also Giegerich 1988). For him the splitting of the atom, creating nuclear fission, was the concretisation of a myth commensurate with the problem of a split god-image 'coming to a head' with the second fish.

In 1945 UFO sightings also began to be reported, signifying, for Jung, symbols of wholeness as unified god-image, a synthesis of opposites in the psyche in compensation for the cleaved god-image as a legacy from the Aeon of Pisces (1963/1995: 366). Their intimation of redemption, as well as their circular shape, connects them to the grail symbol as a 'water drop' from the vessel of Aquarian anthropos. Thus amidst a dark, terrifying and annihilating decade we also witness symbols of hope and completeness. Their opposite projected connotations as menacing and potentially destructive – as evil – also embody the 'dark half' of the self as god-image. The idea of the grail as both dangerous and healing thus finds expression in this singular image of contrary meanings.

Moving on to 1950, we get the Assumption of Mary, the mother of God's bodily ascension into heaven. Here is a further image of Jung's anticipated coniunctio associated with the New Age in that the feminine is finally deified. However, for him, this is a problematic coniunctio as it takes place in a transcendent heaven. There is no integration of the chthonic, matter and evil and there is no sense of divine immanence in the human psyche (see chapter 11).

* * *

For Jung there was another interesting synchronicity around this time. Specifically, in 1950, whilst working on the foreword to Wilhelm's English translation of the *I Ching*, he recounted addressing the book in 'personified form' and consulting it as an oracle that it may introduce itself to the English-speaking public. The answer he got was Hexagram 50, Ting/The Cauldron. In interpreting this image, he writes that 'the I Ching is effectively describing itself as "a ritual vessel containing ... spiritual nourishment" and as a medium through which the will of God can be revealed' (1950: 594). Here we see an example of Emma Jung and von Franz's idea that the cultural values of the Orient can lead toward the west's further integration of the figure of Merlin, and hence of the grail (Emma Jung and von Franz 1998: 398; see also Main 2007: 187).

In Jung's more esoteric worldview this is the spiritually nourishing water and enigmatic vessel that unites the opposites (including the opposites of psyche and matter). I therefore speculate that he may well have considered the entrance of the *I Ching* into western culture as being synchronistic with the approach of a new aeon. Perhaps, for him, the rapprochement between Chinese holism (circle) and western causalism (line) was yet another corroborating *coniunctio archetype* constellated at this most propitious of times.

In summary, we see the symbolic interplay of 'sword and vessel' during the 1940s constructed around the idea of a transitional age from Pisces to Aquarius. By this time, perhaps, Jung had manifested an answer to that fateful riddle of his student years, of snapped bread knife and split table. Central to this riddle, its unfolding and its resolution, we also saw the figure of the alchemical Mercurius shape-shifted into key themes and symbols of this transition: the two 'mercurial' fishes; their synthesis into a third thing, grail vessel and its substance, Aquarian anthropos; and, of course, the enigmatic Merlin.

Virgin's milk – *aqua doctrinae*

In late old age in 1958, three years before his death, Jung carved a rock engraving at Bollingen of an anima-like figure milking the mythical winged horse Pegasus, a constellation between (and above) Pisces and Aquarius (see Figure 12.2). In a letter dated 1960, explaining his Bollingen engravings, he writes: 'Nobody is more uncertain about their meaning than the author himself' (1973–75: 615). Continuing, he mentions that originally he saw in the rock the worshipping woman with the silhouette of an old king on a throne behind her. However, as he started carving, the king vanished and the hindquarters of a mare emerged, which he identified with Pegasus. He further explains that 'the milk takes the place of the water of Aquarius which is the alchemical virgin's milk – a synonym for the *aqua doctrinae* as one of the aspects of Mercurius' (ibid.: 615). Of interest here is that every year, typically beginning around 25 July, meteorite showers lasting about three weeks, can be viewed emanating from the constellation Pegasus (Jung was born on 26 July). It is thus relevant to note that he amplifies the meteor, in a letter to Victor White, with the alchemist's *lumen naturae* – 'all the other lights are artificial and manmade' (Jung 2007: 151–2). Further, a month prior to this, he wrote in a letter: 'At the end of this cosmic age Vishnu will change into a white horse and create a new world. This refers to Pegasus who ushers in the Aquarian Age' (1973–75: 615).

The mythical winged horse Pegasus embodies, for him, the spiritual (winged, white) and instinctual (animal, chthonic) polarities of the archetype (1998: 732) and thus represents, in his model, yet another form of the *archetype of the coniunctio.*

Jung's life-myth

Based on the above developments I now attempt to get to the heart of how Jung and significant others (such as his wife Emma and von Franz) might have considered

Figure 12.2 'Anima milking Pegasus' - Engraving at Bollingen (personal photograph).

his 'life-myth'. What follows are speculations informed by preceding developments (including all prior chapters).

* * *

A riddle in terms of paranormal phenomena is posed to Jung, in his student days, by a Merlinesque 'spirit of the unconscious' in the grail-like objects, the shattered knife and split table. Some years later, having achieved worldly success, he embarks on an experimental 'confrontation with the unconscious' as a Perceval-like adventure into the mystery of the unconscious, where he engages with Salome and the Merlinesque Philemon. His experiences in this 'quest' are akin to an initiatory immersion in an ancient mystery cult and a spiritual illumination. This culminates in his discovery by 1920 of the self as 'the ultimate' (grail), with pictorial analogue in such images as his 1920 'Aquarian anthropos', as well as a number of mandalas. This extraordinary experience shifts his identity to a 'Perceval in service of the grail' and toward a merging with the figure of Merlin.

A few years on, by 1928–30, he likens his school to the 'fountain of renewal' as *krater* (vessel). In these seminars he provides a treatment of a 'Fisher King' and, acting as a Merlin, instigates his Perceval-like quest into the mysterious 'forest' of his unconscious. His patient connects with his soul (anima), conquers a 'monster' (tortoise) and thus frees up a divine child – interpreted as the manifestation of the Holy Ghost in his psyche.

From a historical–esoteric perspective this is synchronous with the dawning of the 'Age of the Holy Ghost' in anticipation of the arrival of the new Platonic month: the Age of Aquarius (for more detail, see Jung 2007: 220). Located within the broader spiritual, religious and esoteric traditions of western culture, we see: Old Testament (first Age – Age of Aries), New Testament (second Age – Age of Pisces) and *Liber Novus* (third Age – Age of Aquarius).

In the decade of the 1940s we finally arrive at 'the first star of Aquarius'. In the midst of this ruptured decade Jung undergoes Merlin's triple death and experiences a beatific vision of the *unus mundus* at the 'bottom of a cosmic ocean'. This culminates in visions of the sacred marriage. He has been 'touched' by the numinosum of the grail (the first water drop from the Aquarian anthropos) and undergoes an apotheosis into a pneumatic man. Like Merlin, he is reborn as a 'salmon of wisdom' and is revitalised to complete his 'main business', his *Mysterium Coniunctionis*. The central character here, the Merlinesque alchemical Mercurius, functions as divine agency to weave an alchemical myth that re-unites the opposites that were sundered in the Age of the Fishes. The coniunctio of a restored god-image is thus affected as a synthesis in the Age of the Water-Bearer. Many of Jung's literary and artistic works are thus a form of 'talismanic magic', in the Hermeticist sense, as a pious attempt to aid humanity through a 'perilous crossing' and toward this new renaissance.

In 1958 Jung 'immortalises' an aspect of his life-myth by means of a stone engraving in which the 'mystical waters of alchemy' are milked by his anima from the winged horse Pegasus. Yearly meteorite showers, visible from the constellation Pegasus (beginning the day prior to his birthday), are a synchronistic celestial affirmation of his life-myth in his role of ushering in the Aquarian Age as an epoch in which the grail narrative finds resolution.

* * *

After World War II, Jung realises his astrological timing is problematic. The subsequent Cold War, the threat of nuclear holocaust and the Iron Curtain are stark symbols of a perpetuated *separatio*. Consequently, a few years later, in a footnote in *Aion*, and possibly after communications especially with French astrologers (in letters as yet unpublished), he revises the dawning of the Age of Aquarius to either 1997 or 2154. In a sense, he does not see this as contradicting his initial 1940s timing, as 'there are no lines in the sky'.

Notes

1 Jung makes this association in the *Dream Interpretation Seminars* (see Jung 1984: 605–7).
2 Malcolm Godwin (a non-Jungian) correlates these three Ages to the three 'branches' of the Grail legend: 'The Pagan, or Celtic Age of the Father was represented by the Old law of the synagogue; the Age of the Son was symbolized in the New Testament, while the Age of the Holy Spirit looked towards the dawn of a New Awakening' (Godwin 1994: 15).
3 The table was ninety years old, according to a letter to Rhine (see Jung 1973–75: 180).

4 This event, witnessed by three females (spanning three generations), and the inclusion of Jung as fourth, constellates a compensatory mirror-image of Christian Trinity plus problematic fourth.
5 Consider here the 'cosmic ubiquity' in chapter 1.
6 See chapter 5 for interpretations of the images 'Aquarian Anthropos' and Philemon as new God images commensurate with the Age of Aquarius.
7 Astrologically, during these years, his secondary progressed Sun moved through the area on the ecliptic above the constellation known as the 'Crater' (a constellation associated with the Grail vessel).
8 As noted in a footnote on this page, the word *Jungbrunnen* translates to 'fountain of youth', with a pun on Jung's name.
9 See footnote on page 557 – there is confusion as to the correct order of these two dreams.

Conclusion

A major intention of the research was to determine how the alchemical Mercurius was both experienced and portrayed by Jung based on a range of primary materials, biography and Hermeneutic enquiries. Based on such an investigation, I assembled the idea of a soothsaying meta-narrative in which the grail legend, an alchemical transformation mystery and the astrological precession of the equinoxes all converged at a momentous time in history synchronistic with Jung's life. In this way a life myth was formulated in which his esoteric identity was brought more fully to light, centred on his role as herald and prophet of the Aquarian Age. A number of Jung's synchronistic experiences were also interpreted from this perspective. Overall, each chapter can be considered a self-contained finding that incrementally built upon and corroborated such a perspective.

My method was predominantly constructivist, as opposed to critical and de-constructivist. In the interests of a more rounded viewpoint, and to better orient the research in terms of contemporary Jungian studies, I now include a few critical reflections. In particular, I consider the issues of Jung's esoteric identity, writing style and methodology.

A critical appraisal

Jung mostly cultivated a persona of 'scientist of the psyche' and as 'empiricist first and last' (Jung 1954: 664). However, as I have pointed out, one can also discern a deeply esoteric side of him, with 'secret knowledge' derived from extraordinary personal experiences creatively modulated by intense research into the arcane. As I argued, such a confluence of inner and outer found fertile soil in the myth of an imminent dawning of the Aquarian Age – perhaps *the* most persistent theme that emerged from this research.

In chapter 5, for example, I argued that *The Red Book* could be interpreted as a chronicling of a new spiritual dispensation commensurate with such a New Age in a way that positions Jung as key to the myth of the Aquarian Age. His myth announces a new dawn (*Aurora Consurgens*) in which the numinosum is experienced and integrated within the individual psyche conceptualised as 'the individuation process'; that is, it is refracted and born within individuals receptive to a psycho-spiritual transformation.

Such a viewpoint differs from Giegerich, for example, who refuses to see Jung as a prophet: 'what separates him from the prophet is the moment of negation or reflection that intercepted the immediate flow from the experiences to the announcement' (Giegerich 1999: 66). However, as I have tried to illustrate, Jung's 'reflection and interception' that culminated in his large corpus of work does not detract from the basic myth that he 'bought into' as a transition of the Ages. Instead it can be viewed as being *corroborative*, if we take the trouble to investigate the finer ramifications of this myth. Such an investigation, as I argued, results in a convergence of the grail legend, his alchemical worldview and his understanding of the astrological transition of the Ages. This convergence arises, as I further argued, if we place the figure of the alchemical Mercurius as a central concern, within the context of his life and works.

Such a finding reinforces, in my opinion, the idea that 'esoteric Jung' should be more fully acknowledged (and taken more seriously) in contemporary Jungian schools of thought, and in the academy.

As an example of how this perspective might assist in a more holistic reconstruction of Jung I draw attention to Michael Palmer's accusation that he is one-sided by not engaging religions which have no belief in God (Palmer 1997: 184). In defence I highlight Jung's concept of Mercurius as a self-image that is both an impersonal *unus mundus* as well as a 'personification of the unconscious'. This is but one instance of how his alchemical worldview has not been sufficiently considered, in my opinion, by Jungian scholars of a theological persuasion.

* * *

I now consider Jung's controversial writing style, which has been amply commented upon by post-Jungians. Placing Mercurius centre stage, in particular, reveals Jung's more obscurantist style. Ironically, it is also the qualities of this figure (elusive, ambiguous, tricky, non-rational, etc.) that might offer, to an extent, 'redemption'.

To illustrate, we can consider the two essays that comprised 'The Spirit Mercurius'. A reading of the second essay offers examples typical of everything Jung's critics accuse him of being: obscurantist, haphazard, elusive, contradictory, irrational, impenetrable, etc. A reading of the first essay, on the contrary, illustrates a remarkable lucidity and coherence. Much of his writings on alchemy could be considered a combination of these two styles.

Concerning his difficult style, Jung defends himself. In a letter we read: 'the language I speak must be ambiguous, must have two meanings in order to do justice to the dual aspects of our psychic nature' (1973–75: 70). Elsewhere, he states that 'not everything I bring forth is written out of my head, but much of it comes from my heart also' (1917/1926/1943: 118).

It is in light of such considerations that the literary critic Susan Rowland offers a cogent defence:

> As a literary figure, an author, Jung has had a bad press. His work is said to be opaque, digressive, circular, indulgent, difficult, inconsistent. I would add, 'tricky', and in that word begin to see something other than a problem with his style. For Jung writes not only *about* the psyche but also *from* the psyche. Although we expect someone calling himself a 'scientist' to prioritize rational, linear, logical prose, Jung prefers to *write from different positions* in the psyche. The persona, the ego, the anima, shadow etc. all speak to us directly in the writing. Sometimes Jung writes as trickster. And in particular, Jung tries to write not only *of* the self but also *from* the self.
>
> (Rowland 2006: 1–2)

In particular, we see here the idea of trickster-self as Other (that is, Mercurius) being portrayed as the 'redemption' of Jung's difficult style. Overall, Rowland defends Jung with such arguments and makes a call for scholars to take him more seriously: 'a culture may misread a work. It may fail to experience its true symbolic value until a later evolution of consciousness enlarges public understanding' (Rowland 2005: 9).

Although largely in agreement with Rowland, I also assert that Jung often failed to 'work upon' the material sufficiently to distil an acceptable level of coherence and conceptual clarity. His writings on Mercurius are a good example. This figure is described variously as the self, the psychoid, *unus mundus*, a symbol, archetype of the unconscious, trickster, Merlin, Wotan, God's shadow, 'Mary or the devil', *lapis philosophorum*, and so on. Although such a wide range of terms circumambulates a complex meaning, it is problematic from the perspective of conceptual precision. As a case in point, Jung's concept of the archetype fails to account for the rich historical and cultural nuances that accrue to a symbol.

* * *

Moving to epistemological considerations, we owe a debt to Heisig's erudite and critical appraisal of Jung's multifarious images of God, much of which is equally valid for the theme of Mercurius – a figure described by Jung as 'the shadow of God'.

In his critique Heisig applies typological theory to Jung himself as a means to highlight his shortcomings as a scientist (Heisig 1979/1983: 105).[1] He notes that Jung considered himself to be an introverted thinking type with intuition as the dominant auxiliary function. Jung's descriptions of these, for Heisig, are revealing of his style: 'Introverted thinking shows a dangerous tendency to force the facts into the shape of its image, or to ignore them altogether in order to give fantasy free play', and further 'the introverted intuitive moves from image to image, chasing after every possibility in the teeming womb of the unconscious ... His arguments lack the convincing power of reason. He can only profess or proclaim' (Jung 1920: 381, 400, 402).

Heisig convincingly criticises Jung's methodology as suffering from precisely these typological shortcomings. In this vein he considers Jung's treatment of source materials to be problematic: 'he was too impatient, too much enamoured of great and moving ideas to trouble himself over the high academic standards of the various disciplines into which he ventured for help' (Heisig 1979/1983: 107). Added to this, he also notes a 'certain tone of prophetic authority in Jung's mature style' (ibid.: 106).

Such criticisms are pertinent to Jung's treatment of Mercurius. For example, nowhere in his corpus do we find a clear and systematic treatment of this figure in the 'positivist empiricist' sense. Nowhere do we find a significant amount of data included for the critical reader to form an independent judgement.[2] In general, his 'clinical data sets' are implied as being derived from 'many years of listening to patient's dreams'. When he does reveal such 'raw material' (for example, Pauli's dreams in *Psychology and Alchemy*), we do not hear of any convincing selective rigour.[3] In summary, as Heisig notes: 'Jung's pioneering spirit was impatient with methodological nuance' (ibid.: 123).

To exacerbate matters, from this perspective, the themes that coalesce around Mercurius also steer us into the bombastic regions of Jung's 'prophetic authority' – an inflationary sensibility that overrides detail and precision. Indeed, in his typological model, the positivist empiricist he claimed to be is undoubtedly better suited to someone with extraverted thinking with sensation as the dominant auxiliary function.

Apart from typology, we can also consider Jung's differentiation of a No. 1 and a No. 2 personality as a means to further critique his methods. In considering his career choices, for example, he noted that his No. 1 personality was more interested in the sciences, as opposed to his No. 2 personality's greater interest in history and the humanities. We also read:

> No. 2 had no definable character at all; he was a *vita peracta*, born, living, dead, everything in one; a total vision of life. Though pitilessly clear about himself, he was unable to express himself through the dense, dark medium of No. 1, though he longed to do so.
>
> (Jung 1963/1995: 107)

Such a dialectical tension, we might say, characterised Jung's method throughout his life. In his early career we get the positivist empiricist developing his scientifically acclaimed word association experiments (a No. 1 prominence). Later in life he espouses his 'secret knowledge' and increasingly identifies with the sage (a No. 2 prominence). For example, his writing on Mercurius in later life (post-1928) typifies such a figure-ground shift – the scientific No. 1 has mostly given way to the *vita peracta* of No. 2. The empiricist who isolates and studies a small piece of reality has receded to give way to the Hermeticist whose concern is a meaningful 'big picture' of the world. Using more conventional language, I agree with John Clarke and Ira Progoff, who consider that 'Jung's work is one of the leading instances of a holistic point of view applied to the study of man' (Progoff, cited in Clarke 1992: 48).

Thus, simplistically, we can read Jung on two levels. On the one level we can read him in the way his persona would have us believe; as a hard-nosed scientist who deployed an epistemology rooted in a radical positivist empiricism coupled with a Hermeneutic approach (Clarke 1992: 7, 46). Read on a second level we see a very different 'esoteric Jung' in which *Mercurius as trickster-self* finds prominence. This voice deploys an epistemology with features of Hermeticism, in which the world as a holistic and meaningful interdependence is assumed – the part reflects the whole.

For a good example of how these two methods interpenetrated, we can ponder his hypnagogic-like vision of Mercurius at his Bollingen Tower. Specifically, whilst puzzling over the inconsistent findings of his astrological experiment (his empirical positivistic approach utilising statistics), he sees in the chiaroscuro of sunlight dancing in the foliage the trickster 'spirit of nature' who incites him to rethink his method. In this reconsideration the experiment on married couples could be seen, ironically, rather as a synchronicity, as an *astrological moment* with the coniunctio in the microcosm of married couples reflected in the spirit–matter coniunctio portrayed in the macrocosm – as a major theme of the New Age (see chapter 9). Here his epistemology shifts from empiricist to Hermeticist. His information gathered is the anomalous as a unique personal qualitative experience (below) meaningfully related to the astrological coniunctio (above) conveyed to him by an Other, as Mercurius.

As a reader of Jung, we have to mostly *extract* this side of him in a roundabout way (excursions into seminars, letters etc.), as it would appear he himself was uneasy and perhaps embarrassed by this 'socially unacceptable' side of himself, and hence his 'secret knowledge'. Thus, there is a pervasive reticence to explicitly include astrological considerations in his method. This is ironic considering that his *magnum opus*, as I illustrated, is largely underpinned by the idea of astrological Ages (see chapters 10, 11 and 12).

Similarly, one can critique his oft-stated and persistent Kantian epistemology in which concern is limited to 'manifestations of the psyche' (such as dreams, fantasies, etc.) as his data for empirical investigation; that is, he *excludes* material as well as spiritual realities. Thus he has been criticised for *psychologism*: for example, the reduction of religion to psychological phenomena (Palmer 1997: 168). However, as Aziz and Main have noted, his synchronicity concept – by including 'the world' and 'spirit' – implies a broadening of ontological concerns beyond psychic phenomena (Aziz 1990: 49; also Main 2007: 23ff).

Thus Jung's synchronicity concept, as an attempt to construct a holistic big-picture model of the world that *meaningfully* includes the individual, is another example of how his epistemology shifted, despite himself, from empiricist to Hermeticist. In particular, the concept of Mercurius described as being on the interface of both psychic *and* material realities had the effect, trickster-like, of expanding him beyond the cocoon of such a Kantian worldview. Thus Jung's concept of the archetype shifted from being defined as intra-psychic, in his early career, to psychoid in his later life. Unfortunately, Jung did not possess the philosophical versatility to modify his epistemology to accommodate such important developments.

His progressive ideas on the concept of projection are a further case in point. In his earlier career Jung agreed with Freud's assertion that contents from the unconscious were spontaneously and involuntarily projected onto the outer world. An example would be the transference in which the patient's father complex would be projected onto the analyst. The eventual 'taking back of the projection' (recollection) would be intrinsic to the cure. However some decades later, in 'The Spirit Mercurius', we read of an important development: here he comes full circle by flirting with the idea that perhaps there is, in certain circumstances, a coincidence of psychic projection with the literal world beyond just a projective hook. This is summed up in his phrase: 'so what was all that rustling in the bushes?' (Jung 1943/1948: 200).

Apart from in his synchronicity concept, this notion is not strongly developed. In particular, Jung's predominant view on alchemy is that it represents a process of psychological projection – the substances, chemical reactions, etc. are of no intrinsic interest to him (see chapter 4). As an example to the contrary, where projection and 'world' coincide, I highlight the findings of chapter 2 in which qualities of the substance mercury and its derivatives, as borne out by modern science, were shown to correlate with ancient alchemical notions. Thus, in agreement with significant alchemical tenets, I pointed out that mercury is ubiquitous throughout nature, is a 'living metal', traverses the modalities of earth–air–fire–water, displays an uncanny paradoxical nature and, indeed, can also be transmuted into gold. Based on such findings I agree with Giegerich, who criticises Jung's narrow psychological envisioning of alchemy that mostly precludes any concern with a 'deeper essence' of *real* life that includes world and, indeed, also the 'cosmic dimension' (Giegerich 1999: 156–7).[4]

This said, there is an important astrological exception, which I looked at in chapter 10. In *Aion*, he reveals his astrological worldview that our religious history and our psychic development could have been 'accurately predicted' from a study of the precession of the equinoxes through Pisces (Jung 1951a: 95). Here we see a coincidence of projection and 'world'. However, there are problems with this specific example. As Rowland notes: 'Jung refuses to accept that Christian enthusiasm for fish symbolism is *derived* from study of the zodiac . . . Rather the psyche spontaneously produces fish symbolism' (Rowland 2005: 149). Judging from Jung's published works, letters, seminars, and so on, it is also clear that he did not engage with notable astrologers of the day on such issues. A 'critical friction' is missing. Thus, although he has the courage (post-1944) to write about his 'secret knowledge', a reticence and naivety remains. Indeed, his inconsistency regarding the specific timing of the transition of the Ages (early twentieth century, 1940s, 1950s, 1997, 2154), as well as other observations, expose him as an astrological dilettante. In addition, the broader ramifications of such an astrological worldview are neither developed nor properly included in his analytical psychology. For example, he refrains from explicitly drawing correlations between his four psychological functions and the astrological elements of fire, water, earth and air.

Moving on to works such as *Mysterium Coniunctionis*, we see a further problem. As Giegerich points out, there is an 'abysmal discrepancy' between his writing on alchemy and his application of such ideas to individual therapy: 'the speculative wealth and depth of the alchemical images is simply lost when it is supposed to be relocated in the narrowness of the consulting room . . . one wonders if in this way the rather banally conceived sphere of therapy is not being *inflated*' (Giegerich 1999: 150). For Giegerich, the 'Great Work' or *Opus Divinum* is not so much a personal concern as an artwork belonging to humankind as it is a suprapersonal process, likened to 'the great dream' that speaks through the artist (ibid.: 151). For example, the idea of grappling with a 'dark angel' as emissary from the self (Mercurius) discernible in works such as *Mysterium Coniunctionis* is surely beyond the fate and concern of the average analysand.

To briefly illustrate, I revisit Jung's identification of the Holy Ghost[5] in a dream as found toward the end of the Dream Analysis Seminars (see chapter 12). He identifies the Holy Ghost in his patient's dreams with the 'Jewish hermaphrodite' and the 'man fallen from the yellow triangular air-vehicle'. Further, in the case of the Jewish hermaphrodite, the dreamer unravels memories that lead to an identification with a rather inconsequential person he knows. In the context of a profound new revelation of divinity these dream figures come across as unconvincing, banal and devoid of the numinosity befitting an encounter with a divine being.

* * *

For scholars such as Heisig and Palmer, such concerns are deeply problematic. For Palmer, 'Jung, despite all his protestations to the contrary, cannot claim to be an empiricist if he is not prepared to submit his findings to the scientific possibilities of verifications and falsifications' (Palmer 1997: 171). In agreement, Heisig considers Jung's factual material and explanatory models to be so insecure that 'his actual methods stand condemned' (Heisig 1979/1983: 140). In conclusion, Heisig is of the opinion that Jung is better located in the human rather than the natural sciences (ibid.: 144).

Such a judgement is, in my opinion, both one-sided and severe. For example, we can recall the joint venture of Jung and Pauli (a physicist of Nobel laureate standing). Common to their quest, as I showed in chapter 9, was a desire to find a unified language (a coniunctio) of spirit and matter in a big-picture model of reality. Indeed, as I argued, we witnessed the figure of Mercurius at the heart of such a project, in which we discovered the scientist No. 1 in service of the Hermeticist No. 2. Such a viewpoint also finds sympathy with Giegerich, who asserts that 'psychology . . . has left both science and religion beneath itself, and at the same time contains them both as sublated moments within itself. It is their *successor*'

(Giegerich 1999: 67).[6] This sentiment, in my opinion, is key if we are to progress the Jungian project – we should surely value his expansive and far-reaching intuitive vision and celebrate his questing spirit, yet strive toward a more careful, appropriate and disciplined epistemology. To confine Jung to the humanities, as Heisig suggests, would surely necessitate the tragic sacrifice of such a vision.

As a final sentiment concerning his methods, style and identity I agree with Clarke who suggests 'we should take Jung more seriously, at his word, and work with his claim that what he is offering is a myth, not a final truth, a perspective, not a doctrine' (Clarke 1992: 181).

Further directions

Overall, the most prominent theme that emerged concerned Jung's life myth. Specific areas within this domain included such notions as the return of the feminine, transformation of the king, the coniunctio, and the birth of the *filius philosophorum*. These motifs form a coherent alchemical narrative with resonances not only with the individual psyche but also with major cultural developments.

In the context of our western world, subsequent to Jung's death, we might say that the 'return of the Goddess' has been championed in the New Age movement and that 'transformation of the King' could be a metaphor for patriarchal Christianity as the collective religious dominant undergoing changes and renewal. The coniunctio might be interpreted as the ailing king of Christianity in the dissolving embrace of the Goddess of the New Age. Indeed, with the proliferation of the New Age movement, feminism, holistic science and the liberalisation of the Church, we have undeniably witnessed such elements in our cultural landscape in recent decades (see Tacey 2001).

In light of such considerations, an obvious further direction would entail a contemporary contextualisation along the lines of *his myth in our times*. This might include socio-cultural factors consolidating research into the New Age movement, as well as contemporary Jungian projects such as 'the re-enchantment of modernity' (for example, see Main, in Casement [ed.] 2007; also Main 2008). The notion of Mercurius as a western culture-specific shaman might also be ventured.

Apart from this, further research could follow a range of trajectories. Scholars of the western esoteric tradition might use the present research to better locate Jung. Astrological research might include a critique of Jung's views on precessional astrology, involving a rigorous evaluation of works such as *Aion* and *Mysterium Coniunctionis*. The notion of Mercurius as *world soul* also lends itself to eco-psychological considerations and related cultural problematics. Furthermore, practitioners of Jungian psychology (analysts, psychotherapists, etc.) could use it as a basis to further explore the clinical ramifications of the Mercurius concept. An attempt might also be made to better critique, circumscribe and develop the elusive conceptual contours of this figure.

Finally, explicit inclusion of a more experimental methodology as a complement to established academic practice could be ventured. Engaging with one's unconscious processes and valuing this as an integral part of the research by means of 'alchemical Hermeneutics', for example, would in my opinion add an invaluable perspective. Robert Romanyshyn hints at the worth of this: '... in research with soul in mind the topic chooses the researcher as much as, and perhaps more than, he or she chooses it ... in this complex relation between the researcher and the topic, there lingers the weight of history that waits to be spoken' (Romanyshyn 2007: 4). A range of other 'sympathetic' methodologies might also be ventured (see Vos 2009). One might also attempt the deconstruction of attitudinal bias from a socialised ethos of disenchantment to a return to a child-like wonderment, and an accompanying epistemology. In the words of Richard Tarnas, 'the study of archetypal forms opens the archetypal eye. And thus the open encounter with the potential reality of an *anima mundi* makes possible its actual discernment ... For here, perhaps, we begin to encounter the interior mystery of the cosmos itself' (Tarnas 2007: 487).

Conclusion

Giegerich relates a myth from the *Edda* to illustrate his opinion as to the perennial relevance of Jung's work. In this myth the god Thor travels to Utgard, the region of the 'beyond', and finds himself in a royal hall, amidst giants. In the hall king Utgaroa-Loki, having heard of Thor's famous strength, challenges him to 'lift his cat'. Thor places his arms under the cat and lifts, using all his strength. The cat's back arches, but her head and tail do not leave the ground. In a second attempt Thor nearly succeeds.

The next day, at Thor's farewell, the king revealed there was trickery involved. The cat was actually no cat, but rather a small section of the Midgard Serpent who encircled the earth. The giants were in great fear as had Thor succeeded, the entire Midgard Serpent would have been released, with devastating consequences (Giegerich 1999: 55).

Giegerich invites the serious reader of Jung to be a Thor: 'to try with all his might to lift what at first appears to be an ordinary cat and to experience the incredible weights holding it down – until, finally, he becomes aware of the fact that in reality he is dealing with a section of the world serpent, with a visible shape in which the invisible horizon of everything becomes accessible' (ibid.: 57). As he explains, an approach utilising everyday consciousness sees 'only the cat' and remains in the empirical reality of Midgard. In contrast, a shift of sensitivity allows access to the 'archetypal background' as the otherworldly Utgard in which an 'unfathomable depth' is apperceived – the Great Serpent. Indeed, for Giegerich, this Great Serpent which cannot be lifted is 'the logical life of the soul', 'the Notion' and Mercurius (see ibid.: 57, 60, 66).

As Giegerich further notes, Jung's mid-life 'confrontation with the unconscious' has resonances with such a task, as the eruption of a lava-like 'primal matter' that seized him and which he worked upon, as a life task, into a *lapis* like the alchemist's enigmatic stone (see Giegerich 1999: 60–3). For him this is not only for *his* individuation but rather for *the* individuation, as the latest grappling of the *Opus Divinum* engaged with 'the Great Riddle' (ibid.: 86).

* * *

Finally, as a concluding remark, we might also consider here the distinction between a personal and a cultural individuation in light of synchronicity. In the Jungian idiom, a synchronicity witnessed by two or more people lends itself more easily to a cultural interpretation (intersecting with a personal interpretation). Thus, in Jung's case, the exploding breadknife and table, the cluster of synchronicities during the decade of the 1940s, meteor showers from Pegasus, the triton mark of Hermes on his forehead shortly after his death, all fall under the ambit of shared synchronistic experiences. In my interpretation, these coalesced around a unitary theme characterised by the symbol of the alchemical Mercurius as a mysterious Other refracted into multiple synchronistic contexts throughout Jung's life. Indeed, allowing Hermes into the academy for a moment, we might say that 'what is a unitary event in the unconscious has been refracted into multiple contexts in consciousness, so that the components of the synchronicity are experienced as separated in time and space as well as differentiated into psychic and physical events' (Main 2004: 53).

Notes

1 See also Romanyshyn, who considers Jung's four functions in terms of epistemological strategies (Romanyshyn 2007: 290).
2 For 'clinical data' the closest we get is a series of Pauli's dreams in *Psychology and Alchemy*.
3 He only included a sample of the many thousands of Pauli's dreams.
4 In partial defence of Jung, we should not forget his relationships with Einstein and Pauli. The holistic worldview they constructed, rooted in 'respectable science', had a significant impact on his thinking.
5 See chapters 8 and 11 for background on the Mercurius–Holy Ghost association.
6 We should remember here that Giegerich singles out Jung's psychology, as opposed to the myriad other psychologies.

Bibliography

Anthony, M. (1990) *The Valkyries: The Women Around Jung*, Shaftesbury, UK: Element Books Ltd.

Aziz, R. (1990) *C. G. Jung's Psychology of Religion and Synchronicity*, Albany, New York: State University of New York Press.

Bair, D. (2004) *Jung: A Biography*, New York: Little Brown & Company.

Begg, E. and Rich, D. (1991) *On the Trail of Merlin: A Guide to the Celtic Mystery Tradition*, London: The Aquarian Press.

Bishop, P. (2007a) *Analytical Psychology and German Classical Aesthetics: Goethe, Schiller and Jung*, Volume 1: *The Development of the Personality*, London and New York: Routledge, Taylor and Francis Group.

Bishop, P. (2007b) *Analytical Psychology and German Classical Aesthetics: Goethe, Schiller and Jung*, Volume 2: *The Constellation of the Self*, London and New York: Routledge, Taylor and Francis Group.

Brome, V. (1985) *Jung: Man and Myth*, London: Paladin Books.

Burns, T. and Moore, A. (2007) 'The Hieroglyphic Monad of John Dee Theorems I-XVII: A Guide to the Outer Mysteries', *Journal of the Western Mystery Tradition*, no. 13, vol. 2, Vernal Equinox, online.

Burns, T. and Moore, A. (2010) 'John Dee and Edward Kelley's Great Table (or, What's This Grid For, Anyway?)', *Journal of the Western Mystery Tradition*. no. 18, vol. 2, Vernal Equinox, online.

Burnes, T. and Turner, N. (2007) 'A Translation of Theorems 1–17 of John Dee's *Monas Hieroglyphica*', *Journal of the Western Mystery Tradition*, no. 13, vol. 2, Vernal Equinox, online.

Cambray, J. (2009) *Synchronicity: Nature and Psyche in an Interconnected Universe*, College Station, TX: Texas A&M University Press.

Campbell, J. (1964/1982) *The Masks of God: Occidental Mythology*, Harmondsworth, UK: Penguin Books.

Campion, N. (2008) *A History of Western Astrology: Volume I, The Ancient World*, London and New York: Continuum Books.

Campion, N. (2009) *A History of Western Astrology: Volume II, The Medieval and Modern Worlds*, London and New York: Continuum Books.

Casement, A. (ed.) (2007) *Who Owns Jung?* London: Karnac Books.

Churton, T. (2005) *The Golden Builders: Alchemists, Rosicrucians, and the First Freemasons*, Boston, MA and York Beach, ME: Weiser Books.

Clarke, J. J. (1992) *In Search of Jung: Historical and Philosophical Enquiries*, London and New York: Routledge.

Cobb, C. and Goldwhite, H. (1995) *Creations of Fire: Chemistry's Lively History from Alchemy to the Atomic Age*, New York: Plenum Publishing Company.

Combs, A. and Holland, M. (1994) *Synchronicity: Science, Myth and the Trickster*, Edinburgh: Floris Books.

Copenhaver, B. (1992/2000) *Hermetica: The Greek Corpus Hermeticum and the Latin Asclepuis in a new English Translation with Notes and Introduction*, Cambridge: Cambridge University Press.

Dobbs, B. (1992) *The Foundations of Newton's Alchemy: or, the Hunting of the Greene Lyon*, London and New York: Cambridge University Press.

Donati, M. (2004) 'Beyond Synchronicity: The Worldview of Carl Gustav Jung and Wolfgang Pauli', *Journal of Analytical Psychology* 49: 707–728.

Drob, S. (2005) 'Jung's Kabbalistic Visions', *Journal of Jungian Theory and Practice*, vol. 7, no. 1, 33–54.

Drob, S. (2010) *Kabbalistic Visions: C.G. Jung and Jewish Mysticism*, New Orleans: Spring Journal Books.

Ebeling, F. (2007) *The Secret History of Hermes Trismegistus: Hermeticism from Ancient to Modern Times*, Ithaca, NY and London: Cornell University Press.

Edinger, E. (1995) *The Mysterium Lectures: A Journey through C.G. Jung's Mysterium Coniunctionis*, Toronto, Canada: Inner City Books.

Edinger, E. (1996) *The Aion Lectures: Exploring the Self in C.G. Jung's Aion*, Toronto, Canada: Inner City Books.

Eliade, M. (1956/1978) *The Forge and the Crucible: The Origins and Structures of Alchemy*, Chicago and London: University of Chicago Press.

Eliade, M. C. (1951/2004) *Shamanism: Archaic Techniques of Ecstasy*, Princeton and Oxford: Princeton University Press.

Faivre, A. (1995) *The Eternal Hermes: From Greek God to Alchemical Magus*, (Jocelyn Godwin, trans.) Grand Rapids, MI: Phanes Press.

Fell-Smith, C. (1909) *John Dee (1527–1608)*, The John Dee Publication Project. Accessed from: http://www.john-dee.org/.

Foreshaw, P. (2005) 'The Early Alchemical Reception of John Dee's *Monas Hieroglyphica*', *Ambix*, vol. 52, no. 3, 247–269.

Freke, T. and Gandy, P. (1999) *The Hermetica: The Lost Wisdom of the Pharaohs*, New York: Penguin Putnam.

French, P. (1972) *John Dee: The World of an Elizabethan Magus*, New York: Routledge.

Geigerich, W. (1988) 'The Invention of Explosive Power and the Blueprint of the Bomb', *Spring* 1988: 1–14.

Geigerich, W. (1999) *The Soul's Logical Life*, Frankfurt, Germany: Peter Lang.

Godwin, M. (1994) *The Holy Grail: Its Origins, Secrets and Meaning Revealed*, London: Bloomsbury Publishing.

Goldwater, L. (1972) *Mercury: A History of Quicksilver*, Baltimore, MD: York Press.

Goodrich, N. (1988) *Merlin*, New York: Harper Perennial.

Goodrich, P. and Thompson, R. H. (eds.) (2005) *Merlin: A Casebook*, London: Taylor and Francis Group.

Gray, R. (1952/2002) *Goethe the Alchemist: A Study of Alchemical Symbolism in Goethe's Literary and Scientific Works*, London and New York: Cambridge University Press.

Grimal, P. (1969) *Larousse World Mythology*, London: Paul Hamlyn.
Grinnell, R. (1973/1989) *Alchemy in a Modern Woman: A Study in the Contrasexual Archetype*, Dallas, TX: Spring Publications.
Halifax, J. (1979) *Shamanic Voices: A Survey of Visionary Narratives*, New York and London: Toronto Arkana.
Hannah, B. (1976) *Jung: His Life and Work, A Biographical Memoir*, New York: G.P. Putnam's Sons.
Harpur, P. (1990/2008) *Mercurius: The Marriage of Heaven and Earth*, Glastonbury, UK: The Squeeze Press.
Hayman, R. (1999) *A Life of Jung*, London: Bloomsbury Publishing.
Heisig, J. (1979) *Imago Dei: A Study of C.G. Jung's Psychology of Religion*, Lewisburg, PA: Bucknell University Press.
Hillman, J. (2010) *Alchemical Psychology*, Putnam, CT: Spring Publications.
Hoeller, S. (1989) *Jung and the Lost Gospels*, Wheaton, IL: Quest Books.
Homans, P. (1979/1995) *Jung in Context: Modernity and the Making of a Psychology*, Chicago: University of Chicago Press.
Howell, A. (1990/2006) *The Heavens Declare: Astrological Ages and the Evolution of Consciousness*, Wheaton, IL: Quest Books, Theosophical Publishing House.
Hutton, R. (1993) *The Shamans of Siberia*, Glastonbury, UK: The Isle of Avalon Press.
Jaffé, A. (1989) *From the Life and Works of C.G. Jung*, Einsiedeln, Switzerland: Daimon Verlag.
Jung, C. G. (1917/1926/1943) 'On the Psychology of the Unconscious', in vol. 7, *Two Essays on Analytical Psychology*, London: Routledge & Kegan Paul.
Jung, C. G. (1921) *Collected Works*, vol. 6, *Psychological Types*, London: Routledge & Kegan Paul.
Jung, C. G. (1929) 'Commentary on "The Secret of the Golden Flower" ', in *Collected Works*, vol. 13, *Alchemical Studies*, London: Routledge & Kegan Paul.
Jung, C. G. (1934) 'The State of Psychotherapy Today', in *Collected Works*, vol. 10, *Civilisation in Transition*, London: Routledge & Kegan Paul.
Jung, C. G. (1936) 'Wotan', in *Collected Works*, vol. 10, *Civilisation in Transition*, London: Routledge & Kegan Paul.
Jung, C. G. (1937) 'Religious Ideas in Alchemy', in *Collected Works*, vol. 12, *Psychology and Alchemy*, London: Routledge & Kegan Paul.
Jung, C. G. (1942/1954) 'Transformation Symbolism in the Mass', in *Collected Works*, vol. 11, *Psychology and Religion: West and East*, London: Routledge & Kegan Paul.
Jung, C. G. (1942) 'Paracelusus as a Spiritual Phenomenon', in *Collected Works*, vol. 13, *Alchemical Studies*, London: Routledge & Kegan Paul.
Jung, C. G. (1943/1948) 'The Spirit Mercurius', in *Collected Works*, vol. 13, *Alchemical Studies*, London: Routledge & Kegan Paul.
Jung, C. G. (1944) *Collected Works*, vol. 12, *Psychology and Alchemy* (2nd edn) London: Routledge & Kegan Paul.
Jung C. G. (1945) 'After the Catastrophe', in *Collected Works*, vol. 10, *Civilisation in Transition*, London: Routledge & Kegan Paul.
Jung, C. G. (1945/1954) 'The Philosophical Tree', in *Collected Works*, vol. 13, *Alchemical Studies*, London: Routledge & Kegan Paul.
Jung, C. G. (1946) *The Psychology of the Transference*, in *Collected Works*, vol. 16, *The Practice of Psychotherapy* (2nd edn) London: Routledge & Kegan Paul.
Jung, C. G. (1950) 'Foreword to the "I Ching" ', in *Collected Works*, vol. 11, *Psychology and Religion: West and East*, London: Routledge & Kegan Paul.

Jung, C. G. (1951a) *Collected Works,* vol. 9ii, *Aion* (2nd edn) London: Routledge & Kegan Paul.

Jung, C. G. (1951b) 'On Synchronicity', in *Collected Works*, vol. 8, *The Structure and Dynamics of the Psyche* (2nd edn) London: Routledge & Kegan Paul.

Jung, C. G. (1952a) 'Answer to Job', in *Collected Works*, vol. 11, *Psychology and Religion: West and East*, London: Routledge & Kegan Paul.

Jung, C. G. (1952b) 'Synchronicity: An Acausal Connecting Principle', in *Collected Works*, vol. 8, *The Structure and Dynamics of the Psyche* (2nd edn) London: Routledge & Kegan Paul.

Jung, C. G. (1954) *Collected Works*, vol. 18, *The Symbolic Life*, London: Routledge & Kegan Paul.

Jung, C. G. (1955/1956) *Collected Works*, vol. 14, *Mysterium Coniunctionis: An Enquiry into the Separation and Synthesis of Psychic Opposites in Alchemy*, London: Routledge & Kegan Paul.

Jung, C. G. (1958) 'Flying Saucers: A Modern Myth', in *Collected Works*, vol. 10, *Civilization in Transition* (2nd edn) London: Routledge & Kegan Paul.

Jung, C. G. (1963/1995) *Memories, Dreams, Reflections*, London: Fontana Press.

Jung, C. G. (1973–75) *Letters, Volumes I and II* (G. Adler and A Jaffé, eds., R. F. C. Hull, trans.) London: Routledge & Kegan Paul.

Jung, C. G. (1984) *Dream Analysis: Notes of the Seminar Given in 1928–30* (W. McGuire, ed.) London: Routledge & Kegan Paul.

Jung, C. G. (1996/1995) *The Psychology of Kundalini Yoga: Notes on the Seminar Given in 1932 by C.G. Jung* (S. Shamdasani, ed.) Bollingen Series XCIX. Princeton, NJ: Princeton University Press.

Jung, C. G. (1998) *Visions: Notes of the Seminar Given in 1930–34, in 2 volumes* (C. Douglas, ed.) London: Routledge & Kegan Paul.

Jung, C. G. (2007) *The Jung–White Letters* (C. Lammers and A. Cunningham, eds., M. Stein, consulting ed.) London and New York: Routledge, Taylor and Francis Group.

Jung, C. G. (2008) *Children's Dreams: Notes from the Seminar Given in 1936–1940* (L. Jung and M. Meyer-Grass, eds., E. Falzeder and T. Woolfson, trans.) London: Princeton University Press.

Jung, C. G. (2009) *The Red Book: Liber Novus* (S. Shamdasani, ed., M. Kyburz, J. Peck and S. Shamdasani, trans.) New York and London: W. W. Norton.

Jung, E. and von Franz, M.-L. (1970/1998), *The Grail Legend*, Chichester, West Sussex: Princeton University Press.

Kottler, J., Carlson, J. and Keeney, B. (2004) *American Shaman: An Odyssey of Global Healing Traditions*, New York and Hove: Brunner-Routledge.

Linden, S. (2003) *The Alchemy Reader: From Hermes Trismegistus to Isaac Newton*, Cambridge: Cambridge University Press.

Lindorff, D. (1995a) 'One Thousand Dreams: The Spiritual Awakening of Wolfgang Pauli', *Journal of Analytical Psychology* 40: 555–569.

Lindorff, D. (1995b) 'Psyche, Matter and Synchronicity: a Collaboration between C.G. Jung and Wolfgang Pauli', *Journal of Analytical Psychology* 40: 571–586.

Lopez-Pedraza, R. (1977/2003) *Hermes and his Children*, Einsiedeln, Switzerland: Daimon Verlag.

McGuire, W. and Hull, R. F. C. (eds) (1978/1990) *C.G. Jung Speaking: Interviews and Encounters*, London: Picador.

Maidenbaum, A. and Martin, S. (1991) *Lingering Shadows: Jungians, Freudians and Anti-Semitism*, Boston and London: Shambala.

Main, R. (1997) *Jung on Synchronicity and the Paranormal: Key Readings Selected and Introduced by Roderick Main*, Hove: Routledge.

Main, R. (2004) *The Rupture of Time: Synchronicity and Jung's Critique of Modern Western Culture*, Hove and New York: Brunner-Routledge.

Main, R. (2007) *Revelations of Chance: Synchronicity as Spiritual Experience*, Albany: State University of New York Press.

Main, R. (2008) 'Secularisation and the "Holistic Milieu": Social and Psychological Perspectives', *Religion Compass*, no. 2/3, 365–384.

Main, R. (2010) 'Jung as a Modern Esotericist', in G. Heuer (ed.) *Sacral Revolutions*, London and New York: Routledge.

Main, R. (2011) 'Synchronicity and the Limits of Re-enchantment', *International Journal of Jungian Studies*, vol. 3, no. 2, 144–158.

Main, R. (2012) 'Anomalous Phenomena, Synchronicity, and the Re-sacralisation of the Modern World', in S. Kakar and J. Kripal (eds.) *Seriously Strange: Thinking Anew About Psychical Experiences*, New Delhi: Penguin Viking.

Mansfield, V. (2001) *Synchronicity, Science and Soul-Making*, Chicago and La Salle, IL: Open Court.

Marlan, S. (2005) *The Black Sun: The Alchemy and Art of Darkness*, College Station, TX: Texas A&M University Press.

Meier, C. A. (ed.) (2001) *Atom and Archetype: The Pauli/Jung Letters 1932–1958*, Princeton, NJ: Princeton University Press.

Miller, A. (2009) *Deciphering the Cosmic Number: The Strange Friendship of Wolfgang Pauli and Carl Jung*, New York and London: W. W. Norton & Company.

Mogenson, G. (1999) 'Psyche's Archetypes: A Response to Pietikainen, Stevens, Hogenson and Solomon', *Journal of Analytical Psychology* 44: 125–133.

Monmouth, G. (1966) *The History of the Kings of Britain*, London: Penguin Classics.

Naifeh, S. and Smith, N. (2003) 'Journal Reviews', *Journal of Analytical Psychology* 48: 127–134.

Noll, R. (1997) *The Aryan Christ: The Secret Life of Carl Jung*, New York and Toronto: Random House.

Palmer, M. (1997) *Freud and Jung on Religion*, London and New York: Routledge.

Papadopoulos, R. K. (ed.) (2006) *The Handbook of Jungian Psychology: Theory, Practice and Applications*, New York and London: Routledge, Taylor and Francis Group.

Papadopoulos, R. K. and Saayman, G. S. (eds.) (1984) *Jung in Modern Perspective: The Master and his Legacy*, Bridport, UK: Prism Press.

Peat, D. (1988) *Synchronicity: The Bridge between Matter and Mind*, New York: Bantam.

Phillips, G. (2005) *Merlin and the Discovery of Avalon in the New World*, Rochester, VT: Bear and Company.

Raff, J. (2000) *Jung and the Alchemical Imagination*, Berwick, ME: Nicholas-Hays.

Romanyshyn, R. (2007) *The Wounded Researcher: Research with Soul in Mind*, New Orleans: Spring Journal Books.

Rowland, S. (2005) *Jung as a Writer*, London and New York: Routledge, Taylor and Francis Group.

Rowland, S. (2006) 'Literary *Aion*: Jung and the History of Imagination', *IAJS/IAAP Conference 2005*, Texas.

Ryan, R. (2002) *Shamanism and the Psychology of C.G. Jung: The Great Circle*, London: Vega.

Salaman, A., Van Oyen, D. and Wharton, W. (1999/2004) *The Way of Hermes: The Corpus Hermeticum and the Definitions of Hermes Trismegistus to Asclepius*, London: Gerald Duckworth & Co.

Samuels, A. (1992) 'National Psychology, National Socialism, and Analytical Psychology: Reflections on Jung and Anti-Semitism Part I', *Journal of Analytical Psychology* 37: 3–28.

Samuels, A. (1993) 'New Material Concerning Jung, Anti-Semitism, and the Nazis', *Journal of Analytical Psychology* 38: 463–470.

Sandner, D. and Wong, S. (eds.) (1997) *The Sacred Heritage: The Influence of Shamanism on Analytical Psychology*, New York and London: Routledge.

Schwartz-Salant, N. (1998) *The Mystery of Human Relationship: Alchemy and the Transformation of the Self*, London: Routledge.

Serrano, M. (1977) *C.G. Jung and Herman Hesse: A Record of Two Friendships*, London: Routledge & Kegan Paul.

Shamdasani, S. (1998) *Cult Fictions: C.G. Jung and the Founding of Analytical Pychology*, London: Routledge.

Shamdasani, S. (2005) *Jung Stripped Bare by his Biographers, Even*, London and New York: Karnac Books Ltd.

Sherry, J. (2001) 'The *Schweizer Illustrierte* Interview. A Commentary', *Journal of Analytical Psychology* 46: 359–364.

Smith, M. (2007) *Jung and Shamanism in Dialogue*, New York and Mahwah, NJ: Paulist Press.

Smith, R. C. (1997) *The Wounded Jung: Effects of Jung's Relationships on his Life and Work*, Evanston, IL: Northwestern University Press.

Sparks, G. (2007) *At the Heart of Matter: Synchronicity and Jung's Spiritual Testament*, Toronto, Canada: Inner City Books.

Spencer, N. (2000) *True as the Stars Above*, London: Orion Books.

Spivack, C. (ed.) (1992) *Merlin versus Faust: Contending Archetypes in Western Culture*, Lewiston, NY: E. Mellen Press.

Stein, M. (1983/2004) *In Midlife*, New York: Spring Publications.

Stein, M. (2011) 'Jungian Psychology and the Spirit of Protestantism', *International Journal of Jungian Studies*, vol. 3, no. 2, 125–143.

Stewart, R. J. (2009) *Merlin: The Prophetic Vision and the Mystic Life*, Arcata, CA: J. Stewart Books.

Sumner, A. (2001) 'John Dee', *Journal of the Western Mystery Tradition*, no. 1, Autumnal Equinox, online.

Suster, G. (2003) *Western Esoteric Masters Series: John Dee – Essential Readings*, Berkeley, CA: North Atlantic Books.

Tacey, D. (2001) *Jung and the New Age*, Hove and Philadelphia, PA: Brunner-Routledge.

Tacey, D. (2004/2007) *The Spirituality Revolution: The Emergence of Contemporary Spirituality*, London and New York: Routledge, Taylor and Francis Group.

Tacey, D. (2011) 'Grassroots Spirituality as a Holistic Expression of the Psyche', *International Journal of Jungian Studies*, vol. 3, no. 1, 36–52.

Tandan, M. (2009) *Dreams and Beyond: Finding Your Way in the Dark*, London: Hay House.

Tannen, R. (2007) *The Female Trickster: The Mask that Reveals: Post-Jungian and Postmodern Psychological Perspectives on Women in Contemporary Culture*, London and New York: Routledge, Taylor and Francis Group.

Tarnas, R. (2007) *Cosmos and Psyche: Intimations of a New World View*, London: Plume, published by Penguin Group.

Tolstoy, N. (1985) *The Quest for Merlin*, London: Hamish Hamilton.
van der Post, L. (1976/1985) *Jung and the Story of our Time*, Harmondsworth, UK: Penguin Books.
von Eschenbach, W. (1980) *Parzival* (A. T. Hatto, trans.) St. Ives, UK: Penguin Books.
von Franz, M.-L. (1966/2000) *Aurora Consurgens: A Document Attributed to Thomas Aquinas on the Problem of Opposites in Alchemy*, Toronto, Canada: Inner City Books.
von Franz, M.-L. (1980) *On Divination and Synchronicity: The Psychology of Meaningful Chance*, Toronto, Canada: Inner City Books.
von Franz, M.-L. (1992) *Psyche and Matter*, Boston and London: Shambhala.
von Franz, M.-L. (1997) *Archetypal Patterns in Fairytales*, Toronto, Canada: Inner City Books.
von Franz, M.-L. (1998) *C.G. Jung: His Myth in our Time*, Toronto, Canada: Inner City Books.
von Franz, M.-L. (1999) *The Cat: A Tale of Feminine Redemption*, Toronto, Canada: Inner City Books.
von Franz, M.-L. and Hannah, B. (2004) *Lectures on Jung's Aion*, Wilmette, IL: Chiron Publications.
Vos, A. (2009) 'A Methodology of the Imagination', *Eye of the Heart: A Journal of Traditional Wisdom*, 1–16, accessed from www.imaginalstudies.org.
Williams, D. (1981) *Border Crossings: A Psychological Perspective on Carlos Castaneda's Path of Knowledge*, Toronto, Canada: Inner City Books.
Woolley, B. (2002) *The Queen's Conjuror: The Life and Magic of Dr Dee*, London: Harper Collins.
Zabriskie, B. (2005) 'Synchronicity and the I Ching: Jung, Pauli and the Chinese Woman', *Journal of Analytical Psychology* 50: 223–235.

Index

For Product Safety Concerns and Information please contact our EU
representative GPSR@taylorandfrancis.com
Taylor & Francis Verlag GmbH, Kaufingerstraße 24, 80331 München, Germany

www.ingramcontent.com/pod-product-compliance
Ingram Content Group UK Ltd.
Pitfield, Milton Keynes, MK11 3LW, UK
UKHW011007180926
475701UK00004B/611

* 9 7 8 0 4 1 5 3 6 5 7 6 5 *